# The Piety of Thinking

*Studies in Phenomenology and*
*Existential Philosophy*

GENERAL EDITOR

*James M. Edie*

CONSULTING EDITORS

Essays by *Martin Heidegger*

*Translations, Notes, and Commentary by*

# The Piety of Thinking

JAMES G. HART and
JOHN C. MARALDO

INDIANA UNIVERSITY PRESS
*Bloomington and London*

*Copyright © 1976 by Indiana University Press*

*All rights reserved*

*Published in Canada by Fitzhenry & Whiteside Limited, Don Mills, Ontario*

MANUFACTURED IN THE UNITED STATES OF AMERICA

Library of Congress Cataloging in Publication Data

Heidegger, Martin, 1899–
   The piety of thinking.

   (Studies in phenomenology and existential philosophy)
   1. Phenomenology—Addresses, essays, lectures.
2. Philosophy and religion—Addresses, essays, lectures.
I. Hart, James G., 1936–   II. Maraldo, John C.
III. Title.
B3279.H48P53   1976   193   75-3889
ISBN 0-253-34498-0   1 2 3 4 5 80 79 78 77 76

# CONTENTS

# TRANSLATORS' PREFACE

The title of this book is the choice of the translators. Although Martin Heidegger has never published a work under the title of "The Piety of Thinking," he once wrote: "For questioning is the piety of thinking."[1] In a later explanation he stated that he means pious *(fromm)* "in the old sense," i.e., compliant and obedient *(fügsam)*. In the text cited pious means being obedient to that which thinking must think. Thus the basic gesture of thinking is not questioning but an antecedent listening. All questioning gets off the ground by means of this initial listening, which precedes and guides the question and which the question pursues.[2] The prior listening out of which all questioning arises is that which always withdraws from view. That which withdraws from view in all coming into view and toward which mortals must be pious is, in a special sense, the holy.[3] The essays here translated gather together discussions which deal with Heidegger's specific sense of the piety of thinking as well as that "other" pious speaking about the holy which is possible only through either faith or mythic existence.

The Notes and Commentary place the translated texts within the wider context of Heidegger's thought and relate Heidegger's basic positions to neighboring discussions in phenomenology, language philosophy, theology, and aesthetic theory.

The translations are the result of the collaborative effort of James Hart and John Maraldo. The notes to Professor Heidegger's "Phenomenology and Theology," to his "Review of Ernst Cassirer's *Mythical Thought,*" and to the appended "Conversation with Martin Heidegger" (reported by Professor Hermann Noack) are James Hart's. The notes to Professor Heidegger's points on "The Problem of a Non-Objective Thinking and Speaking in Today's Theology" and to his "Principles of Thought" are John Maraldo's.

Parts I–III of the Commentary are by James Hart. John Maraldo wrote Part IV. We have used existing translations, unless otherwise noted as our own, for quotations appearing in the Commentary and Notes.

We would like to express our appreciation to Professor Anne Carr for many helpful suggestions toward clarifying the Commentary. Our gratitude is also to Professor Thomas Prufer, whose influence is almost omnipresent in the Commentary, although the responsibility is ours. Finally, to Mechthild Hart and Mary Jo Maraldo special thanks are due for counsel, suggestions, and *auxilium coniugis.*

*James G. Hart*
*John C. Maraldo*

# ABBREVIATIONS OF FREQUENTLY CITED WORKS OF HEIDEGGER

| | |
|---|---|
| EH | *Erläuterungen zu Hölderlins Dichtung* |
| EM | *Einführung in die Metaphysik;* translation: *Introduction to Metaphysics* |
| FD | *Die Frage nach dem Ding;* translation: *What is a Thing?* |
| H | *Holzwege* |
| ID | *Identität und Differenz;* translation: *Identity and Difference* |
| PLT | *Poetry, Language, Thought,* translation of works originally appearing in H, VA II and US |
| SG | *Satz vom Grund* |
| SZ | *Sein und Zeit;* translation: *Being and Time;* page references are to those in the German edition which appear in the margins of the translation. |
| US | *Unterwegs zur Sprache;* translation: *On the Way to Language* |
| VA | *Vorträge und Aufsätze* (I–III) |
| W | *Wegmarken* |
| WhD | *Was heisst Denken?;* translation: *What is Called Thinking?* |
| ZSD | *Zur Sache des Denkens;* translation: *On Time and Being* |

# THE
# PIETY OF THINKING

*Essays by Martin Heidegger*

# Foreword to the German Edition of
# Phenomenology and Theology[1]

This little book contains a lecture and a letter.

The lecture "Phenomenology and Theology" was given on March 9, 1927, in Tübingen and was again delivered on February 14, 1928, in Marburg. The text presented here forms the content of the immediately reworked and improved second part of the Marburg lecture: "The Positivity of Theology and its Relation to Phenomenology." In the Introduction to *Being and Time,* §7, one finds a discussion of the notion of phenomenology (as well as its relation to the positive sciences) which guides the presentation here.[2]

The letter of March 11, 1964, gives some pointers to major aspects for a theological discussion concerning "The Problem of a Non-Objectifying Thinking and Speaking in Today's Theology." The discussion took place at Drew University in Madison, New Jersey, on April 9–11, 1964.

These texts were published for the first time in *Archives de Philosophie* XXXII (1969), pp. 356 ff., with an accompanying French translation.[3]

This little book might perhaps be able to occasion repeated reflection on the extent to which the Christianness of Christianity and its theology merit questioning; but also on the extent to which philosophy, in particular that presented here, merits questioning.

Almost one hundred years ago there appeared simultaneously (1873) two writings of two friends: the "first piece" of the

*Thoughts Out of Season* of Friedrich Nietzsche, wherein "the glorious Hölderlin" is mentioned; and the "little book" *On the Christianness of Today's Theology* of Franz Overbeck, who established the world-denying expectation of the end as the basic characteristic of what is primordially Christian.[4]

To say both writings are unseasonable also in today's changed world means: For the few who think among the countless who reckon, these writings intend and point toward that which itself perseveres before the inaccessible through speaking, questioning, and creating.

For a discussion of the wider realm of investigation of both writings, cf. M. Heidegger, "Nietzsche's Statement: 'God is Dead,' " in *Holzwege;*[5] and "European Nihilism" and "The Ontological-Historical Determination of Nihilism" in *Nietzsche* II.[6]

# *Phenomenology and Theology*[1]

The popular understanding of the relationship between theology and philosophy is fond of opposing faith and knowledge, revelation and reason. Philosophy is that interpretation of the world and life which is removed from revelation and free from faith. Theology, on the other hand, is the expression of the credal understanding of the world and life—in our case a Christian understanding. Taken as such, philosophy and theology give expression to a tension and a struggle between two world-views. This relationship is not decided by scientific argument but by the manner, the extent, and the strength of the conviction and the proclamation of the world-view.

We, however, see the problem of the relationship *differently* from the very start. It is for us rather a question about the *relationship of two sciences.*

But this question needs a more precise formulation. It is not a case of comparing the factual circumstances of two historically given sciences. And even if it were, it would be difficult to describe a unified state of affairs regarding the two sciences in the midst of their divergent directions. To proceed on a course of the factual relationship would yield no *fundamental* insight as to how theology and philosophy are related to one another.

Thus what is needed as a basis for a fundamental discussion of the problem is an ideal construction of both sciences in terms of their ideas. One can decide their possible relationship to one another from the possibilities they both have as sciences.

Posing the question like this presupposes that we have established the idea of science in general, as well as how to characterize the modifications of this idea which are possible in principle. (We cannot enter into this problem here; it would have to be taken up in the prolegomena to our discussion.) We offer as a guide the following formal definition of science: science is the founding disclosure, for the sheer sake of disclosure, of the self-contained regions of whatever is, or, as the case may be, of Being.[2] Every region of objects, according to its subject matter and the mode of Being of its objects, has its own mode of possible disclosure, evidence, founding and its own conceptual formation of knowledge. It is evident from the idea of science as such—insofar as it is understood as a possibility of Dasein[3]— that there are two basic possibilities of science: sciences of whatever is, or ontic sciences; and *the* science of Being, the ontological science, philosophy.

Ontic sciences make a theme of any given being, which in a certain manner is already disclosed prior to the scientific disclosure. We call the sciences of whatever is given—of a *positum*—positive sciences. Their objectification of whatever it is that they thematize is a direct continuation of the prescientific attitude toward this being. Ontology, or the science of Being, on the other hand, demands a fundamental shift of view: from whatever is to Being. And this shift nevertheless keeps whatever is in view, but for a modified attitude. We shall not go into the question of the method of this shift here.

Within the circle of actual or possible sciences of whatever is—the positive sciences—there is between any two only a relative difference, based on the different relations which orient a science to a specific region of being. On the other hand, every positive science is *absolutely,* not relatively, different from philosophy. Our thesis, then, is that *theology is a positive science, and as such, therefore, is absolutely different from philosophy.*

Hence one must ask how theology is related to philosophy in the light of this absolute difference. It is immediately clear from the thesis that theology, as a positive science, is closer to chemistry and mathematics than to philosophy. Put in this way, we have the most extreme formulation of the relationship between theology and philosophy—one which runs counter to the popular view. According to this popular view, each of the sciences (philosophy and theology), to a certain extent, has as its theme the same area: human life and the world. But they are guided by different points of view. The one proceeds from the principle of *faith,* the other from the principle of *reason.* However, our thesis is: Theology is a positive science and as such is absolutely different from philosophy.

The task of our discussion will be to characterize theology as a positive science and, on the basis of this characterization, to clarify its possible relationship to philosophy, which is absolutely different from it.

Note that we are considering theology here in the sense of Christian theology. This is not to say that Christian theology is the only theology. The central question is whether, indeed, theology is a science. This question is deferred here, not because we wish to evade the problem, but only because that question cannot be asked intelligently until its essential idea is elucidated in a broader context.

Before turning to the discussion proper, we wish to submit the following considerations. In accordance with our thesis, we are considering a positive science, and indeed one of a particular kind. Therefore a few remarks are in order about what constitutes the positive character of a science as such.

Proper to the positive character of a science is: first, that a being which in some way is already disclosed is to a certain extent come upon as a possible theme of theoretical objectification and inquiry; second, that this given *positum* is come upon in a definite prescientific manner of approaching and proceeding with that which is. In this manner of procedure, the specific content of this region and the mode of Being of the particular entity show themselves. That is, this disclosure is prior to any theoretical consideration, although it is perhaps implicit and not thematically known. Thirdly, it is proper to the positive character that this prescientific behavior toward whatever is given (nature, history, economy, space, number) is also already illuminated and guided by an understanding of Being—even if it be nonconceptual. The positive character can vary according to the content of that which is, its mode of Being, the manner in which it is prescientifically disclosed, and the manner in which this disclosedness belongs to it.[4]

The question thus arises: Of what sort is the positive character of theology? Apparently this question must be answered before we are in a position to determine its relation to philosophy. But setting down the positive character of theology will not yet sufficiently clarify its status as a science. We have not yet arrived at the full concept of theology as a science, but only at what is proper to it as a positive science.

If thematizing is supposed to adjust the direction of inquiry, the manner of investigation, and the terminology *(Begrifflich-keit)* to the particular *positum,* it is more to the point here to set down the specific scientific character of theology along with its specific positive character. Therefore, only by setting down the positive *and* the scientific character of theology are we brought nearer to this discipline as a positive science and given the basis for characterizing its possible relationship to philosophy.

Thus our consideration contains a threefold division:

*a*) the positive character of theology;

*b*) the scientific character of theology;

*c*) the possible relation of theology, as a positive science, to philosophy.

## *a*) THE POSITIVE CHARACTER OF THEOLOGY

A positive science is the founding disclosure of whatever is given and in some way already disclosed. The question arises: What is already given for theology? One might say: What is given for Christian theology is Christianity as something that has come about historically, witnessed by the history of religion and culture and presently visible through its institutions, cults, communities, and groups as a widespread phenomenon in world history. Christianity: the given *positum;* and hence theology: the science of Christianity. That would evidently be an erroneous characterization of theology, for theology itself belongs to Christianity. Theology itself is something which everywhere in history gives testimony to its intimate connection with Christianity itself. Evidently, then, theology cannot be the science of Christianity as something that has come about in world history, because it is a science which itself belongs to the history of Christianity, is carried along by that history, and influences that history.

Is theology therefore a science which itself belongs to the history of Christianity in the way that every historical discipline is itself an historical appearance, namely, by representing the historical development of its consciousness of history? If this is the case, then we can characterize theology as the self-consciousness of Christianity as it appears in world history. However, theology does not belong to Christianity merely because, as something historical, it has a place in the general manifestations of culture. Rather, theology is a knowledge of that which initially makes possible something like Christianity as an event in world history. Theology is a conceptual knowing of that which first of all allows Christianity to become a radically historical event, a knowing of that which we call absolute Christianness. Thus we maintain that what is given for theology (its *positum*) is Christianness. It decides the form theology will take as the positive science which thematizes it. The question occurs now, what does "Christianness" mean?

We call faith Christian. The essence of faith can formally be sketched as a mode of human existence which, according to its own testimony—itself belonging to this mode of existence— arises not from Dasein or spontaneously through Dasein, but rather from that which is revealed in and with this mode of existence, from what is believed. For the "Christian" faith, that which is primarily revealed to faith, and only to it, and which, as revelation, first gives rise to faith, is Christ, the crucified God. The relationship of faith to the cross, determined in this way by Christ, is a Christian one. The crucifixion, however, and all that belongs to it is an historical event, and indeed this event gives testimony to its specifically historical character only in the scriptures. One "knows" about this fact only *by believing.*

That which is revealed in faith is, in accordance with its specific "sacrificial" character, imparted specifically to people actually existing in history (whether contemporaneous or not) or to the community of these individuals existing as a community. The imparting of this revelation is not a conveyance of information about present, past, or imminent happenings; rather, this imparting lets one partake of the event which is revelation (= what is revealed) itself. But the part-*taking* of faith, which is realized only in existence, is *given* only through faith. Furthermore, this "part-taking" and "having part in" the event of the crucifixion places one's entire human existence— as a Christian existence, i.e., one bound to the cross—before God. And thereby the existence struck by this revelation becomes aware of its forgetfulness of God. Thus—and again I speak only of an ideal construction of the idea—being placed before God means that existence is reoriented in and through the mercy of God grasped in faith. Thus faith understands itself only in believing. In any case, the believer does not come to know anything about his existence in faith by way of a theoretical confirmation of his inner experiences. Rather, he can only "believe" his existential possibility as one which human existence itself is not master over, in which it becomes a slave, is brought before God, and is reborn. Accordingly, the proper meaning of faith for factual existence is: *Faith = Rebirth*. And rebirth does not mean a momentary outfitting with some quality or other, but a way in which a factual, believing human being historically exists in *the* history which begins with the occurrence of revelation; in *the* history which, in accord with the very meaning of the revelation, has a definite uttermost end. The occurrence of revelation, which is passed down to faith and which accordingly occurs through faithfulness itself, discloses itself only to faith.

Luther said, "Faith is permitting ourselves to be seized by the things we do not see" (Erlangen Ausgabe WW, vol. 46, p. 287). Yet faith is not something which merely reveals that the occurring of revelation is something happening; it is not some more or less modified type of knowing. Rather, faith is an appropriation of revelation, which co-constitutes the Christian occurrence, that is, the mode of existence which specifies a factual Dasein's Christianness as a particular form of historicity. *Faith is the believing-understanding mode of existing in the history revealed, i.e., occurring, with the Crucified.*

The totality of this being which is disclosed by faith—in such a way, indeed, that faith itself belongs to the context of its disclosure—constitutes the *positum* which theology comes across. *Presupposing* that theology is enjoined on faith, out of faith, and for faith, and *presupposing* that science is a *freely* performed, conceptual disclosure and objectification, theology is constituted by thematizing faith and that which is disclosed through faith, that which is revealed. It is worthy of note that faith is not just the manner in which the *positum* objectified by theology is already disclosed and presented; faith itself is a theme for theology. And not only that. Insofar as theology is enjoined upon faith, it can find sufficient motivation for itself only through faith.[5] If faith would totally oppose a conceptual interpretation, then theology would be a thoroughly *inappropriate* means of grasping its object, faith. It would lack something so essential that without this it could never become a science. What is necessary for theology, therefore, can never be deduced from a purely rationally constructed system of sciences. Furthermore, faith not only motivates the penetration of an interpretive science; at the same time, faith, as rebirth, is *the* history which theology, for its part, is supposed to promote. Theology has a meaning and a value only if it functions as an ingredient of faith, of this particular kind of historical occurrence.

By attempting to elucidate this connection (between theology and faith), we are likewise showing how, through the specific positive character of theology, i.e., through the Christian occurrence disclosed in faith as faith, the scientific character of the science of faith might be sketched out.

## *b)* The Scientific Character of Theology

Theology is the science of faith.

This says several things:

1) Theology is the science of that which is disclosed through faith, of that which is believed. That which is believed in this case is not some coherent order of propositions about facts or occurrences which we simply agree to—which, although theoretically not self-evident, can be appropriated because we agree to them.

2) Theology is accordingly the science of believing comport-

ment itself, of faithfulness—a revealed faithfulness, which cannot possibly be any other way. This means that faith, as believing comportment, is itself believed, itself belongs to that which is believed.

3) Theology, furthermore, is the science of faith, not only insofar as it makes faith and that which is believed its object, but because it itself arises out of faith. It is the science which *faith* motivates and justifies.

4) Theology, finally, is the science of faith insofar as it not only makes faith its object and is motivated by faith, but because this objectification of faith itself properly has no other purpose than to help cultivate faithfulness itself.

Formally considered, then, faith as the existing relation to the Crucified is a mode of historical, human existence, of historically being in a history which discloses itself only through and for faith. Therefore theology, as the science of faith, that is, of an intrinsically *historical* mode of Being, is to the very core an historical science. And indeed it is a unique sort of historical science in accord with the unique historicity involved in faith, i.e., with "the occurrence of revelation."

As faith's conceptual interpretation of itself, that is, as historical knowledge, theology aims solely at that transparency of the Christian occurrence which is revealed and delimited by faithfulness itself. Thus the goal of this science is concrete Christian existence itself. Its goal is never a valid system of theological propositions about general states of affairs within one region of Being among others. The transparency of faith-full existence is an understanding of existence and as such can relate only to existing itself. Every theological statement and concept addresses itself *in its very content* to the faith-full existence of the individual in the community; it does *not* do so subsequently, for the sake of some practical *"application."* The specific content of the object of theology demands that the appropriate theological knowledge never take the form of some free-floating knowledge of arbitrary states of affairs. Likewise, the theological transparency and conceptual interpretation of faith cannot found and secure faith in its legitimacy, nor can it in any way make it easier to accept faith and remain constant in faith. Theology can only render faith more difficult, that is, more certain that faithfulness cannot be gained through the science of theology, but solely through faith. Hence theology can permit the serious character of faithfulness as a "graciously bestowed" mode of existence to become a matter of conscience. Theology "can" perform this; i.e., it is capable of this, but it is *only possibly* that it may have this effect.

In summary, then, theology is an *historical science,* in accordance with the *positum* objectified by it. It would seem that with this thesis we are denying the possibility and the necessity of a *systematic* as well as a *practical* theology. However, one should note that we did not say that there is only "historical" theology, to the exclusion of "systematic" and "practical" theology. Rather our thesis is: Theology as such is historical, regardless of how it may be divided into various disciplines. And it is precisely this characterization which enables one to understand why and how theology originally divided into a systematic, an historical (in a narrower sense), and a practical discipline—not in addition to but in keeping with the specific unity of its theme. The philosophical understanding of a science is, after all, not achieved by merely latching on to its factual and contingent, pre-given breakdown and simply accepting the technical division of labor in order then to join the various disciplines together externally and subsume them under a "general" concept. Rather, a philosophical understanding requires that we question beyond the factually existing division and ascertain *whether* and *why* this division is demanded by the essence of the science and to what extent the factual organization corresponds to the essential idea of the science as it is determined by its *positum.*

In reference to theology it thus becomes evident that, because it is a conceptual interpretation of Christian existence, the content of all its concepts is essentially related to the Christian occurrence as such. *To grasp the import and the specific mode of Being of the Christian occurrence, and to grasp it as it is testified to in faith and for faith, is the task of systematic theology.* If indeed faithfulness is testified to in the *scriptures,* systematic theology is in its essence *New Testament theology.* In other words, theology is not systematic in that it first breaks up the totality of the content of faith into some collocation, then reclassifies this within the framework of a system and finally proves the validity of the system. It is not systematic by constructing a system, but on the contrary by avoiding a system, in the sense that it seeks solely to bring clearly to light the intrinsic *systema* of the Christian event as such, that is, to place the believer who understands conceptually in the history of revelation. The more historical theology is, i.e., the more immediately the historicity of faith is put into words and conceptualized, the more is it "systematic" and the less likely is it to become the slave of a system. The radicality with which one is cognizant of this task and its methodological exigencies is the criterion for the scientific level of a systematic theology. Such a task will be more certainly and purely accomplished the more theology permits its concepts and conceptual schemes to be determined by the mode of Being and the specific sense of *that which* it objectifies. The more unequivocally theology disburdens itself of the application of some philosophy and its system, the more *philosophical* is its own radical scientific character.[6]

On the other hand, the more systematic theology is in the way we have designated, the more immediately does it found the *necessity of historical theology in the narrower sense* of exegesis, church history, and history of dogma. If these disciplines are to be genuine *theology* and not special areas of the general, profane historical sciences, then they must permit themselves to be guided in the choice of their object by what we have properly called systematic theology.

Furthermore, the Christian occurrence's interpretation of itself as an historical occurrence also implies that its own specific historicity is appropriated ever anew, along with the new awareness of the possibilities of faith-full human existence. Now because theology, as a systematic as well as an historical discipline, has for its primary object the Christian occurrence in its Christianness and its historicity, and because this occurrence specifies itself as a mode of existence of the believer, and existing entails action, *praxis, theology in its essence is a practical science.* As the action of God on faith-full men it is already "innately" homiletical. And for this reason alone is it possible for theology itself to be a practical discipline and to organize itself, as in fact it does, into homiletics and catechetics. Thus

its practical constitution is not due to any accidental require-
ments which demand, say, that it apply its theoretical propositions to a practical sphere. *Theology is systematic only when
it is historical and practical. It is historical only when it is
systematic and practical. And it is practical only when it is
systematic and historical.*

All of these characteristics essentially hang together. The
contemporary controversies in theology can turn into a genuine
exchange and fruitful communication only if the problem of
theology as a science is followed back to the central question
which derives from considering *theology as a positive science:*
What is the ground of the specific unity and necessary plurality
of the systematic, historical, and practical disciplines of theology?

We can add a few clarifications to this sketchy outline of the
character of theology by showing what theology is *not.*

Etymologically regarded, theo-logy means: science of God.
But God is in no way the object of investigation in theology, as,
for example, animals are the theme of zoology. Theology is not
speculative knowledge of God.

And we hit upon the conception of theology no better when
we expand the theme and say: The object of theology is the
all-inclusive relationship of God to man and of man to God. In
that case theology would be the philosophy or the history of
religion, in short, *Religionswissenschaft.* Even less is it the
psychology of religion, i.e., the science of man and his religious
states and experiences, the analysis of which is supposed to
lead ultimately to the discovery of God in man. One could,
however, admit that theology does not coincide in general with
speculative knowledge of God, the scientific study of religion,
or the psychology of religion—and still want to stress that theology represents a special case of the philosophy and history of
religion, namely, the philosophical, historical, and psychological science of the Christian religion.

Yet it is clear from what we have said that systematic theology is not a form of the philosophy of religion applied to the
Christian religion. Nor is church history a history of religion
limited to the Christian religion. In all such interpretations of
theology the idea of this science is abandoned from the very

beginning. That is, it is not conceived with regard to the specific positive character of theology, but rather is arrived at by way of a deduction and specialization of nontheological sciences— philosophy, history, and psychology—sciences which, indeed, are quite heterogeneous to one another. Of course, to determine where the limits of the scientific character of theology lie, i.e., to determine how far the specific exigencies of faithfulness itself can and do press for conceptual clarification and still remain faith-full, is a difficult central problem. It is tied most closely to the question about the original ground of the unity of the three disciplines of theology.

In no case may we delimit the scientific character of theology by using an *other* science as the standard of evidence for its mode of proof or as the measure of rigor of its terminology. In accord with the *positum* of theology (which is disclosed only in faith), not only is the access to its object unique, but the evidence for the demonstration of its propositions is quite special. Its proper conceptuality and terminology can grow only out of itself. There is certainly no need for it to borrow from other sciences in order to augment and secure its bits of evidence. Nor indeed can it attempt to substantiate or justify the evidence of faith by relating items of knowledge gained from other sciences. *Rather, theology itself is founded primarily in faith,* even though its statements and procedures of proof derive from the formally free operations of reason.[7]

Likewise, the inefficacy of the nontheological sciences with respect to what faith reveals is no proof for the correctness of faith. One can have the "faithless" sciences assault and be shattered by faith only if one already faith-fully holds fast to the truth of faith. But faith misconceives itself if it then thinks that it is first proven right or even thereby fortified when the other sciences are shattered by it. The material legitimacy of all theological knowledge is grounded in faith itself, originates out of faith, and leaps back into faith.

On the grounds of its specific positive character and the form of knowing which this determines, we can now say that theology is a fully autonomous ontic science. The question now arises: How is this positive science, with its specific positive and scientific character, related to philosophy?

## *c)* THE RELATION OF THEOLOGY AS A POSITIVE SCIENCE TO PHILOSOPHY

If faith does not need philosophy, the *science* of faith as a *positive* science does. And here again we must distinguish: The positive science of faith does not need philosophy for the founding and primary disclosure of its *positum*, Christianness, which founds itself in its own manner. The positive science of faith needs philosophy only in regard to its scientific character, and even then only in a uniquely restricted, though basic, way.

As a science theology must be able to demonstrate and to form concepts which are appropriate to that which it has undertaken to interpret. But is it not the case that that which is to be interpreted in theological concepts is precisely that which is disclosed only through, for, and in faith? Is not that which is supposed to be grasped conceptually something essentially inconceivable, and consequently something whose content is not to be fathomed, and whose legitimacy is not to be founded by purely rational means?

Nevertheless, something can very well be inconceivable and never primarily disclosed through reason without thereby excluding a conceptual grasp of itself. On the contrary: if the inconceivable as such is to be disclosed properly, it can only be by way of the appropriate conceptual interpretation—and that means pushing these concepts to their very limits. Otherwise the inconceivability remains, as it were, mute. And this interpretation of faith-full existence is the task of theology. And so, why philosophy? Whatever is discloses itself only on the grounds of a preliminary (although not explicitly known), preconceptual understanding of what and how it is. Every ontic interpretation operates within the basic context of an ontology, firstly and for the most part hidden. But can such things as the cross, sin, etc., which manifestly belong to the ontological context of Christianness, be understood as to what they are and how they are, except through faith? How does one ontologically disclose the what (the essence) and the how (the mode of being) underlying these fundamental notions of Christianness? Is faith to become the criterion of knowledge for an ontological-philosophical explication? Are not the basic theological concepts completely withdrawn from philosophical-ontological reflection?

Of course one should not lose sight here of something essential: the explication of basic concepts, insofar as it proceeds correctly, is never accomplished by explicating and defining isolated concepts with reference to themselves alone and then operating with them here and there as if they were playing chips. Rather, all such explication must take pains to envision and hold constantly in view in its original totality the primary, self-contained ontological context to which all the basic concepts refer. What does this mean for the explication of basic theological concepts?

We characterized faith as the essential constitutive element of Christianness: faith is rebirth. Though faith does not bring itself about, and though what is revealed through faith can never be founded by way of a rational knowing as exercised by the autonomously functioning reason, nevertheless the sense of the Christian occurrence of rebirth is that one's pre-faith-full, i.e., unbelieving, human existence is sublated *(aufgehoben)* therein.[8] Sublated does not mean done away with, but raised up, kept, and preserved in the new creation. One's pre-Christian existence is indeed existentielly, ontically, overcome in faith. But this factual overcoming of one's pre-Christian existence (which is the sense of faith as rebirth) means precisely that one's overcome pre-Christian existence is ontologically included within faith-full existence. To overcome does not mean to dispose of, but to have at one's disposition in a new way. Hence we can say that precisely because all basic theological concepts, considered in their full regional context, include meanings which are existentielly (factually) powerless, i.e., *ontically* sublated *(aufgehoben)*, they have as their *ontological* determinants meanings which are pre-Christian and which can thus be grasped purely rationally.

All theological concepts necessarily contain that understanding of Being which is constitutive of human Dasein, insofar as it exists at all.[9] Thus, for example, sin is manifest only through faith, and only the believer can factually exist as a sinner. But if sin, which is the phenomenon contrary to faith as rebirth and hence a phenomenon of existence, is to be interpreted in theological concepts, then the *content itself* of the concept, and not just any philosophical preference of the theologian, calls for a return to the concept of guilt. And guilt is an original ontological determination of Dasein.[10] The more radically and appropriately the basic constitution of human existence is brought to light in terms of genuine ontology, e.g., the more the concept of guilt is grasped in its origin, the more clearly can it function as a guide for the theological explication of sin.

But if one takes the ontological concept of guilt for a guide, then it seems that it is primarily philosophy which decides about theological concepts. And, then, is not theology being led on the leash by philosophy? Not at all. For sin, in its essence, is not to be deduced rationally from the concept of guilt. Even less so should or can the basic fact of sin be rationally demonstrated, no matter how it is approached, by way of this orientation to the ontological concept of guilt. Not even the factual possibility of sin is in the least bit evidenced in this way. Only one thing is accomplished by this orientation; but that one thing is indispensable for theology as a science: The theological concept of sin as a concept of existence acquires that correction (i.e., co-direction) which is necessary for it insofar as the existential concept has pre-Christian meanings. But the primary direction (derivation), the source of its Christian meaning, is given only by faith. *Therefore ontology functions only as a corrective to the ontic, and in particular pre-Christian, meanings of basic theological concepts.*

Here one must note that this correction does not found anything, in the way, for example, that the basic concepts of physics acquire from an ontology of nature their original foundation, the demonstration of all their inner possibilities, and hence the full range of their truth. Rather, this correction only formally points out; that is to say, the ontological concept of guilt as such is never a theme of theology. Also the concept of sin is not simply built up from the ontological concept of guilt. Nevertheless, the latter is determining in one respect, in that it formally points out the ontological character of *the* region of Being to which the concept of sin as a *concept of existence* must necessarily adhere.

In formally pointing out the ontological region, there lies the directive not to construct philosophically the specific theological content of the concept but rather to allow it to arise out of and within the specific existential dimension of faith which was pointed out. Thus formally pointing out the ontological concept does not serve to bind but, on the contrary, to release and point to the specific credal source of the disclosure of theological concepts. The function of ontology here is not to direct, but only, in "co-directing," to correct.

*Philosophy is the ontological corrective formally pointing out the ontic and, in particular, the pre-Christian content of basic theological concepts.*

But it is not of the essence of philosophy, and it can never be established by philosophy itself or for its own purpose, that it must have such a corrective function for theology. On the other hand, it can be shown that philosophy, as the free questioning of purely self-reliant human existence, does of its essence have the task of directing all other nontheological, positive sciences to their ontological foundation. As ontology, philosophy does provide the possibility of being employed by theology as a corrective, in the sense we have discussed, if indeed theology is to be factual with respect to the facticity of faith. The demand, however, that it *must* be so employed is not made by philosophy as such but rather by theology, insofar as it understands itself to be a science. In summary, then, the precise formulation is:

*Philosophy is the possible ontological corrective which can formally point out the ontic and, in particular, the pre-Christian content of basic theological concepts. But philosophy can be what it is without functioning factually as this corrective.*

This peculiar relationship does not overlook but rather takes into account the reminder that *faith,* as a specific possibility of existence, is in its innermost core the mortal enemy of the *form of existence* which is an essential part of *philosophy* and which in fact is ever-changing.[11] Faith is so absolutely the mortal enemy that philosophy does not even begin to want in any way to do battle with it. This factual *existentiell opposition* between faithfulness and a human's free appropriation of his whole existence is not first brought about by the sciences of theology and philosophy but is *prior* to them. Furthermore, it is precisely this *opposition* which must bear the *possibility of a community of the sciences* of theology and philosophy, if indeed they are to communicate in a genuine way, free from illusions and weak attempts at mediation. Accordingly, there is no such thing as a Christian philosophy; that is an absolute "square circle." On the other hand, there is likewise no such thing as a neo-Kantian, or axiological, or phenomenological theology, just as there is no phenomenological mathematics. Phenomenology is always the name for the procedure of ontology, which essentially distinguishes itself from all other, positive sciences.

It is true that someone engaged in research can master, in addition to his own positive science, phenomenology as well, or at least follow its steps and investigations. But philosophical knowledge can become genuinely relevant and fertile for his own positive science *only when,* within the problematic which stems from deliberation on the ontic correlations in his area, he comes upon the basic traditional concepts and, furthermore, questions their suitability for that which is made the theme of his science. Then, proceeding from the demands of his science and from the horizon of his own scientific inquiry, which lies, so to speak, on the frontiers of his basic concepts, he can search back for the original ontological constitution of that which is to remain and become *anew* the object of his science. The questions which arise in this way methodically thrust beyond themselves insofar as that about which they are asking is accessible and determinable only through ontology. To be sure, scientific communication between positive scientists and philosophers cannot be tied down to definite rules, especially since the clarity, certainty, and originality of critiques by scientists of the foundations of their own positive sciences change as often and are as varied as the stage reached and maintained by philosophy in clarifying its own essence. This communication stays genuine, lively, and fruitful only when the respective positive-ontic and transcendental-ontological inquiries are guided by an instinct for the issues and by the certainty of scientific good sense, and when all the questions about dominance, pre-eminence and validity recede behind the inner necessities of the scientific problem itself.

# The Theological Discussion of "The Problem of a Non-Objectifying Thinking and Speaking in Today's Theology"— Some Pointers to Its Major Aspects[1]

What is it that is worth questioning in this problem? As far as I see, there are *three themes* which must be thought through.

1. Above all else one must determine *what* theology, as a mode of thinking and speaking, is to place in discussion. That is the Christian faith, and what is believed therein. Only if this is kept clearly in view can one inquire how thinking and speaking are to be formulated so that together they correspond to the proper sense and claim of faith and thus avoid projecting into faith ideas which are alien to it.[2]

2. Prior to a discussion of *non*-objectifying thinking and speaking, it is ineluctable that one state what is intended by *objectifying* thinking and speaking. Here the question arises whether or not all thinking and speaking are objectifying by their very nature. Should it prove evident that thinking and speaking are by no means in themselves already objectifying, then this leads to a third theme.

3. One must decide to what extent the problem of a non-objectifying thinking and speaking is a genuine problem at all, whether one is not inquiring here about something in such a way that only circumvents the matter, diverts from the theme of theology and unnecessarily confounds it. In this case the convened theological dialogue would have the task of clearly seeing that it was on a path leading nowhere. This would—so it seems—be only a negative result of the dialogue. But it only seems that way. For in truth this would necessitate that theol-

ogy once and for all get clear about the requisite of its major task not to borrow the categories of its thinking and the form of its speech from philosophy or the sciences, but to think and speak out of faith for faith with fidelity to its subject matter. If this faith by the power of its own conviction concerns man as man in his very nature, then genuine theological thinking and speaking have no need of a special accruement to reach people and find a hearing among them.

These three themes have to be placed in discussion in more detail. I for my part, proceeding from philosophy, can only give some pointers with regard to the second topic. For it is the task of theology to place in discussion the first theme, which necessarily underlies the entire dialogue if it is not to remain up in the air.

The third theme comprises the theological consequences of the first and second, when they are treated sufficiently.

I shall now attempt to give some pointers for treating the *second* theme—but this again only in the form of a few questions. One should avoid the impression that dogmatic theses are being stated in terms of a Heideggerian philosophy, when there is no such thing.

## SOME POINTERS WITH REGARD TO THE SECOND THEME

Prior to placing in discussion the question of a *non*-objectifying thinking and speaking in theology, it is necessary to reflect on what one understands by an *objectifying* thinking and speaking, as this problem has been put to the theological dialogue. This reflection necessitates that we ask:

Is objectifying thinking and speaking a particular kind of thinking and speaking, or does all thinking as thinking, all speaking as speaking, necessarily have to be objectifying?

This question can be decided only if beforehand the following questions are clarified and answered:

*(a)* What does objectifying mean?
*(b)* What does thinking mean?
*(c)* What does speaking mean?

(d) Is all thinking in itself a speaking, and all speaking in itself a thinking?

(e) In what sense are thinking and speaking objectifying, and in what sense are they not?

It is of the nature of the matter that these questions interpenetrate when we place them in discussion. The entire weight of these questions, however, lies at the basis of the problem of your theological dialogue. Moreover, these same questions—more or less clearly and adequately developed—form the still hidden center of those endeavors toward which the "philosophy" of our day, from its most extreme counter-positions (Carnap ⟶ Heidegger), tends. One calls these positions today: the technical-scientistic view of language and the speculative-hermeneutical experience of language.

Both positions are determined by tasks profoundly different from one another. The first position desires to subjugate all thinking and speaking to a sign-system which can be constructed logically or technically, that is, to secure them as an instrument of science. The other position has arisen from the question: what is it that is to be experienced as the proper matter of philosophical thinking, and how is this matter (Being as Being) to be said?[3]

Hence neither position is concerned with a philosophy of language as a separate province (in the way we have a philosophy of nature or of art). Rather, both positions recognize language as the realm within which the thinking of philosophy and every kind of thinking and saying move and repose. Insofar as the Western tradition has tended to determine the nature of man as that living being which "has language," as *zoon logon echon* (even man as an acting being is such only as one that "has language"), the debate between the two positions has nothing less at stake than the question of man's existence and its determination.

It is up to theology to decide in what manner and to what extent it can and should enter into this debate.

We preface the following brief elucidation of questions (a) to (e) with a remark that presumably led to the occasion for proposing the "problem of a non-objectifying thinking and speaking in today's theology." I mean the widespread, uncritically accepted opinion that all thinking, as representing, and all speaking, as vocalization, are already "objectifying." It is not possible here to trace this opinion in detail back to its origins. The determining factor has been the distinction, set forth in an unclarified manner long ago, between the rational and irrational. This distinction in turn is brought to bear in the jurisdiction of a reasonable but itself unclarified thinking.

Recently, however, the teachings of Nietzsche, Bergson, and the "life-philosophers" set the standard for the claim of the objectifying character of all thinking and speaking. To the extent that, in speaking, we say "is" everywhere, expressly or not, when Being means presence, which in modern times has been interpreted as objectivity—to that extent thinking as re-presenting and speaking as vocalization have inevitably served to solidify the "life-stream" flowing in itself, and thus to falsify it.[4] On the other hand, such a consolidation of what is permanent, even though it falsifies, is indispensable for the preservation and continuance of human life. The following text from Nietzsche's *Will to Power,* no. 715 (1887/88), may suffice to document this variously modified opinion: "The means of expression in language cannot be used to express 'becoming'; to posit continually a more crude world of what is permanent, of things etc. (i.e. of objects) is part of our *irredeemable need for preservation.*"

The following pointers to questions *(a)* through *(e)* are themselves to be understood and thought through as questions. For the phenomenon most worthy of thought and questioning remains the mystery of language—wherein our entire reflection has to gather itself—above all when it dawns on us that language is not a work of human beings: language speaks. Humans speak only insofar as they co-respond to language. These statements are not the offspring of some fantastic "mysticism." Language is a primal phenomenon whose *proprium* is not amenable to factual proof but can be caught sight of only in an unprejudiced experience of language. Humans may be able to invent artificial speech constructions and signs, but they are able to do so only in reference to and in terms of an already spoken language. Thinking remains critical also with respect to primal phenomena. For to think critically means to distinguish *(krinein)* constantly between that which requires proof for its justification and that which, to confirm its truth, demands a simple catching sight of and taking in. It is invariably easier to set forth a proof in a given case than, in a differently presented case, to venture into catching sight of and holding in view.[5]

*(a)* What does it mean to objectify? To make an object of something, to posit it as object and represent it only as such. And what does object mean? In the Middle Ages *obiectum* signified that which is thrown before, held against our perceiving, imagination, judging, wishing, and intuiting. *Subiectum,* on the other hand, signified the *hypokeimenon,* that which lies present before us from out of itself (and not brought before us by representation), whatever is present, e.g., things. The signification of the words *subiectum* and *obiectum* is precisely the reverse of what subject and object usually mean today: *subiectum* is what exists for itself (objectively), and *obiectum* is what is merely (subjectively) represented.

As a consequence of Descartes' reformulation of the concept of *subiectum* (cf. *Holzwege,* p. 98 ff.), the concept of object *(Objekt)* also ends up with a changed signification. For Kant object means what exists as standing-over-against *(Gegenstand)* the experience of the natural sciences. Every object stands over against, but not everything standing-over-against (e.g. the thing-in-itself) is a possible object. The categorical imperative, moral obligation, and duty are not objects of natural-scientific experience. When they are thought about, when they are intended in our actions, they are not thereby objectified.

Our everyday experience of things, in the widest sense of the word, is neither objectifying nor a placing-over-against. When, for example, we sit in the garden and take delight in a blossoming rose, we do not make an object of the rose, do not even make it something standing-over-against, i.e. something represented thematically. When in tacit saying *(Sagen)* we are enthralled with the lucid red of the rose and muse on the redness of the rose, then this redness is neither an object, nor a thing, nor a standing-over-against like the blossoming rose. The rose stands in the garden, sways perhaps to and fro in the wind. But the redness of the rose neither stands in the garden, nor can it sway to and fro in the wind. All the same we think it and say of it by naming it. There is accordingly a thinking and saying that in no manner objectifies or places-over-against.[6]

The statue of Apollo in the museum at Olympia we can indeed regard as an object of natural-scientific representation; we can calculate the physical weight of the marble; we can investigate its chemical composition. But this objectifying thinking and speaking does not catch sight of the Apollo who shows forth his beauty and so appears as the visage of the god.

(b) What does it mean to think? If we heed what has just been set forth, it will be clear that thinking and speaking are not exhausted by theoretical and natural-scientific representation and statement. Thinking rather is that comportment which lets itself be given, by whatever shows itself however it shows itself, what it has to say of that which appears. Thinking is not necessarily a representing of something as an object. Only the thinking and speaking of the natural sciences is objectifying. If all thinking as such were objectifying, then it would be meaningless to fashion works of art, for they could never show themselves to anyone: one would immediately make an object of that which appears and thus would prevent the art work from appearing.

The assertion that all thinking as thinking is objectifying is without foundation. It rests on a disregard of phenomena and belies a lack of critique.

(c) What does it mean to speak? Does speaking consist only in the fact that it converts thoughts into vocables, which one then perceives only as vowels and consonants that can be identified objectively? Or is the vocalization of speech (in a conversation) something entirely different from a series of acoustically objectifiable sounds furnished with a signification by means of which objects are spoken about. Is not speaking, in what is most proper to it, a saying, a manifold showing[7] of that which hearing, i.e. heeding what appears, lets be said?

Can one, if we keep only this carefully in view, still assert uncritically that speaking, as speaking, is always objectifying? When we speak condolence to a sick person and speak to him heart to heart, do we make an object of this person? Is language only an instrument that we employ to manipulate objects? Is language at all within the human being's power of disposal? Is language only a work of humans? Or is it language which "has" human beings, insofar as they belong to, pay heed to language, which opens up world to them and at the same time thereby their dwelling in the world?

(d) Is all thinking a form of speaking and all speaking a form of thinking? The questions placed in discussion up to now direct us to surmise that thinking and speaking belong together (form an identity).[8] This identity was testified to long ago, insofar as *logos* and *legein* simultaneously signify talking and thinking. But this identity has still not been adequately placed in discussion and commensurately experienced. One principal hindrance is concealed in the fact that the Greek explication of language, that is to say the grammatical interpretation, is oriented to stating something about things. Later, modern metaphysics re-interpreted things to mean objects. This suggested the erroneous opinion that thinking and speaking refer to objects and only to objects.

If, on the other hand, we keep in view the decisive matter at stake, namely that thinking is in each case a letting be said of what shows itself, and accordingly a co-responding (saying) to that which shows itself, then it will become evident to what extent poetizing too is a pensive saying. And the proper nature of this saying, it will be admitted, cannot be determined by means of the traditional logic of statements about objects.

It is this insight into the interrelation of thinking and saying which lets us see that the thesis—thinking and speaking as such necessarily objectify—is untenable and arbitrary.

(e) In what sense do thinking and speaking objectify, and in what sense do they not? Thinking and speaking objectify, i.e., posit as an object something given, in the field of natural-scientific and technical representation. Here they are of necessity objectifying, because scientific-technological knowing must establish its theme in advance as a calculable, causally explicable *Gegenstand,* i.e., as an object as Kant defined the word. Outside this field thinking and speaking are by no means objectifying.

But today there is a growing danger that the scientific-technological manner of thinking will spread to all realms of life. And this magnifies the deceptive appearance which makes all thinking and speaking seem objectifying. The thesis that asserts this dogmatically and without foundation promotes and supports for its part a portentous tendency: to represent everything henceforth only technologically-scientifically as an object of possible control and manipulation. This process of unrestrained technological objectification naturally also affects language itself and its determination. Language is deformed into an instrument of reportage and calculable information. It is treated like a manipulatable object, to which our manner of thinking must conform. And yet the saying of language is not necessarily an expressing of propositions *about* objects. Language, in what is most proper to it, is a saying *of* that which reveals itself to human beings in manifold ways and which speaks to human beings insofar as they do not, under the dominion of objectifying thinking, confine themselves to it and close themselves off from what shows itself.

That thinking and speaking are objectifying only in a derivative and limited sense can never be deduced by way of scientific proof. Insight into the proper nature of thinking and saying comes only by holding phenomena in view without prejudice.

Hence it just might be erroneous to suppose that only that which can be objectively calculated and proven technically-scientifically as an object is capable of admitting Being.

This erroneous opinion is oblivious of something said long ago that Aristotle wrote down: *esti gar apaideusia to me gignoskein tinon dei chetein apodeixin kai tinon ou dei.* ". . . for not to know of what things one should demand demonstration, and of what one should not, argues want of education" (Meta. 1006a6 ff.; W. D. Ross's translation).

Now that we have given these pointers we may turn to the third theme—the decision whether and to what extent the theme of the dialogue is a genuine problem—and say the following:

On the basis of the deliberations on the *second* theme, the problem put by the dialogue must be expressed less equivocally. It must, in a purposely pointed formulation, read: "The problem of a non-technological, natural-scientific thinking and speaking in today's theology." From this more commensurate reformulation, it is very clear that the problem as stated is not a genuine problem insofar as it is geared to a presupposition whose nonsense is evident to anyone. Theology is not a natural science.

Yet the problem as stated conceals the positive task for theology. That task is for theology to place in discussion, within its own realm of the Christian faith and out of the proper nature of that faith, what it is to think and how it is to speak. This task also includes the question whether theology can still be a science—because presumably it should not be a science at all.

## ADDITION TO THE POINTERS

An example of an outstanding non-objectifying thinking and speaking is poetry.

In the third of the *Sonnets to Orpheus,* Rilke says in poetic speech by what means poetic thinking and saying is determined. "Gesang ist Dasein"—"Song is Existence" (cf. *Holzwege,* p. 292 ff.). Song, the singing saying of the poet, is "not coveting," "not soliciting" that which is ultimately accomplished by humans as an effect.

Poetic saying is "Dasein," Existence. This word, "Dasein," is used here in the traditional metaphysical sense. It signifies: Presence.

Poetic thinking is being in the presence of . . . and for the god. Presence means: simple willingness that wills nothing, counts on no successful outcome. Being in the presence of . . . : purely letting be said the god's presence.

Such saying does not posit and represent anything as standing-over-against or as object. There is nothing here which could be placed before a grasping or comprehending representation.

"A breath for nothing."[9] "Breath" stands for a breathing in and out, for a letting be said that responds to the word given us. There is no need for an extensive discussion to show that underlying the question of a thinking and saying commensurate to the matter at stake is the question of the Being of whatever is and shows itself.

Being as Presence can show itself in various modes of being present. What is present does not have to stand-over-against; what stands-over-against does not have to be empirically perceived as an object. [Cf. Heidegger, *Neitzsche,* vol. II, sections VIII and IX.]

# Review of Ernst Cassirer's
# Mythical Thought[1]

This volume of Cassirer's major work is dedicated to the memory of Paul Natorp. The title, *Mythical Thought,* could mislead
the reader into thinking that the dominant theme of the investigation was the differentiation of mythic thought operations
from the purely logical ones. Instead of this, however, the non-
autonomy of mythic "thought" as an "operation of the understanding" is to be shown by the demonstration that it is
grounded in a specific "form of life" together with an appropriate "form of intuition." "Thought" here means to include all
forms of attending to something *("Sinnen und Trachten"),*
each of which, of course, have their own "form of thought" (i.e.,
manner of interpretation and specification). The intention of
the investigation, consequently, is to pursue the disclosure of
"myth" as a unique possibility of human Dasein which has its
own kind of truth. By posing the question in this manner Cassirer explicitly takes over the view of Schelling that "everything in mythology is to be understood as myth expresses it, not
as if something else were thought or something else were said"
*(Einleitung in die Philosophie der Mythologie,* S.W. 2. I, p. 195).
Myth, "the destiny of a people" (Schelling), is an "objective
process" to which Dasein itself is subjected, against which it
can become free, but never in such a way that it can dispense
with it. Although Cassirer clings to the basic view of Schelling
that in myth there is "no defect of spirit," that it is not a mere
appearance but rather has its own "formative power," never-

theless he considers the task of a philosophy of myth to be quite different from the speculative metaphysics of Schelling. But, of course, neither is an empirical-psychological "explanation" of myth ever able to achieve a philosophical understanding. Cassirer attempts, therefore, a "phenomenology of mythic consciousness," along with maintaining the "objectivity" of myth and rejecting the merely psychological interpretation. This is regarded as an expansion of the transcendental problematic as understood by neo-Kantianism, namely, to grasp the unity of "culture," and not only "nature," as the law-structure *(Gesetzlichkeit)* of spirit. The "objectivity" of myth lies in its properly-understood "subjectivity"; it is a unique spiritual "creative principle of world-formation" (p. 14).

In accordance with this position, which is given in the Introduction, Cassirer gives an interpretation of myth as a "form of thought" (Section I, pp. 27–70), as a "form of intuition" (Section II, pp. 71–152), as a "form of life" (Section III, pp. 153–232), and concludes everything with a characterization of "The Dialectic of Mythic Consciousness" (Section IV, pp. 233–261).

The analysis of the mythic form of thought begins with a general description of the way in which objects stand over against mythic consciousness. The object-consciousness of mathematical physics as understood by the Kantian interpretation of Hermann Cohen serves as a guide to the characterization: There is an active forming of a passively given "chaos of sensation" into a "cosmos." A basic feature of the mythic object-consciousness is the absence of a clear delineation between dreaming and waking experiences, between the imagined and the perceived, between the original and the copy, between word (signification) and thing, between wished-for and actual possession, between living and dead. Everything is on the equal ontological footing of the immediately present with which mythic Dasein is captivated. This object-consciousness lays claim to having an "explanation" and an "understanding" which are proper and adequate to it. The co-presence of something with something else "provides" the explanation: The swallow makes the summer. This phenomenon of "accompaniment" has the character of magical power. (See below.) What functions as "accompanist" is not just anything at all but is rather determined by the guiding context of the magical experience. As capricious as these magical "reality contexts" may seem, e.g., for a theoretical consideration of nature, they nevertheless have their own truth. Mythic thought knows nothing of the analytical break-down of the real into series of causes. The interwovenness of magical reality is clearly seen in the understanding of the relationship of the whole and the part. The part "is" the whole itself, i.e., it has its magical power unimpaired. Each "thing" within the totality of magical powers bears within itself its membership with the others. In mythic thought "the law of the concrescence or coincidence of members of relations" is valid (p. 64).

In the second section Cassirer shows the effect of this form of thought on the understanding of space, time, and number. A chapter with the title "The Basic Opposition" (pp. 73–82) precedes this "Theory of the Forms of Myth." Already the discussions of the characteristics of mythic object-consciousness showed how mythic Dasein is seized by, fascinated with, and overcome by what is present. Presence directly involves an overpowering. And in this is found the note of the extraordinary, i.e., the incomparable in contrast to what is everyday. But the everyday is not a *nihil negativum.* It has its own characteristic of being, i.e., its character of being common within the horizon of an overpowering uncommonness. This "primordial division" of holy and profane is the basic articulation of the real to which mythic Dasein "relates," regardless of the meaning-content of the being. This ontological characteristic of the mythic "world" and of mythic Dasein itself is the meaning of the mana-representation. The mana-representation has, in research in mythology during the recent decades, come forth with increasing clarity as one of the basic categories, if not *the* basic category, of mythic "thought." Mana does not signify a definite circle of objects. Nor does it admit of being a certain kind of "spiritual" power. Mana is the most general ontological characteristic, the "how" or the manner in which the real seizes upon human Dasein. The expressions "mana," "wakanda," "orenda," "manitu," are interjections in the immediate state of being overtaken by that which is insistently crowding against (pp. 76 ff., 158 ff., and 185). [See also E. Cassirer, *Lan-*

*guage and Myth,* trans. by Susanne Langer (New York: Dover & Harper, 1946), where a still more lucid interpretation of the notion of mana is given in connection with the problem of language.]

In the original captivation by the mana-reality, mythic Dasein realizes the articulation in which Dasein as such always moves, namely the interpretation and "determination" of space, time, and number. The specific mythic modalities entailed by these "representations" are also characterized by the author by means of distinguishing these phenomena from the conceptual interpretation which these phenomena have enjoyed in contemporary mathematical-physical theory.

The "basic feeling of the holy" and the accompanying "primordial division" mark out the basic sense of space as well as the kind of individual setting of limits within this basic sense of space. The original division of space, in which space is first of all disclosed, distinguishes two "regions": a "holy" region, which is singled out, correspondingly cared for and protected, and a "common" region, which is available at all times to everyone. Space is never given beforehand "in itself" in order then to be mythically "construed." Rather, mythic Dasein discovers "space itself" first of all in the above-mentioned manner. Thereby is the mythic spatial orientation everywhere guided by the opposition of day and night, which, in turn, discloses itself primarily in a mythic fashion, i.e., this opposition brings under its spell all Dasein by reason of the unique power of mana. Insofar as this uncovered spatiality codetermines the possible abode of Dasein, space, however it is factually divided, can be seen to fall into a schema of the most variegated relationships of Dasein. (Consider, for example, the intricate arrangement of classes involved in the totemic mode of perception.) Mythic Dasein thereby creates for itself a total orientation which is uniform and easily managed.

Time is a still more original constituting factor for mythic Dasein than is space. With this characterization, Cassirer provides a foundation for the popular notion of time and understands the "temporal" property of myth to be a "being in the time (era)," e.g., of the gods. The "holiness" of the mythic real is determined by its origin. The past as such shows itself to be the genuine and ultimate Why of all beings. In the periodic recurrence of the seasons and in the rhythm of phases and stages of life the power of time discloses itself. The individual segments of time are "holy times." The behavior toward them is far removed from any mere reckoning of time; rather, it is regulated by specific cults and rites (e.g., initiation rites). The ordering of time is, as the ordering of destiny, a cosmic power and reveals in its orderliness a permeating obligation which binds all human deeds. The regulations by the calendar and by moral obligations are fused in the power of time. The fundamental mythic-religious relationship to time can accentuate a single temporal direction. The variations of the different feelings for time and the corresponding indications of conceptions of time account for "one of the profoundest differences in the character of individual religions." Cassirer shows (pp. 119 ff.) the main features of the typical views of time among the Hebrews, Persians, Indians, Chinese, and Egyptians as well as in Greek philosophy.

Even the numbers and the relationships of numbers are, in mythic Dasein, understood from out of the basic characteristic of everything which in any way is, i.e., from out of the power of mana. Every number has its "individual physiognomy," its own magic power. Sameness of number, regardless of content, is regarded as one and the same thing, according to the "principle of concrescence." "All magic is in large part number magic" (p. 144). Numerical specification does not mean classification in a series but rather membership in a definite power-region of the extraordinary. The number is the mediatrix which joins together the totality of mythic reality in the unity of a power-full world order. Even though mythic doctrines of numbers are quite varied and even though the mythic preference for individual numbers (e.g., three, seven) is not everywhere uniform, nevertheless certain original designations for the holiness of special numbers can be shown to derive from the fundamental structure of the particular mythic spatiality and temporality. For example, the holiness of four can be shown to be related to the four directions of the sky. Also the holiness of the number seven goes back to the powerfulness of time disclosed in the phases of the moon. This phenomenon leads also to the divisions into the quarters of the twenty-eight day month. In the mythic preference for the number three, on the other hand, the original personal relationship of father, mother, and child shows itself, just as in language the dual and trial forms refer back to the relationship of I, you, and he. These are originally powerful relations, the number character of which remains still completely caught in the web of mythic efficaciousness.

From the analysis of the mythic world of objects, from the manner of its disclosure and specification, the inquiry turns to "subjective reality" and its disclosure in mythic existence. Cassirer begins this discussion with a fundamental and pertinent criticism of "animism," a concept which still dominates in the most diverse ways ethnological investigations. The world of mythic Dasein cannot be simply construed out of the prevailing notions of the soul. The reason, first of all, is that the "subject" as such remains concealed. But insofar as mythic Dasein is at all known to itself, it is not interpreted on the basis of a thing-like version of the world. Mythic Dasein understands both object and subject and their relationship to one another within the horizon of that which announces itself as having the character of the real, that is, in terms of mana. And it is a question here of showing how mythic Dasein, which in its "indefinite feeling for life" remains bound to everything which is, realizes a "confrontation" between world and I which is proper to its own specific mode of being, i.e., rooted in its "doing." The region of the real primarily disclosed and delineated in doing reveals by way of a peculiar reflexivity that doing itself is invested with various "capabilities." Within the horizon of the magical power one's own doing is also a magical effecting. "The first energy by which man places himself as uniquely his own self and as autonomous in opposition to things is the force of desire" (p. 157). "The fullness of the forms of the gods which he creates for himself not only guides him through the sphere of objective being and events but above all leads him through the sphere of his own will and accomplishment and illuminates this sphere from within" (p. 203). The further process of the disclosure of "subjectivity" and its comportments is realized in the transition from the nature myths to the culture myths, to, finally, the stage of the manipulation of tools, which is more or less free from magic. At this stage of the process the ontological context of things by itself becomes manifest as more independent in that man frees himself from magical bondage to the things and, by stepping back from the world, it is possible for him to meet things "objectively."

Consequently, as it is not the case that the subject discovers himself in a pure going out and return from things which are simply standing over-against him, so it is not the case that an articulated I-Thou relationship or some particular form of society is primarily constitutive for the disclosure of subjectivity. Totemism, which is often falsely set forth as the basic phenomenon of mythic Dasein, does not admit of being sociologically explained. Rather, all social structures, the individuals given with the structures, and totemism itself as well stand in need of a "founding" in the original manner of being of mythic Dasein and the view of mana dominating it. The real problem of totemism is that not only man and animals or, as the case may be, plants in general, stand in certain interweaving relationships but also special groups have their special totemic animal. Farmers, shepherds, and hunters have their own proper dependence upon plants and animals which manifests itself immediately as a magical relationship. But at the same time, by means of the above mentioned reflexivity, this relationship to plants and animals makes possible the explicit realization of the pertinent sphere of human life as such. Totemism is not occasioned by special kinds of plants and animals but originates out of the elementary relationships of man to his world.

Only when we take as the basis the mana-representation can we grasp how the individual self-consciousness is developed and how the "concept" of the soul comes to be articulated. What are later distinguished as body and soul, life and death, are indeed for mythic Dasein also always already real, but they are real in the mode of magic power according to which the deceased also *is* and manifests a spiritual power even though the person in question can no longer be bodily encountered. Precisely within the unity of magical efficacy can the individual powers of the soul or "souls" come forth as separated and live along side one another. Correspondingly the "development" of an individual Dasein is distributed among various subjects, among whom specific transitional phases occur. In the situation of oppression by a magical power, Dasein's "own" soul can stand in opposition as an "alien" power. Also in the case where the notion of protective spirits is alive, one's own self is, as it were, still a power which takes care of the individual I. Not until higher stages are reached does the magic demon become *daimonion* and genius so that finally Dasein is no longer determined by an alien power but by what it itself is able to do freely by itself for itself as a moral subject.

If the powerfulness and uncommonness of the divine primarily and thoroughly dominate mythic Dasein, then the basic posture toward reality can never be a mere looking on but it likewise must initiate activity which unfolds as cult and rite. All mythic narrative is always a supplementary account of sacred actions. In sacred actions, on the other hand, mythic Dasein presents itself in immediacy. The earlier a cult develops the more does sacrifice move into the center position. Sacrifice is indeed a renunciation, but at the same time it is a self-performed action which prepares the way for a certain release from the exclusive power of the magical forces. Herein is disclosed the free power of Dasein, and at the same time the gap between man and God is widened in order to require a renewed overcoming on a higher level.

Thus it becomes evident that myth is a unified formative force with its own laws. Mythic forms disclose an inner dialectic in which earlier forms are developed and transformed but not simply cast away. The mythic "process" is realized in Dasein without reflection. When this process has run its course it becomes eventually mature enough for its own self-conquest. Cassirer attempts to show this dialectic in the various attitudes which myth itself takes toward its own picture of the world (pp. 235 ff.).

——————

This present brief account must forego a discussion of the rich ethnological sources and material from the history of reli-

gions upon which Cassirer bases his interpretation and which
he brings into his analysis with his unique gift for a lucid and
adroit presentation. The Warburg Library in Hamburg provided the author, with its abundant and rare collection as well
as its general facilities, an extraordinary aid in the research
(Foreword, p. xviii). From among the analyses of mythic
phenomena we may especially call attention to the function of
the tool in the disclosure of the world of objects (pp. 212 ff.) and
the function of sacrifice (pp. 221 ff.).

The position we take toward the above characterized philosophy of myth must arise from three considerations. First, we
must ask, what does this interpretation achieve for the foundation and direction of the positive sciences of mythic Dasein
(ethnology and the history of religions)? Then there must be an
examination of the foundations and methodological principles
upon which rests the philosophical essence-analysis of myth.[2]
Finally the basic question arises concerning the constitutive
function of myth in human Dasein and in the totality of whatever is.

As for the first question, Cassirer's work is manifestly a valuable achievement. It brings the problematic of the positive
investigation of myth to a basically higher level through the
manifoldly executed demonstration that myth does not admit
of being "explained" by a reduction to a definite sphere of objects within the mythic world. The criticism directed against
naturalistic, totemistic, animistic, and sociological attempts at
explanation is everywhere clear and penetrating. The critique
is founded on an anticipatory specification of myth as an autonomously legislative form of the functioning of spirit. If this
understanding of myth can assert itself in empirical research,
a safe guide is thereby gained for the initial acquisition and
interpretation of freshly discovered material as well as for the
digestion and penetration of results already acquired.

However, if this present interpretation of myth is to be judged
not only with respect to its function as a guide for the positive
sciences but also with respect to its own philosophic content,
then the following questions arise: Is the pre-specification of
myth as a kind of functioning of the formative consciousness
adequately based? Wherein lie the foundations of this admit-

tedly ineluctable base? Are these foundations themselves satis-
factorily established and worked out? Cassirer's founding of his
guiding pre-specification of myth as a formative force of the
spirit ("symbolic form") is essentially an appeal to Kant's
"Copernican turn," according to which all "reality" is to be
regarded as a structure of formative consciousness.

First of all, it can, with good reasons, be doubted whether
Cassirer's interpretation, and in general the neo-Kantian epistemological interpretation, of what Kant means by the "Copernican turn" gets at the center of the transcendental problematic as an ontological problematic in its essential possibilities.[3]
But leaving that aside, does the critique of pure reason admit
to being simply "expanded" to a "critique of culture"? Is it so
certain, or rather is it not highly questionable, whether the
foundations for Kant's very own transcendental interpretation
of "nature" have been explicitly disclosed and founded? What
about the unavoidable and omnipresent task of working out the
ontological understanding and mode of being of that which,
indefinitely enough, is sometimes called "consciousness,"
sometimes "life," sometimes "spirit," sometimes "reason"? But
still before all questions about a possible leaning on Kant in the
sense of an "expanding" of his problem, it is important first to
clarify the basic and pressing problems which the position of
myth, as a form of functioning of "spirit," contains in itself.
Only from the vantage point of this consideration can it be
decided whether and how far such an appropriation of the
Kantian questions, or, as the case may be, of the schemata, is
intrinsically possible and justified.

The interpretation of the essence of myth as a possibility of
human Dasein remains accidental and directionless as long as
it is not founded on a radical ontology of Dasein in the light of
the problem of Being in general. The basic problem arising in
this context cannot be discussed here. It may be enough, by way
of an immanent critique of the Cassirerian interpretation of
myth, to make evident the ineluctability of some of the chief
problems and thereby to provide philosophical precision and
clarification of the task which Cassirer has set for himself.
Cassirer himself emphasizes that his investigation is "merely
a first beginning" (p. xviii).

The neo-Kantian orientation to the problem of consciousness is so disadvantageous that it, in fact, hinders a firm footing at the center of the problem. The layout of the book already shows this. Instead of placing the interpretation of mythic Dasein in a central setting of the ontological constitution of this being, Cassirer begins with an analysis of the mythic object-consciousness, its form of thought and form of intuition. Of course Cassirer sees with full clarity that the form of thought and the form of intuition must be pursued back to the mythic "form of life" as the "spiritual-primordial level" (pp. 69 ff.). However, the explicit and systematic elucidation of the origin of the forms of thought and intuition out of the "form of life" is not carried through. The indefiniteness of the systematic place of the representation of mana, to which Cassirer repeatedly returns when dealing with all essential mythic phenomena, shows that these original connections remain in the dark, that indeed the problem of the possible intrinsic connection of form of life, form of intuition, and form of thought is not posed. The representation of mana is not treated among the forms of thought, nor is it shown to be a form of intuition. It is thematically discussed in the transition from the form of thought to the form of intuition under the title of "The Basic Opposition"—which expresses more an embarrassment rather than presenting a structural determination of this "representation" which derives from the structural whole of mythic Dasein. At the same time, however, the mana-representation is referred to as a "fundamental form of thought." Cassirer's analysis of the mana-representation remains, of course, important when contrasted with the customary interpretations insofar as he understands mana not as a being among other beings but as the "how" of all the mythic real, i.e., as the Being of beings. But now there arises the central problem inasmuch as it must be asked: Is this fundamental "representation" in mythic Dasein simply present before us *(vorhanden)*, or does it belong to the ontological constitution of mythic Dasein? And, if the latter, as what? In the mana-representation there is disclosed nothing other than that understanding of Being which belongs to Dasein as such but which is specifically modified according to the basic mode of being of Dasein—in this case mythic Dasein—and which anticipatingly illuminates thought and intuition.[4] But this consideration urges the further question: Which is the mode of being of mythic "life" which enables the mana-representation to function as the guiding and illuminating understanding of Being? The possible answer to this question of course presupposes a previous working out of the basic ontological constitution of Dasein. If this basic constitution is to be found in "care," understood ontologically (see *Sein und Zeit*, pp. 180–230), then it becomes clear that mythic Dasein is primarily determined by "thrownness." Here we can only hint that and how a justified articulation of the ontological structure of mythic Dasein is founded in "thrownness."[5]

In "thrownness" mythic Dasein, in its manner of being-in-the-world, is delivered up to the world in such a way that it is overwhelmed by that to which it is delivered up. Overwhelmingness can disclose itself as overwhelmingness only in the case of a being-delivered-up-to. . . . In such a case of being delivered up to that which is overwhelming, Dasein is captivated and can experience itself only as belonging to and related with this reality. In thrownness, accordingly, all disclosed beings have the ontological feature of overwhelmingness (mana). Indeed, if the ontological interpretation is pursued to the specific temporality which founds thrownness, then it can be made ontologically understandable why and how the Real, in the form of mana *(mana-haft Wirkliche)*, discloses itself in a specific present "moment of vision" *("Augenblicklichkeit")*.[6] In thrownness there is a unique case of being-driven in which there is an openness for whatever may be surprisingly extraordinary. Thus the specific "categories" of mythic thought must be "deduced" with the mana-representation serving as the guide.

Another issue deriving from this inseparable cluster of phenomena is the question concerning mythic Dasein's basic comportment and its comportment to itself. The "first energy" (powerfulness) by which mythic Dasein discloses its own being is, according to Cassirer, the energy of desire (p. 157). But why is it the first? It is a question of showing how this desire is rooted in thrownness and of pointing out how mere desire, on the basis of a unique survey of possibilities which does not overlook any of them, can have this power to be efficacious in this way.[7] Only when desire itself is antecedently understood within the context of mana *(mana-haft)* can it disclose itself as such an "efficacy." But if desire is to constitute the "confrontation" between world and I, then one must also consider that such comportments of mythic Dasein are always only ways in which the transcendence of Dasein to its world is uncovered and never ways in which transcendence is first produced. The "confrontation" is founded in the transcendence of Dasein. And mythic Dasein can identify itself with "objects" only because it, as a being-in-the-world, comports itself to a world. But how this transcendence, rightly understood, belongs to Dasein must be shown. The position of a chaos of "sensations" which are "formed" is not only insufficient but it obscures the original phenomenon of transcendence as the condition for the possibility of any form of "passivity." Hence in Cassirer's talk of "impressions" there is a basic confusion: Sometimes a pure felt affection is meant and other times the circumstances of being captivated by the real, perceived under the aspect of mana, is meant. In mythic Dasein, mana, of course, is not grasped as a mode of Being, but rather it is represented mana-ly *(mana-haft)*, i.e., as a being. Thus even the ontic interpretations of mana are not completely false.

Cassirer speaks often, in the context of the formative power of myths, of the mythic fantasy. However, this fundamental capacity is left completely unclarified. Is it a form of thought, or a form of intuition, or both, or neither of the two? Here an orientation focused on the phenomenon of the transcendental power of the imagination and its ontological function within the *Critique of Pure Reason* and *Critique of Judgment* could have at least made clear that an interpretation of the mythic understanding of being is much more intricate and steep than one would gather from Cassirer's presentation.[8]

Finally, reference can be made to the methodological maxim which served as a guide in Cassirer's attempt to interpret the phenomena of Dasein: "The basic rule which governs all development, namely, that spirit achieves true and complete inwardness only in expressing itself" (p. 196; cf. pp. 156, 185, 199–200, 217). Here also there is need of a foundation for the claim made for this rule and an answer given to the basic question, what is the ontological constitution of human Dasein which accounts for the fact that it, as it were, comes to its proper self only by way of a detour through the world? What do selfhood and self-autonomy mean?

But even with all these considerations, the fundamental philosophical problem of myth is not yet reached, namely, in what way does myth in general belong to Dasein? In what respect is it an essential phenomenon within a universal interpretation of Being as such and its conjugations?[9] Whether a "philosophy of symbolic forms" is sufficient for solving or working out these questions need not be discussed here. A position can be taken toward this matter not only when all "symbolic forms" are presented but also and especially when the basic concepts of this system are worked out and brought to their ultimate foundations. (One can now consult the quite general and free-floating discussions of Cassirer in his lecture, "The Problem of Symbol and Its Place in a System of Philosophy." [*Zeitschrift für Aesthetik und allgemeine Kustwissenschaften,* XXI (1927), pp. 295 ff.].

The critical questions here brought forward cannot detract from the merit of Cassirer's work insofar as it is the first attempt since Schelling to place myth as a systematic problem within the range of philosophy. The investigation will remain a valuable point of departure for a renewed philosophy of myth even without its incorporation within a "philosophy of symbolic forms." It will have this value, of course, only when it is grasped more decisively than up till now that even such a rich and accommodating presentation of the phenomenon of spirit for the contemporary mind is not yet philosophy. Philosophy's plight emerges only when its fundamental problems, stemming from antiquity, still unmastered and elementary, are once again taken hold of.

# *Principles of Thinking*[1]

The principles of thinking guide and regulate the activity of thinking. Hence they are also called the laws of thought. Among them are the principles of identity, of contradiction, and of the excluded middle. The laws of thought are commonly accepted as valid for any and every kind of thinking, no matter what it is that is thought, and regardless of how the thinking proceeds. The laws of thought have no need to take into account either the content or the objects thought about or the form, i.e., the kind of thought procedure. Empty of content, the laws are pure forms. In these forms of thought, concepts are formed, judgments passed, and conclusions drawn. The forms of thinking, being empty, can be presented as formulas. The formula for the principle of identity reads: $A = A$. The principle of contradiction is: $A \neq A$. The principle of the excluded middle exacts: either $X = A$ or $X \neq A$.

There is a peculiar interplay among the formulas for the laws of thought, and attempts have been made to deduce one from another. This occurred in several ways. The principle of contradiction, $A \neq A$, is represented as the negative form of the positive principle of identity, $A = A$. And contrariwise, the principle of identity, insofar as it rests on a covert opposition, is the as yet unexpanded form of the principle of contradiction. The principle of the excluded middle either follows then as the immediate consequence of the first two principles or is conceived of as their intermediate link. But no matter how the laws of thought are treated, they are taken to be self-evident, often to be necessarily so. For, viewed correctly, the principles are not amenable to proof. Is not proof itself already an activity of thought? Proof is therefore already subject to the laws of thought. How could it purport to place itself above them, in order to justify their truth beforehand? Even if the question whether the laws of thought are provable or not appears out of place to us, there is still a danger that in considering the laws of thought we become entangled in a contradiction. We find ourselves in a peculiar situation with respect to the laws of thought. For whenever we attempt to call the principles of thinking to mind, they inevitably become a theme of our thinking—and its laws. Behind us, in back of us as it were, the laws of thought lie ever ready and guide every step of our thinking about them. This directive is immediately evident and appears to check every attempt to properly think the laws of thought in a single move.

But that appearance vanishes as soon as we notice what befell the history of Western thought. In the reckoning of the historical disciplines,[2] the incident lies barely over a century and a half ago. Through the endeavors of the thinkers Fichte, Schelling, and Hegel, upon Kant's preparation,[3] thought entered another dimension—in certain respects the highest dimension—of its possibilities. Thinking became deliberately dialectical. In the domain of this dialectic, but set astir even more by its unplumbed depths, the poetic recollection of Hölderlin and Novalis also arose. The complete theoretical-speculative development of the dialectic to a self-contained area reached its culmination in the work of Hegel entitled *Wissenschaft der Logik—The Science of Logic*. The incident by which thinking entered the dimension of a dialectic is an historical one. Hence it seems to lie behind us. It seems this way because we are used to picturing history from the viewpoint of the historical disciplines. In the course of the following investigation our relation to history will continually play a part. Therefore, in prelude, we take note of the following:

As long as we picture history from the viewpoint of the historical disciplines, it appears as occurrence—and an occurrence appears in the passage of before and after. We even find ourselves in a present permeated by flowing occurrence. From out of this present, we charge what is past to the account of what is present. For the sake of what is present we plan the future—what is to come. Picturing history thus as the passage of occurrences prevents us from experiencing just how much authentic history, properly speaking, is always an attending present *(Gegen-wart)*. By present we do not mean what happens to be here now, for the moment. The attending present is that which tends toward us, awaits us, waits on whether and how we expose ourselves to it or seal ourselves off from it. What tends or comes toward us is the future—rightly thought of as what is to come *(Zu-kunft)*. It holds sway over the attending present as an imposition which engages our being here, our existence, which disposes us to feel one way or another toward it, that we might suppose what it summons from us. Only in the mien of such supposition does questioning thrive, the essential questioning which is a part of the growth of every solid work, no matter of what field. A work is a work only by speaking toward the imposition of what is to come, thereby setting free the hidden presencing of what has been, delivering it to us. Great tradition comes upon us as future—what is to come. Reckoning with what is past will never make tradition what it is: imposition, summons. Just as every great work is itself responsible for the awakening and formation of the generation that will set free the world hidden in that work, the growth of the work in turn must hear ahead to the tradition it is responsible for.[4] What one is apt to call creative or ingenious in a work does not arise from a surge of feelings or ideas out of the unconscious; rather, it is an alert obedience to history, an obedience that rests in the pure freedom of being able to hear.

Authentic history is an attending present. The attending present is the future coming as the imposition of the originating, i.e., of the already abiding, presencing, and of its hidden gathering. The attending present is the summons upon us of what has been. It is not true that there is never really anything new in history, if this statement means everything is always "the same old thing." But if "nothing under the sun is new" means that there is only the old within the inexhaustible transforming power of the originating, then the statement hits upon the essence of history. History is the advent of what has been. What has been, i.e., what already is, and only it, tends toward us, comes upon us. What is past, on the other hand, goes away from us. In the reckoning of the historical disciplines, history is the past and the present is what is actual and relevant. But current affairs remain eternally futureless. The historical disciplines inundate us with information; yet seldom do we gain insight into history. Newspapers, radios, television, and paperbacks are the currently standard, worldwide forms for accounting for the past, i.e., making it actual and relevant. It would be blind of us to reject these procedures—and equally blind to promote them blindfolded instead of giving some thought to their essential presencing. For such procedures belong to our history, to what tends toward and comes upon us.

Now we apply the term historical to that incident whereby thought entered the dimension of a dialectic. What does it mean to say that the dialectic is a dimension? First of all, it is not yet clear what the dialectic is and what the talk of dimension here means. We know of dimensions and the like from the realm of space. Dimension can mean extent, as in the phrase, an industrial plant of large dimensions, i.e., measurements. We also speak of the familiar three-dimensional space. A plane, in contrast to a line, has another dimension. But another dimension is not merely adjoined to the line; rather, a plane, in relation to the linear manifold, is another domain assimilating the linear manifold and providing its measure. The same holds true for a solid body compared to a plane. Solid, plane, and line each contain their own measure. If we no longer restrict ourselves to space, then dimension proves to be the domain of a measure—whereby measure and domain are not two different or distinct matters but rather one and the same. Each and every measure yields and opens a domain wherein the measure is at home and thus can be what it is.

When we characterize the dialectic as a dimension of thinking and are even compelled to recognize it as the highest dimension of thought in the history of metaphysics, we mean the following: By becoming dialectical, thinking reaches a hitherto closed domain of measure for defining its own essential presencing. By way of the dialectic, thought attains to that domain within which it can fully think itself. Thinking thereby first comes to itself. Within the dimension of dialectic it becomes evident, and demonstrably so, that thought entails not only the possibility but also the necessity of thinking itself, reflecting itself in itself. Why and in what manner thinking is reflection is fully apparent only in the dimension of a dialectic.

Yet by necessarily thinking itself, thought as representation in no way severs itself from its objects. Rather, only by thinking itself can it mediate and adequately unite with its objects. For this reason the dialectical process of thought is not a mere psychologically observable series of representations in the human consciousness.[5] The dialectical process is the fundamental movement in the whole of the objectivity of all objects, i.e., in Being—as it is understood by the moderns. That Western thought attained the dimension of a dialectic prescribed for it ever since Plato is an incident in world history. In various shapes and forms this incident comes upon the people of this age, wherever they turn, as the present.

Of what significance is this incident for the task which engages us here—for thinking about the laws of thought? In all brevity, the summary answer is that the entrance of thought into the dimension of a dialectic made it possible to push back the laws of thought to the domain of a more fundamental measure. In the range of the dialectic the principles of thinking assume a transformed shape. Hegel has shown that the laws of thought we mentioned earlier posit more—and posit something else—than what our usual representative thinking finds in the formulas right away. For it finds nothing in them. The formula for the principle of identity, $A=A$, for example, is commonly understood to be void of any meaning. Yet Hegel has shown that this statement, $A=A$, could not even posit what it does if it has not already pierced through the empty sameness of A with itself and at least opposed A to itself. The statement could not even be a statement, i.e., something that is always a connection, if it had not already relinquished that which it purports to posit—namely, A as the completely empty and hence unexpandable sameness of something with itself; A as identity in the abstract. Thus Hegel can say, *"The form of the statement in which identity is expressed, therefore, contains more* than simple, abstract identity" (*Wissenschaft der Logik,* Book II, Lasson, Vol. 2, p. 31).

Hegel's *Logic,* however, not only made visible the richer truth of the laws of thought now returned to their foundation; he also convincingly demonstrated that our usual thinking does not even follow the laws of thought—rather it continually contradicts them—exactly where it passes itself off as correct thinking. Yet this proves to be just a consequence of the state of affairs in which everything that is has contradiction for its foundation. Hegel expressed this idea often and in various ways. For example: "It [contradiction] is the root of all movement and vitality; something moves, has drive and is active only to the extent that it contains a contradiction in itself."

More familiar—because more accessible and hence quoted more often—is Hegel's thought about the relationship between life and death. Death is commonly thought of as the annihilation and devastation of life. Death stands in contradiction to life. Contradiction tears life and death apart; contradiction is the rupture of both. However, in the Preface to the *Phenomenology of Mind* Hegel writes: "But the life of the mind is not one that shuns death, and keeps clear of destruction; it endures its death and in death maintains its being. It only wins to its truth when it finds itself in utter desolation [i.e., in contradiction]" (J. B. Baillie's translation). One of Hölderlin's later poems, "In lieblicher Bläue blühet" ("In lovely blueness blooms"), closes with the words, "Life is death, and death is also a life." Here the contradiction is unveiled as that which unites and abides. This seems to be contradicted by what Novalis writes in one of his fragments (*Wasmuth,* vol. 3, p. 1125): "To annihilate the principle of contradiction is perhaps the supreme task of higher logic." But this thinking poet means to say: the principle of ordinary logic, namely the law of a contradiction to be avoided, has to be annihilated, thus establishing contradiction as the primary trait of all that is real. Novalis is saying here exactly the same thing that Hegel thought: annihilate the principle of contradiction, and salvage contradiction as the law of the reality of the real.

Hegel's dialectical interpretation of the laws of thought has them say more than their formulas state, and what the formulas state is never followed by dialectical thinking. Some remarkable matters come to light here; inadequately known and not experienced decisively, these matters have not yet been heard by our usual thinking. That of course should come as no surprise to us. When Hegel himself calls that part of his *Logic* which treats of the laws of thought the "most difficult" (Encycl. §114), how should we, without any preparation, find our way into that dimension in which the dialectic renders the laws of thought and their foundation worthy of questioning?[6]

To be sure, as soon as there is talk of dialectic today one takes note of the fact that there is a dialectical materialism. One takes this to be a *Weltanschauung* and passes it off as ideology. But such observation only evades our reflection instead of recognizing that today dialectic is a global reality—perhaps *the* global reality. Hegel's dialectic is one of the ideas which, intoned from afar, "direct the world"—as powerful in those places where dialectical materialism is refuted with a slight twist of the same style of thinking as in those places where it is believed. Behind this ideological confrontation, as one is wont to call it, the struggle for the rule of the earth rages on. And behind this struggle there prevails a strife in which Western thought is entangled with itself. It is beginning to expand into its ultimate triumph, which is: having forced nature to yield atomic energy.[7]

Is it then so out of place or bizarre for us to attempt to think —about thought, and to reflect on its principles? Perhaps we will thereby pursue thought to its foundation. Or perhaps we will only come across its tracks, so that we might still get wind of that power of thought which infinitely—by its very essence —eclipses every possible quantum of atomic energy. For nature could never appear as a store of energy as it is now represented if atomic energy were not elicited, i.e., set up by thought. Atomic energy is the object of the calculations and controls accomplished by a scientific technology called nuclear physics. However, that physics has succeeded in framing nature in this manner is a meta-physical incident, if not something else besides.[8] But suppose that thinking beings were obliterated by means of atomic energy—where then would thought linger? What is more powerful: the energy of nature in the shape of machines and technology, or thought? Or does neither of the two, which in this case are coupled, take precedence? Does anything at all remain if all mortal human beings on earth "are" obliterated?

More pervasive than the power of the energy of nature and the thinking of nature has been and remains to be the thought which a thinking follows by pursuing nature to the point of atomic energy. Such thoughts do not first come to be by way of mortal thinking. Rather our mortal thinking is always summoned by that thought to correspond to it or to renounce it. We human beings do not come upon thoughts; thoughts rather come to us mortals, whose being is founded upon thinking. But who is it that thinks these thoughts that call upon us—so we will ask, taking this to be a proper question just because it immediately occurs to us. Us—who are we—when we mean ourselves so directly? How can we expect to enter into such thoughts if we are not versed in the principles of thinking?

"Principles of Thinking"—we begin with a clarification of the title of the essay. Clarification can open the way for the ensuing course of thought. Clarification seeks what is clear and pure. We say that air and water are pure insofar as they are not turbid but clear. But there is also such a thing as pure gold, which is thoroughly opaque. That which is pure and clear is not turbid in the sense that it contains no admixture of what does not belong to it. We clarify and purify the title "Principles of Thinking" in order to keep all that does not belong at a distance. We do so by arriving at those determinations which the title of this study intends to convey. The clarification of the title thus puts us on the path of a thinking which follows upon thought. "Principles of Thinking" means first of all: laws for thinking. Thinking, with all its judgments, concepts, and conclusions, is subject to and regulated by the laws. Thinking is the object of the principles. "Principles of Thinking" means principles for thinking; the "of thinking" in the title is a *genitivus obiectivus.*

But at the same time a second point is shown: Statements of the sort $A = A$ and $A \neq A$ are basic forms of thought, statements by means of which thought achieves its own form. The principles thus prove to be the object posited by thinking. Thinking declares itself to be the subject of the positing of the principles. Kant, following the procedure of Descartes, made clear in the *Critique of Pure Reason* how all thinking is essentially an "I think. . . ." Everything represented in thought, as a representation, refers back to an "I think"; or to put it more exactly, everything represented is already covered by the reference to "I think." If this reference back to the same I that thinks did not pervade our thinking throughout, we would never be able to think anything. For all thought, the I in "I think" must be the same, at one with itself.

Fichte formulated this matter as "I=I." In distinction to the formula for the principle of identity, A=A, which formally holds for whatever can be represented, the content of the statement "I=I" is determined like the statement we can make of any particular tree, for example: "the tree = the tree." But then in his *Wissenschaftslehre* of 1794, Fichte shows that the statement "the tree is the tree" can by no means be ranked equal to the statement "I am I." Of course not, we will say, since a tree and my "I" are two different matters in content. Yet all statements of the form "the tree = the tree," "the point = the point," "I=I," come under the formally empty and hence most general statement "A=A." Exactly this, however, is ruled out by Fichte. Rather the statement "I am I" is the assertion for that deed of the I, i.e., of the subject, by means of which the statement "A =A" is first posited. The statement "I=I" is more comprehensive than the formally general statement "A=A"—a remarkable state of affairs. And we do not exaggerate when we claim that to this day we have not clarified what this matter touches upon, which for thinking means we have not found its originating character worthy of questioning.

Thought is first of all not the object of the principles but rather their subject. In the title "Principles of Thinking," the "of thinking" is a *genitivus subiectivus*. Yet the principles are also for the sake of thinking and engage it. The "of thinking" is also a *genitivus obiectivus*. For this reason we now say more carefully: the title "Principles of Thinking" conveys something equivocal. Hence it places us before the following interlinked questions: Can and should we restate our title univocally and accordingly interpret it either as a *genitivus obiectivus* or solely as a *genitivus subiectivus?* Or should we leave this "either . . . or" be and instead vouch for a "both one and the other"? But "both one and the other" is only a pretence for not pursuing the thought. "Both one and the other" cannot be the answer to what is at stake: to think in a way that follows upon thought and its principles. It is only an approach to the question: How about thinking itself, if it is to be both the subject and the object of its principles?

"Principles of Thinking"—even a crude clarification of the title leaves us with an uneasiness[9] which we no longer wish to still. Let us follow the course of our thought once more—this time along a different path—so that the principles of thinking might arouse us to reflect on them. We ask: Is the principle of identity in the formula A = A valid because thinking, as "I think . . ." posits it; or must thinking posit this principle because there is an identity of A with A? What does "is" mean in this instance? Do the principles of thinking derive from thinking? Or does thinking derive from what is posited by the principles? What does "posit" mean here? Positing can mean assuming that such and such is the case. But the positing of the principles is evidently no mere assumption. The principles stipulate something as a priori valid for all cases. They are accordingly pre-suppositions. True, but this word too is used vaguely and carelessly, without giving thought to what or who it is that does the "positing," or how it is done, or in advance of what the laws thus posited are "pre-posited."

Yet the principles of thinking posit what they do as irrefutable laws of thought. They form as it were the citadel wherein thought secures in advance all that it undertakes. Or are the principles of thought—if we think of what Hegel said about them—not at all a secure fortress for thought? Do the principles themselves stand in need of security and shelter? Where might they be secure? Whence do they arise? Which is the place of the origin of the principles of thinking? Anyone who would claim that today this question is clearly decided is a swindler who would pass off as science something that is not and cannot be science—because no science can locate the place where the origin of the principles of thought might be placed in discussion. Let us readily admit: the origin of the principles of thinking, the place of the thinking that posits them, the essence, i.e., essential presencing of this place and its locality—all that remains in the dark for us. This darkness is perhaps always in play, in all thinking. Human beings cannot avoid it. Rather, they must learn to recognize the dark as the ineluctable and to keep at a distance those prejudices which destroy the lofty sway of the dark. The dark has nothing to do with pitch blackness as the complete, sheer absence of light. The dark is rather the secret mystery of what is light. The dark keeps what is light in its presence; what is light belongs to it. The dark therefore has its own clearness and purity. Hölderlin, who truly knew ancient wisdom, says in the third stanza of his poem "Andenken" (Commemoration):

> But may one hand me,
> Full of dark light
> The sweet-scented cup.[10]

Light is no longer a clearing when what is light is diffused into a mere brightness, "brighter than a thousand suns." It is hard to keep the dark pure and clear, to preserve it from admixture with a brightness that does not belong to it and to find the only brightness that does. Lao Tzu says (Ch. 17), "one aware of his brightness keeps to the dark." To that we add the truth that everyone knows but few realize: Mortal thinking must descend into the dark of the depths of the well if it is to view the stars by day. It is harder to preserve the clearness of the dark than to produce a brightness which would seem to shine as brightness only. What would seemingly only shine does not illuminate. And according to the textbook presentation of the doctrine of the laws of thought, it would seem that the content of these laws and their validity are immediately apparent to anyone.

Yet even the first clarification of the title "Principles of Thinking" led us directly into the dark. Whence the principles arise, whether from thought itself, or from that which thinking basically has to think about, or from neither of these two sources directly at hand—this remains hidden from us. Hegel's dialectical interpretation of thinking, moreover, forced the laws of thought to relinquish their hitherto valid form and role.

Above all, however, the entrance of thinking into the dimension of a dialectic deters us from speaking in the future so casually of "thinking" in general, as if there were only one kind. At any rate no one kind of thinking has a hegemony. Thought becomes a product of sheer fantasy when we represent it as a universally human faculty. But if we recall that in our time an equiform manner of thinking is commandeering world history all over the globe, then we must be equally determined to keep in mind that this equiform thinking is only the standardized and utilitarian form of that historical mold which we call Western. We have hardly begun to come to know how singular is its historical destiny; it is seldom enough that we are inclined to acknowledge it. Karl Marx, in one of his early, posthumously published works, declares that *"all of so-called world-history* is nothing but the production of human beings by means of human work, the coming to be of nature for human beings" (*Die Frühschriften* I, 1932, p. 307).

Many will reject this interpretation of world history and its underlying conception of human nature. But no one can deny that today technology, industry, and economy, setting the standards for the work of the self-production of human beings, determine the reality of all that is real. Nevertheless, this observation only serves to exclude us from that dimension of thought within which Marx's assertion moves: world history is "the work of the self-production of human beings." For here the word "work" *(Arbeit)* does not mean mere activity and accomplishment. The sense is rather that of Hegel's concept of work, thought of as the basic trait of the dialectical process, by means of which the Becoming of the real unfolds and perfects its reality. Marx, in contrast to Hegel, sees the nature of reality not in an absolute mind that comprehends itself but in human beings producing themselves and their means of living. That puts Marx in an extreme opposition to Hegel, but this very opposition binds Marx to Hegel's metaphysics. For the life and prevailing force of reality is, everywhere, the work process as a dialectic, which means, as thinking, insofar as what is actually productive in any production is and remains thinking—be it understood and performed as metaphysical and speculative or as scientific and technical, or as a crude mixture of both. Every production is in itself re-flection, thinking.

If we dare, as our title suggests, to give thought to thinking in general, then talking about thinking in general makes sense only if we experience thinking everywhere and exclusively as that which determines our historical human existence. As soon as we attempt to think about this thinking in a fundamental way, we find ourselves channelled into the network and the relations of our history, and hence of present world history. Not until we are sufficiently experienced in our thinking, in the scope of its essential presencing, will we be able to acknowledge another thinking as strange and to listen to it as estranging in its abundant strangeness.

Yet the thinking which, itself historical, determines world history today, does not stem from today. It is older than the merely past, and drifts our way in its most ancient thoughts out of a nearness whose tracks we fail to catch wind of, because we believe that what really, essentially concerns us is what is current and actual.

# Appendix: Conversation with Martin Heidegger, Recorded by Hermann Noack[1]

In the beginning of December, 1953, Martin Heidegger spent two days as a guest of the Protestant Academy at Hofgeismar. Here there took place among a small circle of directors of study-groups and colleagues a conversation with Professor Heidegger concerning certain questions which were occasioned by his philosophical writings and which were focused on the relationship between thinking and faith or between philosophy and theology. Heidegger's readiness to participate in this discussion fulfilled the long-cherished wish to arrange a personal meeting between him and the Protestant Academy, which, since its incipiency, has been nurtured in its philosophical and theological investigations by his thinking. Thus this conversation was to provide the opportunity, by way of direct questions and answers, to clarify issues and to mark off the territories of disagreement. Heidegger agreed emphatically to the preparatory character of this first meeting. When one takes into account this goal, the meeting may be judged to have been a good beginning.

Participants in the conversation were, besides Professor Heidegger, Professor Landgrebe, Professor Metzke, Doctor Krämer, Doctor Müller-Gangloff, Doctor Müller-Schwefe, and Professor Noack.

After the introductory clarification of certain concepts and passages in Heidegger's writings, the discussion moved toward the decisive problems which indicated the differences in basic positions. Of course, the fertility of Heidegger's philosophical mode of inquiry in *Being and Time* and later writings and the importance of his criticisms of traditional philosophy were generally recognized and presupposed. However, in assessing their consequences for the relationship of faith and thinking (theology and philosophy), both in terms of "systematic" and historical considerations, the views were divergent. The very first question asked by Metzke struck at the heart of the discussion and determined its entire course. In order to assure an overview in the report, I will not give a play by play account of individual questions and answers. Rather, I will present in context what came out in the course of the contributions of the conferees, keeping as close as possible to the original formulations. Thereby the meaning and importance of the individual contributions will be more intelligible without neglecting the various responses and objections of the conferees, especially because these may be explicitly given in particular instances.

Metzke took off from Heidegger's thesis that the thinking of Being "is addressed" and "is laid claim to" (Heidegger speaks, e.g., of the "unspoken word" of Being). Metzke, basically in agreement with this view, observed that thinking does not simply begin with itself and it cannot think from merely out of itself. Genuine philosophical thinking obtains primarily when thinking holds to that which makes a claim on it. What concerns a philosopher is therefore everything which concerns a human being in a way which excludes mere caprice. Such a claim does not proceed from "Being as such" but always from particular and concrete, or even the very most concrete, Being. We know that apparently totally "incidental" encounters are the very essence of life and can become an impulse to change completely one's thought and life. The Christian proclamation made a claim and was an impulse of this sort because it radically placed in question the thought of persons coming into contact with it. The historical factuality of this event is in no way a lessening of its ontological claim. Rather, the proclamation uncovered what was never previously experienced or thought. The alleged connection in Greek thought (especially in Heraclitus and Parmenides, to whom Heidegger has recourse) between thinking and Being, the supposed indestructible relationship of humans (Dasein) to the truth ("manifestness") of Being, is contested. The proclamation leaves no doubt that the original breach in that unity was not grasped in its depth and gravity. Therefore one must take quite seriously the statement of Paul concerning the "foolishness of philosophy" (1 Corinthians, 1:20), which Heidegger also refers to in the "Introduction" to "What is Metaphysics?".[2] The Christian proclamation therefore speaks of something absolutely new in the ontological relationship of human beings and connects this to a unique historical event: the revelation of God in Jesus Christ.

When someone called to "faith" is addressed by this message and called upon to make a decision, then it is impossible that his "thinking" overlook the claim of the Gospel. For "that which is most worthy of questioning" for philosophical thinking is thereby decisively enhanced in that it, as e.g., Nicholas of Cusa says, should hold fast to the *maximum concretum,* in the face of which the arbitrariness of interpretive thinking comes to an end.

Western philosophy to this day has not done justice to this "claim." It still treats the "essence of man" as if there never occurred an event which changed this essence. Nevertheless one can name a list of thinkers in history who, like Nicholas of Cusa, openly received this impetus and seriously wrestled with the problem which the Christian proclamation burdened them with—for example Paracelsus, I. G. Hamann, Kant, and Hegel. The way the latter permitted "spirit" to come to itself only through history, and therefore enabled the unity of Being and thinking to be realized historically, shows that he knew something of truth as an "historical event" even though he overcame the process again in a dialectical system. Such a thinking, which so esteems the concrete and historically unique over against the trans-temporal, has been made possible only through Christianity. And such a thinking is not merely a "worldly" and "historical" effect which is unessential for Christian existence. On the contrary, it is still our task to do justice to the Christian "claim" in terms of thinking. For it must also disturb the thinking of philosophers that the Christian bears witness to a definite reality and makes what are for him most essential truth-claims. The confidence and hope of faith has actually created a new relationship of humans to history. And, as a result, the future horizon for Western thought is determined.

Landgrebe found himself very close to these considerations of Metzke. He similarly interpreted the word of Paul concerning the "foolishness of philosophy." The proclamation of the New Testament rejects the presupposition of Greek thought that thinking can move in a realm of the abiding and unchangeable and therein take hold of Being as Being. In contrast to the Aristotelian immutability of essence (of *to ti en einei*) there is the event-character of revelation and of truth "becoming flesh."

If philosophy is, according to Heidegger's *Being and Time,* a "hermeneutic of the facticity of Dasein," then foremostly faith is to be included among the "basic dispositions" *(Grundbefind-lichkeiten),* in which there is originally disclosed to us the "that" of our "being-in-the-world." Faith should take priority over the thinking of the pre-Socratics and the word of the poet. The "historicity" of Dasein obtains also from such basic experiences and they are historically demonstrable. The Christian proclamation is likewise an historical event whose effect in world-history is visible. It is capable of being grasped quite differently from the "historical destining disclosure of Being"[3] which puts us at the limit of inquiry. It is possible to show how, through the meeting of the Christian "claim" with the prevailing ancient interpretation of Being, there resulted ultimately the self-understanding of the modern as an "autonomous subject." Therefore we are compelled to consider philosophically the truth-claim of the Christian proclamation, which entered into a world already interpreted with the concepts of antiquity and enlisted in an historical struggle with antiquity over its explication of the meaning of Being.

Other participants shared the view of Metzke and Landgrebe that the fact as well as the "offensive" content of the Christian belief in a revelation should deeply disturb philosophical thought—primarily in its question concerning the "meaning of Being" (Heidegger) and that *de facto* post-Christian philosophical thought already is beholden to the Christian claim.

Müller-Schwefe attacked Heidegger's explication of Heraclitus and Parmenides. Its assertion that thinking and Being form a unity is only an anticipation of what should be. Humans only apparently succeed in achieving binding unity with the origin of their existence through magical conjurations. But according to the Bible this unity is a pure gift.

Here Heidegger objected: The New Testament inquires about *whence* the unity originates; Heraclitus *in what* it consists. According to Heraclitus the human being could not fall out of the unity, i.e., from the "truth," as the unconcealment of Being. Of course, there prevails a certain unrest; but the falling out of the truth of *logos* (Heraclitus, *Fragments* 1, 2, 17, 19, 34, among others) means only the privation of "not-hearing," not a negation. The Greeks also understand the belonging-together of Being and thinking as the "apportionment," as the "historical destining disclosure of Being" *(Moira)*.

Müller-Schwefe responded that indeed Greek thought did represent this view but the Christian proclamation reveals that *de facto* the human being has fallen from this unity. In the face of this claim philosophical thinking must be taken aback. After the opening up of the new dimension of faith it is no longer possible to continue to think in the same way. Even art changes: tragedy loses its cultic sense, poetry becomes a venture of secular humanity. One sees how the Christian faith had an effect on thought in the fact that, e.g., since Augustine there is such a thing as a philosophy of history. This means, among other things, that the human being no longer understands himself from out of the past but primarily from out of his future.

The believer knows that through God's word even the language of man is liberated to "authenticity." He confesses that he is commissioned also to place poetry and thinking under the obedience of faith (2 Corinthians, 20:5).

What has been reported thus far was, for the most part, a response to Heidegger's differing views. I myself asked him in the beginning for an explication of two texts which apparently are of decisive importance for his judgment of theology and its relation to philosophy (or, the metaphysics of the West). In the "Introduction" to "What is Metaphysics?" he speaks of the "foolishness of philosophy" which theology must take seriously; and in the "Letter on Humanism"[4] one reads: "Only out of the truth of Being" is it possible to think of the "essential-presencing *(Wesen)* of the holy" and the "essential-presencing of the divinity," and only "in the light of the essential-presenc-

ing of the divinity can there be thought and stated what the
word 'God' is supposed to mean." Furthermore, we read that
limits are set for "thinking as thinking" by that which "is to be
thought," i.e., by the truth of Being, with respect to deciding the
issue of theism or atheism.[5] I remarked that these statements
encourage the interpretation that Heidegger's thinking moves
in a dimension which alone makes room for doing genuine
theological "thinking" once again—inasmuch as theology at a
very early stage fell under the spell of "metaphysics," which is
inappropriate for speaking about the truth of revelation. Heidegger did not contest this, but he literally said: "Within thinking nothing can be achieved which would be a preparation or
a confirmation for that which occurs in faith and in grace.
Were I so addressed by faith I would have to close up my shop.
—Within faithfulness one still thinks, of course; but thinking as
such no longer has a task." "Philosophy engages in a kind of
thinking of which man is capable on his own. This stops when
he is addressed by revelation." "Today thinking has taken the
most tentative form imaginable."

Theologians, Heidegger continued, have simply too little
trust in their own standpoint and have too much to do with
philosophy. The impetus from the side of thinking can only be
an indirect one. Theologians should abide in the exclusiveness
of revelation. For Luther, to whom Metzke referred several
times because his *Commentary on Romans* shows how the
traditional concepts of philosophy were shattered, there was no
question of the "claim" (of philosophy). For him Paul's Epistle
to the Romans was a revelation from the start; there he heard
the word of God. When a thinker listens to a poet like Hölderlin
there is something completely different—a listening in another
region of "manifestness," the founding of which, in contrast to
the already decided revelation of the word of God, the poet
himself essentially participates in. The thinker speaks of the
"manifestness of Being"; but "Being" is an untheological word.
Because revelation itself determines the manner of manifestness and because theology does not have to prove or interpret
"Being," theology does not have to defend itself before philosophy. Of course the "thinking" of theology is not only "receptive"
but also explicative. But "thinking" should not be equated with

"judging" but rather it is to be understood as Parmenides originally experienced it.

The Christian experience is so completely different that it has no need to enter into competition with philosophy. When theology holds fast to the view that philosophy is foolishness, the mystery-character of revelation will be much better preserved. Therefore, in the face of a final decision, the ways part.

With respect to the text referred to from the "Letter on Humanism," what is being discussed there is the God of the poet, not the revealed God. There is mentioned merely what philosophical thinking is capable of on its own. Whether this may also be of significance for theology cannot be said because there is for us no third case by which it could be decided. That also holds for this discussion. But this does not mean that we must all simply withdraw into our mutual positions! There are historical encounters which entail passing closely by one another without indifference. But the Christian faith does not need to consider itself as an "historical destining disclosure of Being," nor does it have need of treating the mystery of the incarnation with concepts such as the "ontological difference" (between "beings" and "Being"). We understand one another better when each speaks in his own language.

In connection with this sharp separation of philosophical and theological assertions (which occasioned Müller-Schwefe to ask whether we still speak in one language at all), Heidegger contested also that it could be shown that the Christian faith had an essential influence on philosophy. The previously reported answers to his repeated question, What was changed in the thinking of Western philosophy (metaphysics)?, did not satisfy him. Either, he emphasized, it is a matter of theology or nothing in principle has been changed with respect to the essence of philosophical thinking, even, e.g., in the case of the concept of Being in Hegel.

On the other hand, Heidegger denied that philosophy has any significance for theology. The thinking of philosophy is and remains the thinking of Being, i.e., of that which is most worthy of being questioned. Faith, on the other hand, is ultimately protected in the sense that it enjoys confidence. This, of course, can falter, but basically it holds steady. Indeed, because so many cannot endure the questioning of philosophy—and "as is well known philosophy can only question"—they therefore convert. But "questioning is the piety of thinking."

This view of the protectedness of faith was contradicted. Krämer recalled the theological distinction between *certitudo* (certainty) and *securitas* (security). Part of the certitude of faith is to endure the uncertainty and "temptation" *("Anfechtung")* of thinking. Müller-Schwefe likewise referred to the complete "unprotectedness" of the Christian confession in its Protestant understanding. It is not merely that we have an interest in getting the issues clear with respect to philosophical thinking because, as Heidegger seemed to believe, we want to have an apologetical conversation with the unbelievers; but it is also because we are thinkers and believers in a single person and we are "tempted" by thinking. We hold the conversation within ourselves. Certainly it is true that thinking and faith do not lie on the same plane and cannot be harnessed under the same yoke. But the "hidden God" has destined us to endure the questions of philosophy. This situation tends toward the "fulfillment of time." Heidegger rightly warns of false mixtures and hasty resolutions. But if he means that theologians should not attempt to win over the philosophers, one can respond that the theologian is questioned by the philosophers themselves and he must answer. This "responsibility" cannot be taken away from the theologian, and a man like Karl Heim was concerned his life long to follow the directive of 2 Corinthians and, indeed, as Krämer added, without succumbing to the danger of "Thomism."

However, precisely for these reasons Krämer objected to the views of Metzke. We should not go so far in our insistence that philosophical thinking take account of the Christian "claim" as to create the appearance that the "foolishness of philosophy" is something to be overcome. Revelation is and remains inaccessible to thinking. The shape of this truth is so ambiguous that thinking can never be led to acknowledge revelation on its own terms. When, however, one is doing philosophy in faith and is listening to the message of faith, not only is he able to introduce into thinking the general possibility of a concrete disclosure of the meaning of Being, but he must pronounce the name of Jesus Christ and thereby become a theologian, as in the case of Augustine or Thomas. Faith must be on guard (as Heidegger emphasizes) not only against making it too easy for thinking but also against watering down its own claim. Faith and thinking cannot be made to coincide. We live, according to the New Testament's message, in an aeon which is only approaching "fulfillment." Even Christianness and its theology stand under the shadow of our "broken" existence. According to 1 Corinthians, 15, theology will cease at the time of the fulfillment. Until then, faith, thought, poetry, creativity, etc. remain as possibilities of human beings living among one another. These possibilities have a most fundamental justification; but they also have their limits. In the light of faith they are "dangerous" only when they do not candidly keep to their proper limits. But the tension which their particular "claims" create for us must be endured by faith. For, after all, revelation involves the imperative "Rejoice!" as well as "fear and trembling." It is to grace alone that we owe our joy. "Fear and trembling" remind us that we stand in continuous temptation which is to be overcome only in faith. It was already mentioned that Heidegger did not claim to see a temptation for faith in the questioning and doubting of thinking. This "temptation originates rather from the content of revelation itself." But "fear and trembling" before the "wrath of God" are ultimately enveloped in a trust which neither the thinker nor the poet as such knows.

A difference of views came to light surrounding the meaning of an "historical event" for the ontological understanding of Dasein; or, in terms of Heidegger's later thought, there was a difference of opinion concerning the meaning of an "historical destining disclosure of Being," such as "the forgetfulness of Being" of metaphysics and the "turn about" in the "thinking of the truth of Being." I therefore asked Heidegger how the historicity of the historical destining disclosure of Being relates to the factual (and historically knowable) history of humans. He answered that the historical destining disclosure of Being, i.e., the "manifestness" or "unconcealment" of a meaning of "Being" at a particular time, always precedes, "as if it were on dove's feet" (Nietzsche), the factual history. This he elucidated by discussing the fate of translations of the Greek word *theoria*. The transformation of meaning which was attached to the various translations was not the "cause" of the basic changes in philosophical thinking but rather was already a symptom of the ontological-historical transformation in the understanding of Being. And this owes its origin not to human ideas but to the "clearing" of Being itself which defines Da-sein. It is this which also always opens up the space of human freedom in which failure, neglect, and going astray take place.

Landgrebe raised the question several times of whether, in man's factual understanding of Being and of himself, the historical presuppositions for the opening up of a new ontological clearing can be exhibited (e.g., as in the transition to modernity's conviction that what is central to man is the autonomy of reason). Heidegger responded that such a view would imply a causal explanation of history which is as little possible and just as slippery as the causal calculations of natural events by contemporary physics. With respect to the encounter of Christian faith with ancient philosophy, a topic also introduced by Landgrebe, Heidegger stated that the historical destining disclosure of Being, which is to be concomitantly thought of with the "facticity of Dasein," had already had its say at the time of the encounter. Müller-Schwefe suggested: If, then, the "how" of the "historical destining disclosure of Being" is inexplicable, then one can theologically speak of the historical destining disclosure "of the hidden God." I believe, however, that the discussion showed that this assertion is not able to be made for thinking in Heidegger's sense. Thinking knows nothing of a "revealed God" and cannot recognize in the Christian proclamation any "historical destining disclosure of Being" because the content of revelation consists in statements about "a being" (God as creator and lord of the world). Therefore the "foolishness" of which Paul speaks may be said to be reciprocal for faith and thinking.

In order to elucidate what is called "thinking," i.e., what it means and what it demands, Heidegger read his interpretation of *Fragment* VIII, 34–38, of Parmenides.[6] Thinking means neither

1. something happening in the mind or soul (psychological view), nor
2. an objectifying representation (epistemological view), nor
3. a turning to the supra-sensible (metaphysical view).

The way thinking belongs to Being is not in any of the above senses an identity but refers to the "pre-possession" of thinking by Being which is achieved in the "saying" *(legein)*, i.e., "in the letting lie before us of what is present in its presencing." Thereby "Being" is always to be thought within the "twofold" of "being(s)" and "Being." Heidegger answered in the affirmative to my question whether this relation of Being, thinking, and saying holds for all dimensions and therefore also for theology. But he adhered to his position that the twofold, which to begin with is hidden in the historical destining disclosure of Being, remains what is properly questionable and worthy of thought for thinking, whereas for faith this questionableness is taken away. Here, he continued, it is not a matter of personal decisions but rather of decisions of world-history *(weltge-schichtliche Entscheidungen)*. Even "thinking," as it arose among the pre-Socratics, was a unique "flash" of Being. (If we call it "philosophy," then there is not its like in India or China or anywhere else.) Everything which we are inclined to regard as a "necessary element of the culture" can one day pass away. So, e.g., the "objectifying" knowledge of physics rests upon the historical destining disclosure of Being in terms of the "objectivity" of so-called "nature," the mastery of which is the goal of research and that is fast reaching its limits today.

Thinking remains always on the path upon which it is sent and destined (*"geschickt"*). And if Protestant theology knows that it can only be "on the way" in its explication of revelation, and therefore never exempt from the "temptation" of thinking, then the conversation between thinking and faith continues. We have learned from the present meeting; but later on we should think about what was still not said.

Several questions, which in the course of the discussion were peripherally treated, among them Heidegger's interpretation of Hölderlin, may be left out of this retrospective review, which intends to report only the results of the discussion surrounding the central theme. An attempt will be made to summarize.

If the relation of truth (as "unconcealment") and *logos* (as a speaking which preserves [what is unthought]) holds for all dimensions, then that may not be a "third cause" superior to thinking and faith; but it is a statement about the essence of all "unconcealment" which is as important as the other statement intending universal validity: "The manner of unconcealment is determined by that which is itself self-manifesting." Thus there appears the opposition between: the unconcealment of "Being" in beings, in "that which emerges" (i.e., the *physis* of the pre-Socratics) and the manifestness of God in beings as his creation.[7] Insofar as both of these do not exclude one another, the thinking (of philosophy) does not have to close its shop if and because faith abides in the light of revelation.[8] For even then there remain open questions (as Heidegger admitted) which cannot be answered by faith alone. The revelation of the New Testament confirms quite explicitly that humans are left free to reflect on and understand whatever is, in which Being discloses and hides itself, in all its modes (as "nature," "history," "work of art," etc.). Thinking is a "foolishness" for faith (according to 1 Corinthians, 1:20–21 and 2:7–15) only because the "wisdom of this world . . . does not recognize God in his wisdom" without revelation. Proceeding from a thinking in obedience to faith (2 Corinthians, 10:5) does not necessarily result in a "Christian philosophy" in the sense of dogmatic pre-decisions. A thinking which explicates revelation would always be theology.

It must give philosophy pause that there is something such as faith in a divine revelation—a revelation occurring in an historically unique and concrete event. And this faith, even if not beyond temptation, is "certain" of its truth. Even one who is not "claimed" and bound by this proclamation can think about and understand the nature of this manifestness. What is impossible for thinking, within the limits proper to it as thinking, is to confess to faith. But that which in the thinking of Heidegger is called the "historical destining disclosure of Being" and the "forgetfulness of Being" can, as the "homelessness" of the remoteness and "darkness of God" (M. Buber), become dangerous for faith, even a faith tried by philosophical and scientific knowledge.

Despite the fact that the divergent views approached one another in these quite essential areas, many questions remained open. This made a continuation of the discussion within a larger circle desirable.

# TRANSLATORS' COMMENTARY

*by James G. Hart*
*and John C. Maraldo*

# COMMENTARY

Martin Heidegger has said of his research in 1923:

> I was concerned neither with a new direction in phenomenology nor, indeed, with anything new. Quite the reverse, I was trying to think the essence *(Wesen)* of phenomenology in a more originary manner, so as to fit it in this way back into the place that is properly its own within Western philosophy.[1]

In order to place Heidegger's attempt to think the holy, we shall do well to retrace his placing of the essence of phenomenology. We shall review briefly both phenomenology's essence and that essence of which phenomenology speaks (Part I). This will enable us to relate the holy to world and to theology's incapacity to think this relation (Part II). After having thought the relation of world to the holy, we can see how things within world relate to the holy. This puts us in position to think about the transformation of the world (Parts III and IV).

# Part I · Hermeneutical Phenomenology and Eidetic Phenomenology

## §1. The Phenomena Themselves

Since the time of Edmund Husserl's *Logical Investigations* (1900), phenomenologists have rallied around the shibboleth "die Sachen Selbst," the phenomena or issues themselves. However, what precisely the issues or the phenomena of phenomenology are is not agreed upon. Nevertheless, phenomenologists have made a common front against ontologies which, mistrusting the realm of perception and reflection, reduce perceptual experiences to categories appropriate to a restricted realm of experience, e.g., laboratory experimental situations operating within the authoritative schema of stimulus, response, reward, and reinforcement. Common to phenomenologists is a commitment to that which shows itself to perceptual and reflective experience. That which shows itself need not be the case, i.e., it can be a "mere appearance," or it can be apparent as something manifesting itself through something which it itself is not (e.g., a symptom). All such distinctions, however, still depend on that which shows itself. The basic context for the language of appearing, i.e., of "that which shows itself," is not the issue of the immediacy of sense data, nor is it an ontology of relations. It is the position that whatever we deal with or come to know must, in some way, be made present.

## §2. The Essential Phenomena

A basic theme is provided by the following picture: We apprehend something obscurely from an unfavorable angle of vision. In order to get a full, lively view, we must draw near the remote object and alter our angle, thereby fulfilling or revising our original hunches and anticipations. This is to bring the object into the light and let the object speak for itself in a lively way or "in person" and "in the flesh." This is to allow the thing to become present, to shine in itself, and to remove it from its original obscurity.

In its earliest days, phenomenology was described by Husserl as a science of essences and not of mere facts. This meant that what was relevant for phenomenology was not just any thing that appeared or could be brought to light but rather that which was "essential" in what showed itself. In our prepropositional experience of things, we not only experience a "this here," a fact, but we also tacitly experience a "what." All experiencing is an experiencing of something as something. If we experience something, it looks like . . . or appears as. . . . Experience has an implicit, meaningful content which, when articulated, can be described by saying that we see, e.g., the hammer as a hammer, not that we see it stupidly or vacuously. Note that it is difficult, if not impossible, to describe the vacuous experience. If we confess that we stupidly saw an object not as a hammer but (as) a shiny, metal, wooden, and unfamiliar object, we nevertheless would be describing an experience of "essential meanings" (as shiny, as metal, as unfamiliar, etc.). The tacit seeing or experience of something as . . . is called by Heidegger the "hermeneutical as."[2] Phenomenology, as an essential or "eidetic" science, is to prescind from the factual, individual, and incidental features of experienced phenomena and seek out the essential qualities. This prescinding from the incidental and focusing on essentials was called the eidetic reduction.

## §3. *Eidetic Analysis, Essence, and Essentiality*

For eidetic phenomenology, the primary phenomena to be brought into the light are the basic essences, categories, and types of objects and experiences. The realm of essences is as capable of being brought to light as a particular material object or an intentional act. The difference is between bringing this material object into view, seeing it from all sides, etc., and bringing into view the material object as a material object; between recalling distinctly what I did yesterday and distinctly presencing recalling or remembering as such.

In the perception of either the concrete material thing or the explicable essence, there is given-*with* a surrounding fringe of indeterminateness which is capable of being specified and determined. This "horizon" of perceivable background or explicable meanings is initially obscure and remote from a lively, lucid presence. In eidetic analysis, one begins with a general felt-meaning or inkling of the given-with fringe and attempts to bring it into lively presence. This initially unfilled and obscure fringe of meaning contains an authoritative matrix of rules for determining the properties of the essence.[3]

The phenomenological technique of free imaginative variation involves imaginatively conceiving which elements are indispensable and which are incompatible in the constitution of this being-such or whatness. This is always performed by appealing to the authoritative given-with horizon. We can entertain a multitude of possible properties for a centaur (as such), but there is a prescribed range of meanings outside of which we are not permitted to roam. Thus though I may ascertain that femininity as femininity is not specified by any particular color of eyes or bodily silhouette, I am not free to ascribe to it the virtues of a bulldozer or a locomotive. There is a "legal space" (Husserl) to which we are bound, and essence-analysis brings the particular *eidos* to the space where it properly belongs.

What separates early phenomenology from later phenomenology is, for the most part, the status given this legal space. For early phenomenology, essence is always the essence *of something* and is no more to be separated from that of which it is an essence than a surface is to be separated from that of which it is a surface.[4] Each object or phenomenon "presenting itself" (whether it be concrete or abstract, particular or universal) has one and only one essence. Thus two empirical objects may have completely similar essences but not the identical same essence. The "idealization" of the essence achieved through essence-analysis (also called ideation) gives the essence a "second existence": Although the essence of the object is inseparable from the object of which it is an essence—and when the object perishes the essence of the object likewise perishes—the idea of the object perdures (but merely as an idea).

One can shift the question from that proper to essence-analysis—as in, What is the essence of . . . , i.e., the being-such or being-so of an object?—to the whatness, i.e., the such-ness or so-ness itself. We are not only able to reflect on and speak about the redness of a red thing or the horseness of a horse, we are also able to reflect on and speak about the redness itself or horseness itself. Here we move into an objective realm of universal and timeless meaning structures (called *eide* or *essentialities*) which are *ante res* and the foundation of all essences and logical spaces. This *kosmos noetos* has its own kind of ideal being, which is not to be confused with the merely intentional or "ideal" existence of the essence achieved in ideation. Rather, all ideation and essence-analysis rests on the objective legislating spaces of the *kosmos noetos*.

## §4. Regional Ontologies and Positive Sciences

The metaphor of a legal space which prescribes the properties of an essence and the proper *topos* of an essence in relation to other essences points to the basic meaning-spaces or regions wherein every essence ultimately resides. For the early phenomenologists known as the Munich-Göttingen Circle, essence-analysis was the ultimate task of philosophy. Eidetic intuition presences the ultimate meaning-*topoi* wherein all experienced meanings find their normative possibilities.[5] The fruits of such analysis would bring to light, e.g., how moral blame and praise as such presuppose (in the praised or blamed "object") responsible action, which in turn presupposes freedom, which in turn presupposes a form of self-consciousness; or it would show how brightness as brightness is founded in color, which, in turn, is founded in the extension of a material thing.

All sciences of facts are founded in regional ontologies.[6] This means that the various sciences presuppose basic generic categories which determine the content and approach of the sciences. Thus history, the social and behavioral sciences, the natural sciences, etc. are all *positive* sciences insofar as they *posit as given* an area of investigation and are heedless of the defining fringe of essential founding meanings. This positing, on the one hand, facilitates the unencumbered pursuit of study within the predefined region. It frees the inquiry from having to bother with justifying or elucidating basic presuppositions. On the other hand, this positing means that all sciences, except for regional ontologies, are basically naive about their subject matter. For example, a mathematician, in order to ask what a number is or what mathematics as such is, would have to leave the practice and region predefined by mathematical science. As a practicing mathematician he could no more raise these questions than a philologist could raise the question of the essence of language within the confines of the preoccupations and practices of philological research.[7]

## §5. The Importance of Eidetic Phenomenology for Heidegger

Shortly after the appearance of *Being and Time*, Heidegger was widely acclaimed as an eidetic phenomenologist of the regions of human being or spirit and history. In the later writings one finds numerous sketches of eidetic studies of, e.g., dwelling, language, building, technology, poetry, and the work of art. In this present volume he offers an eidetic of Christian faith and theology as well as suggestions toward an eidetic of primitive mythic existence. Of course, to see Heidegger merely as an eidetic phenomenologist is to miss his basic position and

the sense of his eidetic studies. However, without an understanding of his own appreciation of eidetic analyses, the basic
themes cannot be grasped. If one grasps the essence of eidetic
phenomenological *praxis,* one is in a position to see in what
sense Heidegger's thought is a phenomenology of phenomenology and a phenomenological philosophy.[8]

Without eidetic analysis and regional ontological reflection
there can be no revolution and advance in the sciences. All
decisive transformations in the positive sciences find their basis in the eidetic examination of the basic guiding concepts and
postulates.[9] For example, Newton's first law of motion and
Galileo's law of falling bodies went in advance of all modern
experimentations and dealings with material bodies. This going in advance is a pregrasp or an anticipation in that it prede-
termines how the specific realm of phenomena will appear. As
being in advance it is prior, i.e., before what follows; in this
sense it is a priori. The priority of the a priori is that of the
essence of the thing. What enables the thing to be what it is is
prior when one considers the essential issue and nature of the
thing. This is true even though we grasp the antecedent prior
meanings subsequently, i.e., when we take notice of certain
properties of the thing.[10] The greatness of the modern natural
sciences lies in the fact that the formative researchers were all
philosophers. It is false to suppose that Aristotle and the
scholastics had theories and Galileo and the moderns had facts.
The great researchers grasped that there are no brute facts but
only facts in the light of guiding concepts. The revolutions and
advances occur with the radical examination of the basic guiding concepts. Thus the subsequent discovery of the presuppositions of Aristotle's theory of inertia does not lessen its a-priority
with respect to the ancient world's grasp of the motion of
material bodies. Nor does it lessen the anticipatory power of
the basic concept in determining the approach to and investigation of material bodies by the ancients. Analogously, when a
phenomenologist discloses that promising as such entails a
performative speech act which effects an obligation for the
promiser and claims by the promisee, this (subsequent) elucidation of the essential properties of promising does not mean
that the essence of promising was not prior with respect to the

theme itself or that it did not hold sway in all our pre-phenomenological promisings.

Because what is prior with respect to the essential matter itself is subsequent in the course of our getting to know (thematically) the matter, the convenient but false view frequently arises that the essentially prior is in fact something subsequent and thus of no consequence. This widely circulated view corresponds to a certain blindness toward the essences of things and the prescriptive force of the knowledge of essences. Such "essence-blindness" is always a hindrance to the development of a science.[11]

## §6. Everyday Being-in-the-World

The point of departure for essence-analysis is the prepropositional perception of something *as* something. In the eidetic reduction, however, an attitude is assumed (i.e., objectification and thematizing of what is given as . . .) which is not characteristic of how we are for the most part in our everyday dealings with the world. It is in this prephenomenological or preanalytical attitude that we first experience things as. . . . This "everydayness" must first of all be brought to light.

Objects are given to us in our everyday intercourse with them for the most part as *pragmata:* things ready to hand and at our disposal for the sake of. . . . This mode of givenness is only possible if we antecedently experience that for the sake of which they are and the possible role they might play in our lives. This antecedent for-the-sake-of-which of the things we encounter in our everyday dealings is always already known. However, it itself cannot be said to appear in the same way as the ready-to-hand things appear. At first glance we are inclined to say that the instruments at our disposal are nearer and more present than that-for-the-sake-of-which, which seems remote and absent. And this is, indeed, the case if we always understand what is present or near to be an object, either as ready to hand or simply as present before us. And yet, if it is true that the system of references and instrument-contexts is that which makes it possible for objects to be given as ready to hand for our disposal and use, the reference system may be said to be more proximate and to have a mode of presencing itself not characteristic of objects. If the context for the sake of which we encounter things may be said to be more proximate, it may be said to be a condition for the possibility of the "immediate" everyday mode of givenness of things. It is a condition in the sense that it mediates the mode of givenness of things. Its proximity or nearness with respect to things is, as mediating, an immediate mediation. It is immediate in that it is always already achieved and in play. As mediation it is always to be recovered and taken into account. This immediate mediation Heidegger calls "world."[12]

## §7. *Language and the* Praxis *of Eidetic Intuition*

"World," as the ultimate for-the-sake-of-which which releases everyday things in a network of meanings, is no less operative in our impractical, theoretical posture toward things present before us in essence-analysis. This is witnessed by the practice of the experts, e.g., Husserl, Scheler, and Conrad-Martius, etc. Here we do not find an immediate intuition of the timeless essence but a labored analysis mediated by the horizon of authoritative indeterminate meanings. "It is not as if a particular Dasein, untouched and unenticed by this already unfolded world, was placed before the free space of a 'world' in itself and only needed to look at what it encountered."[13]

The effort of eidetic phenomenology to thematize aims at the releasing of the innerworldly meanings in terms of their proper network of relations and involvements. But this freeing of innerworldly meanings is possible only on the basis of the defining, prescriptive, yet indeterminate whole (project) which is prior. The elucidating explication of something as something, i.e., the unpacking of the relations and involvements of the essential meanings, is only possible on the basis of the antecedent priority (a priori) of the essential meanings. But these meanings themselves are not isolated autonomous essentialities. Rather, prior to them and giving the realm of regional meanings their own proper *topoi* is world as that in which the human being always already finds himself as a "thrown project." We "always already" have been (*perfect* tense) in that which is *prior* to objects present before us and ready to hand. World has thus an *a priori perfect* character.[14]

This "wherein" of world which lets all things be encountered is opened and held open by language. Language is not the subsequent linguistic expression of what appears. Rather, it goes in advance of what appears and holds open the space in which things appear.[15] The understanding of the specifics of this position requires the elucidation of the two theses that *(a)* language always goes in advance of us and *(b)* language opens world.

The sense of "language" in "language goes in advance of us" and "speaking is listening to what language has to say" is brought to light when we have something important to say and cannot find the right words. In such a case we pause and appeal to our silent felt *habitus* of the language. Thereby, without reflecting on it we touch upon language as the immediate mediation of all particular speeches.[16]

This example shows the prelinguistic character of the mediation of language. That is, we do not appeal to any explicit words, nor do we imagine any grammatical constructions or syntactic rules in searching for the right word. Instead we appeal to the felt *habitus* or to characteristic learned activities by which we are in the world. Thus language functions prelinguistically in the sense that we do not use words and sentences when we appeal to language in our thinking and speaking. We are rather listening to language when we are looking for the right word or letting something come to presence. This is not an appeal to an unmediated and absolutely prelinguistic dimension which somehow is alive to the innerworldly meanings waiting to be expressed or presenced. Were it not for the felt *habitus* of our native language, either things would not be present at all or they would come to presence in some other way.

This prelinguistic sense of language parallels the extended sense of language suggested by Wittgenstein's notion of forms of life which found language games. What founds the *habitus* of a language is the training and instruction of the child which enables him to learn the language. For example, the child comes to learn the game of "naming." These learned games themselves are not properly linguistic but are that by which properly linguistic activity begins. These forms or basic patterns function transcendentally with respect to subsequent linguistic behavior, i.e., they establish the frameworks and horizons of meaning.

Does such early learning entail modes of givenness mediated by the meaning-context of world? Before the acquisition of language can we presume in the child a preanalytic undiscriminating awareness of the logical or essential spaces of which adults are more perspicuously aware?[17] How we answer these questions specifies the sense to be given the thesis that "language holds world open." *On the Way to Language* (1959) involves a shift from *Being and Time* (1929), where discourse, understanding, and emotive finding oneself *(Befindlichkeit)* were held to be coprimordial in holding world open. The priority of the project of possibilities, i.e., world, subordinates language to understanding. Hearing and speaking are rooted in this pregrasp of world. This view puts Heidegger in a better position to handle the arguments that language ability entails innate a priori capacities which are in some way operative and illuminating Dasein in the initial learning of a language. In the later writings, however, the view is advanced that we understand because we listen (to language), not that we listen and speak because we understand, i.e., because we project world as the context of references.[18] World is only properly open when Dasein, under the sway of language, acknowledges its peculiar mastery by following its rules and being attuned to its basic forms. When Heidegger maintains that there is no appearance of something as something without language, he is not maintaining that words or linguistic behavior cause things to exist; rather, something appears as something through language. Without the linguistic relationship to things, they fade from presence as something and world collapses.

The open space in which things come to light, world, has its limits in the limits of language. There is no apprehension of the Being of beings, i.e., of that which is most fundamental and that out of which and by which beings show themselves, without language. Language is the house of Being: Being resides in that unsaid silence which breaks its silence and is listened to in thinking, speaking, and writing, i.e., in the coming to presence of beings.

Basic to this view is the refusal to radically separate *langue* and *parole*. Language as the appropriated world-opening *energeia* has a teleology of presencing and therefore cannot be grasped by the paradigm of a worldless text or a self-contained universe of signs, absolved from the question of truth. Rather, language, as that by which beings come to presence, involves responsible appropriation by a speaker.

> Consider saying: "It is true, but I don't believe it." No doubt there are unstated sentences which if stated would be true statements, but the issue is whether this makes sense or shatters: "No sentence is ever stated, yet some sentences are true."[19]

Heidegger's view of language as a letting presence from out of world, like Husserl's transcendental reduction to the living present, moves in a realm which is beyond language as a system of already spoken signs. Language, as *sagen* (i.e., presencing), is to be envisaged at once as that which possesses human beings and goes in advance of them and also as the performance of a speaker. This necessity of a speaker's appropriation implies the capacity to dwell on the mediation by language of whatever is. On the one hand, this is to retrieve the meanings or implications already meant by words and to remind ourselves that we are responsible for these meanings. On the other hand, the retrieval of this mediation provides possibilities for a critical and creative use of language and opening of world. (See Part III of our Commentary.)

The performance of phenomenological analysis bears witness to the way language holds sway over explication. Free imaginative variation involves presencing the phenomenon in a generic way by subsuming it under a word or a concept, e.g., "a promise." The grammatical possibilities of this generic determination may then be explored, e.g., whether it lends itself to being used as an adverb, e.g., "promissorily"; whether it can be used in the imperative form; whether it must be addressed to another who is listening, etc. All good phenomenologists show a sensitive ear for their language and listen to what their feeling for the language dictates as permissible and proper in the course of free imaginative variation.[20]

Although the explication of language usage is indispensable for essence-analysis (thus there is a coincidence between Heidegger's "Language is the house of Being" and Wittgenstein's "The essence is expressed in the grammar"), it is unlikely that Heidegger would hold that all essence experiences are merely linguistic explication. When Wittgenstein reduces all sentences concerning the *depth* of an essence to the depth of the *need* for agreement among sentences, Heidegger could ask: Is there not an experience of essence *of some sort* which has a particular depth and which is not found immediately in sentences but in the establishing of the condition for the possibility of sentences as well as in the introduction or change of language games? For example, not finding the right word in a situation where it is crucial to say exactly the right word is to be in the presence of language as language or world as world. This is to approach the limits of language in the sense that one demands that its mediating role be recovered or mediated. To be in the limit-situation of seeking to mediate that which mediates everything else is to approach the situation proper to the basic sense of anxiety.[21] The sense of essence here is not an eternal *eidos;* nor is it even something as . . . within a language game or world. It is nevertheless an experience of suchness or as . . . in the sense that there is an identifiable meaning, which is to be explicated as: being at the limiting conditions for the possibility of language, meaning, and world. We shall return to this in Part II. The difference between Wittgenstein and Heidegger on this point seems ultimately reconcilable. Wittgenstein is quoted as having said:

> I can well understand what Heidegger means by Being and *Angst.* Man has an impulse to run up against *(anzu-rennen)* the limits of language. Think, for example, of the wonder that anything whatever exists. This wonder cannot be expressed in the form of a question, nor is there any answer to it. All that we can say about it can apriori be only nonsense. Nevertheless, we run up against the limits of

language. This running-up-against *(anzurennen)* Kierkegaard also saw, and indicated in a completely similar way
—as running up against the Paradox. This running up
against the limits of language is Ethics.[22]

In summary: All innerworldly meanings receive essential
elucidation by recourse to that absent, silent context which is
held open by language and out of which something first of all
has meaning. There is no text without a context. Essential understanding is textualizing or thematizing the proper context
of meaning involvements. All phenomenology is properly hermeneutical or explicating phenomenology because it unfolds
texts within their contexts and then pursues the textualizing of
the contexts. But all contexts and texts are within world, which
itself is temporality.[23]

## §8. Essence, World, and Temporality

The basic prejudice of eidetic phenomenology is a variation
of that of Western thought: The meaning of Being is what is
abidingly present. This conviction leads to the ontologizing of
essential spaces in terms of essentialities, which themselves
are to be presenced. These essentialities, which enjoy an ideal
trans- or a-temporality, are considered to be the foundations for
the background of meanings appealed to in explicating something as. . . . But this construction, Heidegger believes, is unmindful of the a priori perfect. Da-sein is always already in the
world, and all making present or essential thematizing is a
"coming back" from that prior context of contexts which is
historical.

The identification of world as the a priori perfect with the
temporality of Dasein on the one hand and with the historical
epochs of the unconcealment of Being on the other means that
the ultimate significance given to essence-analysis by early
phenomenology is called into question. The Munich-Göttingen
Circle saw phenomenology's proper task to be the uncovering
of the *material synthetic a priori* positions concerning states
of affairs which obtain in the regions of experienced beings.
These are material because they obtain in the given objects of

experience themselves and are not to be ascribed to the formal and transcendental constituting activity of the subject; they are synthetic insofar as they are not the result of an immediate analytic explication or definition of the terms *(ex vi terminorum);* they are a priori because they are universal and necessary. Early phenomenology saw philosophy's task to be the elucidation of the timeless meaning-spaces and states of affairs. This was to let things come into their proper meaning-*topos.* It was also to derive from what *is* and is implicitly given an explicit *ought,* i.e., it uncovered the most fitting attitude to assume toward what is.

If, in the course of free imaginative variation, the question should arise: "Could someone have a feeling of ardent love or hope for the space of one second—*no matter what* preceded or followed this second?"[24] early phenomenology would found the necessary negative answer on timeless essentialities which legislate the states of affairs surrounding the meanings of love and hope. Heidegger, on the other hand, would seem to be reluctant to say that this state of affairs could in no way be imagined. Rather, like Wittgenstein, he would seem compelled to answer that this is not what love or hope means (in our language). Given the historical linguistic-cultural situation ("worlding of world"), this *cannot* happen. This non-possibility or necessity that it not be the case is genuinely a part of the fabric of inner-worldly meaning—in this sense it is a material synthetic a priori; nevertheless, it is mediated by world and not founded in essentialities which, in turn, found world.[25]

The sense of the synthetic a priori is thus not due to insight into the states of affairs obtaining between timeless essentialities but, rather, it is the result of having acquired an historical form of life and language. All essential questions of the form "What is . . . ?" or "What is the nature of . . . ?" are dictated by the anticipated answer already possessed by virtue of the fact of having a language and by appropriating ways of looking at things.

Having a language itself enables us to shift ways of looking at things ("conceptual frames"); i.e., we can *learn* and thus have occasion to call into question our set approaches. (As we shall see, this is one of the basic characteristics of what Heidegger calls authentic existence and, later, poetic dwelling.) One need only think of the difficulties of explicating the essence of "religion" from, say, an exclusively Baptist background, or explicating the essence of "the feminine" in the context of middle-class European traditions.[26] Before one has a change in conceptual framework, the explication proceeds as a clear synthetic a priori or, in an extended sense, *ex vi terminorum.* But when, e.g., the great "poetic work" (see our later discussion in Part III) or the learning process begins to bring about a modification in our habitual way of looking at things, we "will admit to being 'uncertain' of even those propositions which, in that frame, are true *ex vi terminorum.*"[27]

The material synthetic a priori which is mediated by world has its strongest case in reference to the life-world of intersubjective experience. But does it apply to logical and mathematical entities and all essential states of affairs? Do we not have regions of meaning which are amenable only to an eidetic phenomenology and not to a hermeneutical phenomenology? That is, are there not regions where historical-contextual explications are irrelevant?[28] Throughout Heidegger's writings (see especially "Principles of Thinking" in this volume) the position is maintained that no realm of meaning is exempt from the immediate mediation of world. There are no timeless principles of thought or principles of meaning. As we shall see, the notions of principle and ground are inappropriate for the ultimate dimensions of discourse. Inasmuch as world is held open by language, Heidegger would side, *ceteris paribus,* with Sellars that

> the conceptual status of descriptive as well as logical—not to mention prescriptive—predicates is constituted, *completely* constituted, by syntactical rules. . . . (While) every conceptual frame involves propositions which, though synthetic, are true *ex vi terminorum,* every conceptual frame is also but one among many which compete for adoption in the marketplace of experience.[29]

It is this necessity among innerworldly meanings, occurring within a space of ungrounded prescriptions, which occasions the description of the "basic" ontological dynamics in terms of *play.* We shall return to this in Part III.

The *praxis* of the phenomenological explication of the synthetic a priori, as well as all other forms of presencing, exhibits the justification for identifying world with temporality. This identification is hinted at in the description of world as the a priori perfect. All presencing is a coming back out of that context of involvements in which Dasein always already is and which is "not yet" with respect to what is actually present. And although world as held open by language always goes in advance of Dasein (as a thrown project), this project itself is always from out of Dasein's standing in a "no longer" of handed-down, acquired, and retained meanings. Thus presencing, whether spoken or tacit, is effected by a coming back from that in which Dasein always already is, which itself is always being constituted by extrapolation from out of the linguistic-cultural milieu in which Dasein finds itself.

It is these basic modalities attached to being-in-the-world, i.e., these "temporal ecstasies," which permit an object to appear the way it does. The ready to hand or the present before us are made present inauthentically, i.e., improperly, by Dasein's being unmindful of its being ahead of itself. What we normally mean by time and the various qualitative modifications of the experience of time (e.g., not having enough of it, its standing still, its going fast, etc.) involve the forgetting of the a priori perfect and the consequent picturing of what is present as discrete, cut off from the thrown project out of which it is presenced. Only on the basis of this forgetting can the concernful, awaiting presencing hold the present before it in isolation and treat it in the manner of a series of discrete nows.[30] Time as the flow of nows, as well as the flow of the various modifications of these nows, has no legitimation other than Dasein's temporal ecstasies.

Proper presencing takes the form of a resolve to appropriate Dasein's ownmost possibilities, i.e., its being in world, and to be open for that out of which meanings are presenced. This entails an appropriation of what Dasein always has been, a thrown project, which comes back to itself (its ownmost possibilities) by way of gathering itself out of its fallenness in what is present. (We shall return to this in Part III.)

The thrown project of world deriving from Dasein's temporal ecstasies is the transcendental side of the later references to the historical-epochal disclosures of Being. Although these disclosures necessarily transpire through the *there* of Being which Dasein is, their sense cannot be confined to Dasein's temporality. That out of which meanings come to be present, which is *the* phenomenon of phenomenology, does not have its exhaustive sense in the thrown project which is Dasein.

## §9. The Phenomenon of Phenomenology

Heidegger, with Husserl, holds that the Munich-Göttingen ontological phenomenology of essences does not raise the properly, i.e., most radical, philosophical issues. For Heidegger the task of phenomenology as radical inquiry into what shows itself cannot be merely an account of the various modes of givenness of objects, even if this includes all the basic modalities of being-such or as-such. Nor can it be merely an account of the mode of givenness of constituting consciousness.[31] Phenomenology must rather deal with the question of how being-given is possible at all. This is still phenomenology as the study of what shows itself, but it points to the inherent ambiguity of "what is given" or "what shows itself."[32] Eidetic phenomenology, as we have seen, was committed not only to what was explicitly given but also to the prescriptive horizon of indeterminate given-with meanings. For Heidegger the Munich-Göttingen Circle was not sufficiently attentive to this hidden, obscure background.

Early in *Being and Time* we find a programmatic statement as to what the phenomenon of phenomenology is.

> But what in its essence is *necessarily* the theme of an explicit manifesting? Apparently that which at first and for the most part does *not* show itself. That which remains hidden over against that which first of all and for the most part shows itself—but that which essentially belongs to that which first of all and for the most part shows itself in such a way that it constitutes its meaning and ground (reason).[33]

All presencing or bringing to light is made possible by the a priori perfect of world. World, although it may be considered the immediate mediation (the "Nearest") and that without which things could not show themselves the way they do, remains hidden and absent with respect to what is in the light and present. What is brought into the light is made present from out of the hidden and absent. That which is in the light or the open does not merely set aside the hiddenness but needs it in order to be present as it is, as un-concealed and dis-closed. Human beings must learn to recognize concealment, darkness, and hiddenness as belonging to "Being," i.e., to the process of unconcealment, not as the lightless abyssal night but as shadows belong to light. They

> must learn to recognize the darkness as the ineluctable and to keep at a distance those prejudices which destroy the lofty sway of the dark. The dark has nothing to do with pitch blackness as the complete, sheer absence of light. The dark is rather the secret mystery of what is light.[34]

The phenomenon of phenomenology for early Heidegger is world as the project of Dasein. But the question soon arises whether the anticipation by Dasein of its possibilities (what *Being and Time* calls "understanding") can fully account for absence and hiddenness. In its anticipation, Dasein is always providing itself with expectant types, patterns, and heuristic orientations. But in the process of disclosure, Dasein must always wrest what is to be disclosed from what is hidden. If Dasein's projective understanding is genuinely an understanding, how is it that the horizon is always and essentially hidden? The answer for later Heidegger is that Dasein's transcendence or ex-sistence (the a priori perfect) is not the only source of "truth" as un-concealment *(a-letheia)*. Concealment belongs to Being as Being and not as a mere consequence of human finitude.

> No attempt to ground the essence of unconcealment in "reason," "spirit," "thought," *"Logos,"* or any form of "subjectivity" can rescue the essential-presencing *(Wesen)* of unconcealment. . . . Therefore there is first needed an appreciation of the "positive" in the "privative" essential-presencing *(Wesen)* of *aletheia*.[35]

The phenomenon of phenomenology is that positive privative out of which things come into the open, i.e., that by which
things shine and which is manifest only through shining
things but which itself does not shine. Heidegger uses the metaphor of the "clearing" for the phenomenon of phenomenology.
In order for something to appear in the forest a place must be
cleared, i.e., the thicket must be cleared away and space must
be made. Light itself does not create the clearing but presupposes it: Something shines and is in the light only when it is
already admitted to the open space of the clearing. The metaphor of the clearing accounts for the luminousness of that
which is in the light as well as that by which things are in the
light. Likewise the "friendly struggle" between absence and
presence occurs within the clearing. And the full sense of absence and withdrawal as belonging not to Dasein's finitude but
to Being itself is pointed to by the metaphor because the clearing is within the thicket of a forest. Finally, things only appear
so long as Dasein remains in the neighborhood of the clearing.[36]

The claim that the clearing is *the* phenomenon of phenomenology therefore struggles against the "myth of the given" and
the pervasive teleology of presencing of language as the gathering out of hiddenness and absence into presence and manifestness. The phenomenon of phenomenology is an emptiness. In
what sense?[37] It is not the *emptiness* of the unsaturated intention which is to be saturated or the inadequate givenness which
is to be overcome. (The clearing, e.g., is not *ipsum esse subsistens* which can saturate, in a *visio beatifica,* the restless heart.)
This emptiness is neither the signified absence of a named nor
the signifying absence of any name.[38] Nor is it even the differentiation of filled/empty and presence/absence which keeps
open the space of their interplay and their "friendly struggle."
(See our later discussions of the poetic measure and the "difference" in Part III.) Rather, it is that absence within which all
presencing and absencing occurs. This absence withdraws itself in all acts of presencing just as the way a picture depicts
that of which it is a picture withdraws or is not in the picture,
or the way the mode of projection of a map withdraws and is
itself not part of the map. This absence and withdrawing, like

the "lofty sway of the dark" which is not the lightless abyssal night but the "secret mystery" of what comes into the light, is ~~emptiness~~.

To summarize: The phenomenon of phenomenology is what first makes room for those ontic spaces of essential clarification and for any appearing whatsoever. But this itself cannot be grasped in its priority if it is regarded as a transcendental project of Dasein. Prior to such transcendental thinking is the world-clearing in which Dasein finds itself. All innerworldly beings are manifest, even the human being to himself, only insofar as they are within the clearing. Even the distinction between (appearing) in itself and (appearing) for us is subsequent to the world-clearing. Phenomenology, therefore, is most properly neither eidetic nor transcendental; rather it is "aletheiological."[39]

All bringing into view requires Dasein's compliant attunement to the clearing. This antecedent compliance is the "piety of thinking." We must now turn to other senses of piety and their relationship to the clearing.

# Part II · Phenomenology and Religion

## §1. The Eidetic Phenomenology of Religion

The themes of "world" and "clearing" provide the basis for the critique of the eidetic phenomenology of religion as well as of Christian theology. The former, as a discipline, separates itself from the historical-comparative phenomenology of religions in that it, as a regional ontology of the "divine," is primarily interested in the elucidation of the basic concepts or essential phenomena which guide the research of the historians and comparativists: the holy, cult, prayer, the divine, sin, etc. Its dangers are notorious. In examining an essence, e.g., "sin" or "the feminine," the phenomenologist seeks out the eidetic properties through free imaginative variation. But the cultural limitations of the legislating space for the essence are disclosed as soon as the ethnological-comparative material is brought in to aid the free imaginative variation.[1] The temptations become strong to give up essence-analysis and either pursue a more nominalistic family-resemblance type of classification or seek (universal) structures in the transcendental constants of human ex-sistence, i.e., the ways human beings dwell and cultivate world. This latter was the alternative urged by the early Heidegger.

Max Scheler and Rudolf Otto focused the regional ontology of the divine or "religion" on the phenomenon of the holy.[2] Both Scheler and Otto regarded the holy as a unique ("non-natural") quality of objects, i.e., a value. Indeed, for Scheler the holy is the highest of values. Heidegger's references to the holy, on the one hand, seem consonant with the "qualities" of *mysterium tremendum et fascinans* as "properties" of what is meant by the holy. Yet the holy is not proper to a separate region, nor is it primarily a quality of objects; the reasons for this are to be found in Heidegger's sustained repudiation of value thinking.[3]

Value philosophy is unmindful that it is foremostly world which enables things to appear as they do, i.e., significantly and valuably. The basic premise of value philosophy is that the fundamental level of the phenomenon disclosing itself is its present-before-us thingliness.[4] The ontologizing of values, a species of the ontologizing of essences, assumes that we first have the naked present thing and then subsequently there is affixed to it significance and value. This does not mean that for Heidegger the ordinary commitment to saying "She is noble," "That is beautiful," etc. is to be uprooted. Nor does it mean that what is ordinarily regarded as valuable is in fact worthless. Rather, by focusing the sense of worth and value on that which makes place for such perceptions, Heidegger believes we restore to what we esteem its full worth. Through the appreciation of something as a value, what is esteemed is permitted to become merely an object standing in correlation to the approval of a person. This is, in fact, a subjectivising of what is valued. What something is, in its fullest sense, is not exhausted by its objectness. The weight of its worth is in its meaning-involvement "elsewhere." This is the sense to be given Heidegger's remark: "No one dies for mere values."[5] What we call values may be said to presence world for us in a more urgent way than other things. And it is for world as the on-account-of-which of our life-projects that we might be willing to die. But values themselves *as qualities* of things are *within* world. World itself is therefore not a value.[6] Thus the ranking of what we esteem in terms of value qualities takes no account of the a priori perfect and the clearing by which things are assigned their worth and significance.

Value philosophy expresses the highest measure of confusion and uprootedness and therefore it is not the overcoming of nihilism but its fulfillment. The treatment of God as the highest value is actually a degradation of the essence of God. Furthermore it is the "highest blasphemy against the meaning of Being."[7] How discussion of the holy in terms of a value-quality is a distortion can only be seen after examining how un-*concealment* becomes manifest. Here let it be noted that Heidegger maintains that certain modes of presencing, e.g., great works of art, enable un-concealment to become manifest and thereby make possible the presencing of the holy. When this happens

> dignity and splendor are not properties, next to which and behind which the god stands, but in the dignity and in the splendor the god becomes present. In the reflection of this splendor there radiates, i.e., there is lighted up, what we have called world.[8]

This text indicates how what we call values presence world in an urgent way. The eidetic phenomenology of religion, which focuses on the essential region of divine objects or the holy, is blind to the full sense of the phenomenon of the holy because of its value-oriented approach. Whether the opening up of the full phenomenon justifies the elimination of the nuclear value-quality is not pursued by Heidegger.[9]

## §2. *Christian Theology, Metaphysics, and the Holy*

In "Phenomenology and Theology" Heidegger sketches the eidetic of Christian theology. This secures one sense of theology in Heidegger's writings. Another sense, more important for his philosophical reflections, is Western theology's actual historical form. Theology has yielded to the temptation to be relevant and scientific and has thus perverted itself into a form of competition with philosophy.

> Someone who has experienced theology in his own roots, both the theology of the Christian faith and that of philosophy, would today rather remain silent about God when he is speaking in the realm of thinking.[10]
>
> ... *causa sui:* This is the right name for the God of philosophy. Man can neither pray nor sacrifice to this God. Man

can neither fall to his knees in awe before the *causa sui* nor can he play music and dance before this God.[11]

Heidegger is not "spoken to" by theology. We know from other texts that (at least *qua* thinker) he is not addressed by faith. But here we see that the reason he is not addressed by theology is that it has become wed to metaphysics, which is ill-suited for speaking of religious themes. The philosophical issue is how Heidegger judges metaphysics to be ill-suited for speaking about God or religious themes. The point is not that metaphysics cannot speak religiously about religion, i.e., that it must speak conceptually and abstractly. Rather, Heidegger maintains that *(a)* there is a sense of the holy to which *philosophical* reflection (the "experience of thinking") points and *(b)* Western metaphysics has a basic commitment which blinds it to this experienced meaning. We shall begin with *(b)*.

## §3. *Metaphysics as Onto-theo-logic*

In the earliest stages of Western thought there occurred the fated decision concerning the basic meaning of Being and the basic theme of philosophy. In this epoch Being became identified with *logos* as *legein:* That which lies before us became that which, as lying before, was first of all to be taken into account and upon which everything else rests. That upon which everything else rests is the ground, the basis, the reason.[12] The understanding of Being as *logos* is the understanding of Being as reason or the ground. *Logos* unfolded itself to *principium,* or to what is first and begins.

The lying before us, as that upon which everything rests, shows itself as that which is to be held responsible for something: for the Greeks, *aition,* for the Romans, *causa.* Principles and causes have the character of founding, grounding, providing a reason. In subsequent metaphysics the Being of beings is determined by the quest for reasons, for the ground (of beings). Eidetic phenomenology, no less than logical analysis, is bent on bringing that which shows itself under a category or giving it a basis.

Thus Being as *logos* is logic; and ontology is ontologic as well as onto-theo-logic because it is in search of the most fundamental ground as well as of the highest cause.[13]

> Therefore all metaphysics is at bottom, and from the ground up, what grounds, what gives an account of the ground, what is called to account by the ground, and finally, what calls the ground to account.[14]

In modern thought this basic theme of metaphysics has attained expression in Leibniz's "principle of sufficient reason": Every being has a reason or a ground; nothing is without a ground. But the principle of sufficient reason says nothing about the ground or reason, but rather about what is insofar as it is, or about a being insofar as it is a being. If one takes an interpretative plunge and emphasizes "Nothing *is* without a *ground,*" there is derived: Being and Ground are the Same.

> That is, insofar as Being as Ground presences itself, it itself does not have a ground. But this is not because it grounds itself but because every grounding, and especially that of something by itself, has no place here. All founding and every appearance of something being able to be grounded would degrade Being to a being. Being as Being remains groundless. The Ground or Reason [as themes] . . . remain remote from Being. Being is thus *Ab-Grund* (abyss).[15]

"Being" throughout Heidegger's writings means that which is *the* question (note the temptation to say "most fundamental") of philosophy or *the* phenomenon of phenomenology. "Being" is thus always under an historical determination.[16] The form of this question for Heidegger is how to make present that which withdraws in all making present. We stumble before this task because the only sense of questioning and thinking we are familiar with is onto-theo-logical. Nevertheless, granted the soundness of the claim for the priority of the a priori perfect, it is that which withdraws which is most worthy of being thought and therefore is that which calls for philosophy's reflections. In this sense, that which withdraws may be said to draw us on the way toward it. And this itself is a form of presencing, namely of that which withdraws and hides.

The task is to presence that which is nearer than all that is present and which is prior to all measures, reasons, and grounds. But the attempt to raise the prior question and to formulate it so that it remains this side of the question which identifies the Being of beings with the ground or reason is full of pitfalls—language being not the least treacherous of them. In the Why of metaphysical inquiry, and thereby in the Why of all other inquiries, there is concealed an original determination which always thinks of Being as foundation or ground. Why? never ceases to mean For what reason? On what basis? Thinking which attempts to undo itself from this initial presupposition will then think without the Why. In searching for the measure with which one thinks without the Why, one comes upon a groundlessness wherein the human being is not at all at home. It is *unheimlich,* uncanny, eerie, and unhomey in an essential sense: The modern is at home only when the issue is firmly based; but in this respect he is shortsighted.

## §4. Thinking and Homelessness

Heidegger paraphrases *Fragment* 72 of Heraclitus:

> Mortals are ceaselessly turned to the manifesting-hiding gathering which lights all that is present in its presencing. But still they turn from the clearing and turn only to that which is present. . . . They believe that this traffic with what is present of itself provides them with proper familiarity. . . . But they are unaware of that to which they are entrusted: unaware, forgetful of the presencing which as lighting first of all lets anything present come into view.[17]

In its everydayness Dasein is forgetful of its essential place, i.e., where it most properly "belongs." This is not due to a fall from bliss but is due to the fated event wherein the meaning of Being was established as *logos,* as that which is present before us. Modern nihilism, as the will to power, and technology, as the will to mastery, conquest, production, and consumption, are merely intensifications of this forgetfulness of the a priori perfect and the clearing. Western man, and a fortiori the modern, is, in a technical Heideggerian sense, uprooted and homeless. This homelessness is pointed to and contradicted in the occasional experiences of boredom, uneasiness, and anxiety. Occasionally the familiarity and being at home with things around us disintegrates and we become ill at ease, not at home, with anything. We are not afraid of anything, but rather we are anxious—no particular thing being the cause. Everything and we ourselves sink into an indifference. Things become indifferent not in the sense that they vanish from our surroundings but rather in the sense that they slide away just when they turn to us. We hover over everything and there is nothing that we can fasten onto.[18]

Such experiences point to the human being's "proper" home in the clearing. These are unique experiences in that there is no recognition of some*thing* as . . . , i.e., as a meaning within a context of meanings. Rather, here we have a limiting case for grasping *some*thing as . . . , insofar as there is no further involvement or network of relations to be unpacked. In these cases we are outside of and hovering over all innerworldly things and experience them as not providing a hold. We are immediately and quasi-thematically at that-on-account-of-which, toward which, and out of which, innerworldly things show themselves. World as the immediate mediation, which is ordinarily only subsequently thematically available, is here immediate and prior, resisting thematization within a context of involvements. Its meaning (as . . .) is found precisely in this priority and limiting resistance. This is world's essential presencing *(Wesen).*

For Heidegger these experiences are also occasions in which the groundless ground, the absence and emptiness out of which all unconcealment occurs, is experienced. At the same time there is implied an experience of our mortality: The context of contexts, or world, in which we live our lives as thrown projects, is the total possibility of our life—our hopes, wishes, dreams, plans, etc. But the full possibilities of life always stand in the shadow of our death as our "ownmost" possibility, as the ineluctable horizon of all our projects. In these occasional moments, when all the things in our life lose their taken-for-granted and substantial quality, not only are we confronted with world as world, as our thrown project, but the never completely buried awareness of the scope of this project, i.e., of our being-toward-death, presses upon us. Thus, in the basic human task of experiencing the clearing as the prior measure, death and the unsettling experience of anxiety have a special place.[19] "Death is the still unthought measure of the immeasurable, i.e., of the game with the highest stakes where the human being is brought into play on earth."[20] If world, as the immediate mediation, is the immeasurable, the sense of *this* measure is to be found in the nothingness proper to death's *not* being a being before us and *not* being ready to hand. The "nothing" which is my death cannot be handled in terms of innerworldly categories, e.g., event, change, property, fact, object, privation, etc. The "phenomenal properties" of the death of another are all "this side" of death in its proper sense (as my death), and to apply these categories to death is to miss its proper sense. And to miss the proper sense of death is to miss a paradigm which surmounts the thing-ontology wherein the meaning of what is is determined by the paradigm of what is present before us. ("Being-toward-death may be envisaged as an epoché of the meaning of Being in terms of ready to hand, present before us and Dasein"—Thomas Prufer.) Furthermore, to miss the sense of death is to overlook what is uniquely proper to the human being; i.e., what is his ownmost and therefore where he, upon appropriation, comes into his own, is necessarily the uncanny, that which unsettles us from being at home with things in the world.

It is clear that what is at stake here for Heidegger is more than an eidetic of experiences which some people might be able to recognize. Nor is the absence of this experience to be understood merely as *a* form of repression. Rather, the human being's avoidance of authentic ex-sistence in the clearing provides the generic category for all alienation and repression. All ideological, sociological, and psychological forms of alienation are but aspects of this estrangement. But how does one get to be at home with that which is the eerie *simpliciter?*

## *§5. Thinking and the Holy*

It is in the experience of the Greek tragedians, especially as presented in Sophocles and re-presented in Hölderlin, that Heidegger finds a mode of being-in-the-world which corresponds to the "truth of Being," i.e., to un-concealment. Sophocles' use of *ta deina* in *Antigone* to describe the human being is rendered by Heidegger as "das Unheimliche." Thus Sophocles' statement "Manifold is the uncanny, but still nothing comes forth more uncanny than the human being" expresses for Heidegger Dasein's constitutional incapacity to be at home in the midst of things. His ex-sistence skids away from settling down with innerworldly things and thus he properly dwells in that realm which, being beyond the homey and comfortable, is uncanny and eerie.[21] But this skidding away is resisted and ex-sistence is in-sistent, i.e., it stiffly holds fast to the innerworldly realm of things, needs, goals, plans, etc., forgetful of whence these are allowed to come to presence. Thus Heidegger can say of typical human beings: "The more familiar everything that can be known becomes, the stranger it remains for them without their being able to know it."[22] And:

> The homeless modern, through the success of his ever-increasing accomplishments and organization of the masses, allows himself to flee from his own essential being, in order to imagine this flight as the return home to the true humanity of *homo humanus* and to set it in motion himself.[23]

The first step in overcoming this homelessness is the non-metaphysical thinking of that which withdraws in our presencing of anything. This is a step "back" to that positive privative which is nearer and prior inasmuch as it is the a priori perfect of the clearing. This is called by Heidegger a thinking from out of the truth, i.e., un-concealment, of Being.

> Only thinking which thinks from out of the question concerning the truth of Being inquires more originally than metaphysics can inquire. Only out of the truth of Being is the essential-presencing *(Wesen)* of the holy able to be

thought. Only from out of the essential-presencing of the holy is the essential-presencing of the divinity to be thought. Only in the light of the essential-presencing of the divinity can there be thought and stated what the word "God" is supposed to mean.[24]

The nihilism summed up in Nietzsche's "God is dead" is not a personal attitude to be refuted on the basis of church attendance numbers or apologetic proofs for God's existence. It is an expression of the unfolding of Western metaphysics—which is nearer to us than, and the condition for the possibility for, all the things within our everyday life. Its meaning is thus an after-the-fact description: Man has forgotten his uncanny dwelling and the holy is not in the established places. The really real supersensible world has lost its quickening and life-giving power. Christianity (not necessarily Christian faith) has contributed most to the withdrawal of the holy by becoming onto-theo-logic and a worldly-cultural power.[25] Man's proper existence, to be the most uncanny of beings and to dwell in the proximity of the divine, is so obfuscated that the absence of the divine is not even discerned. An explication of a theme in Hölderlin runs:

> The world's night is spreading its darkness. The era is defined by the god's failure to arrive, by the "missingness of God." But the missingness of God which Hölderlin experienced does not deny that the Christian relationship with God lives on in individuals and in the churches; still less does it assess this relationship negatively. The missingness of God means that no god any longer gathers men and things unto himself, visibly and unequivocally, and by such gathering disposes the world's history and man's sojourn in it. The missingness of God forebodes something even grimmer, however. Not only have the gods and the god fled, but the divine radiance has become extinguished in the world's history. The time of the world's night is the destitute time, because it becomes ever more destitute. It has already grown so destitute it can no longer discern the missingness of God as a missingness.[26]

The return of the divine is not completely up to man. Nevertheless the precondition is that man retrieve his proper place in the clearing. But the still unanswered question is: How does one begin to be at home in that which is the essential unhomey? In the same reflection on Hölderlin, Heidegger writes:

> Because of this missingness *(Fehl Gottes)* there fails to appear for the world the ground that grounds it. . . . The ground is the soil in which to strike root and to stand. The age for which the ground fails to come hangs in the abyss [—is completely without ground]. Assuming that a turn still remains open for this destitute time at all, it can come some day only if the world turns about fundamentally— and that means, unequivocally: if it turns away from the abyss. In the age of the world's night, the abyss of the world must be experienced and endured. But for this it is necessary that there be those who reach into the abyss.[27]

We interpret this difficult text to mean that, for the modern, the ground of the world, as the sense of the divine, has lost its reality. Thus the sense of the missingness of the divine for the modern is that there is no ground to the world. But a change is possible if this commitment and presupposition are completely relinquished: if the sense of world shifts from *both* the sense of its having a ground *and* of its being without a ground (and therefore "meaningless"). In order to experience un-concealment, however, there must be those, the poets, who experience Western man's displacement from world as having a ground, i.e., who experience the abyss. This is preparatory to being at home in the clearing. Hölderlin, according to Heidegger, saw this to be the basic task of his thoughtful poetry. In order to become at home in the clearing, historical man must make a detour and settle among what is uncanny and unaccustomed.[28]

The pattern of Heidegger's basic position is clear: Dwelling in the clearing, the most original and near, enables the "dimension" of the divine to be experienced.

> But the holy, which is the essential space of the divinity, which itself only provides the dimension for the gods and the god, only shines when previously and with long prepa-

ration Being itself has illuminated itself and been experienced in its truth.[29]

The issue is a Heideggerian variation of the eidetic phenomenological theme of essence-blindness. Unless one is open to the unhomey experience of un-concealment—which opens up and provides the measure for the region of the holy —the divine remains missing. In and of itself the experience of thinking is not an experience of the divine or the holy but of absence and withdrawal as such. But inasmuch as the clearing bestows on each real innerworldly thing its meaning and essential space—and therefore, metaphorically, its integrity and wholesomeness—Heidegger can speak of the clearing as the whole-some *(Heil)* or integral. And as the immediate mediation, and therefore never a mere innerworldly being able to be present before us, i.e., as the nearest to which we can never draw near because it is always that which withdraws *(Entzug)*, the whole-someness of the clearing is also the upsetting and displacing *(das Ent-setzliche)*; that is, the clearing is both *Heil* and *das Un-heimliche*.[30] In this way Heidegger has occasion to appropriate the doublet established by the eidetic phenomenology of religion, *mysterium tremendum et fascinans*, in conjunction with the withdrawal and presencing of the clearing.[31]

The thinking which experiences the clearing is also referred to as *the mystery*.[32] In order for a mystery to be known, it must manifest itself in such a way that what is revealed is the concealment as such. But in our most needy day, when no need is experienced, the sense of mystery is that the concealment itself is concealed—and "nevertheless somehow appears."[33] The "somehow appears" refers to how the clearing is that by which everything appears but which itself does not appear amidst that which appears. Only for the experience of thinking is its absence as absence apparent. Otherwise it is mystery as that which hides its hiding.

Theology can be criticized by the experience of thinking because it, as onto-theo-logic, closes itself off from the essential measuring region wherein mystery and the holy are manifest. Heidegger's critique is from the standpoint of un-concealment.

There are no more fundamental reasons. The free open place of the clearing is a "primordial phenomenon."[34] The "argument" against theology is a *petitio principii.*

---

In the following three sections a detour is made from the general presentation in order to consider in greater detail the meeting of faith and primitive mythic existence with Heidegger's thinking. This excursus furthers the commentary provided by the translators' notes to the essays translated in this volume.

## §6. Excursus: Early Heidegger and Early Bultmann

Rudolf Bultmann and Martin Heidegger were colleagues at Marburg from 1923 to 1928. In the formulation of the eidetic (ideal construction) of theology in "Phenomenology and Theology" (translated in this volume) as well as in Bultmann's early writings, we can assume a mutual influence. Here we merely note some of the points of contact.

Bultmann, in a 1930 essay, defended his use of the categories of *Being and Time* and referred to theology as a "positive science," in contrast to philosophy, which has Being for its object.[35] In this essay Bultmann uses the same example as Heidegger (the relationship between sin and guilt) to show how the merely "formally signifying" structure of "natural Dasein" points the way for a theological elucidation of faith-full existence.[36] Although Heidegger would not assent to the tendency in Bultmann's writings to treat the analysis of Dasein as a secularized version of the New Testament view of life, he would acknowledge the influence of the Christian theological tradition on his own analyses.[37]

Very early Bultmann appropriated the notion of Dasein's preunderstanding of Being (as worked out in *Being and Time*) as the transcendental-ontological horizon of all theological concepts. Preunderstanding of Being is the transcendental condition for revelation as authentic self-understanding. This revelation "is an act of God, an occurrence, and not a communication of supernatural knowledge."[38] Heidegger himself does not describe faith-full existence in terms of authenticity, because what is proper to Dasein is not a matter of faith. Whatever is proper to faith-full existence is always apprehended in faith.

When Bultmann raises the Johannine inspired question, How does the world end for the believer? he describes the acquired authentic existence of faith as a de-worlding *(Entweltlichung)*. This veers sharply from the Heideggerian meaning. (See the sense of de-worlding in SZ, pp. 65 and 112.) But Bultmann defended his attempt at synthesis:

> The meaning of the phrase is ontic or *existentiell.* For faith, the "world" (and the theological concept also is possible only on the basis of this existential or ontological concept of world) has come to an end as a specific "how" of human existence (which can also be understood ontologically in its formal meaning).[39]

Thus Dasein is always ex-sistence, i.e., always a being-in-the-world.[40]

A common theme shared by early Bultmann and Heidegger is that faith gives rise to theology. But the relationship of the *intellectum* to the *fides quaerens* is cautiously described. On page 17 of "Phenomenology and Theology" Heidegger holds that "if faith does not need philosophy, the *science* of faith as a *positive* science does." But (on p. 11) we have the statement: *"Presupposing* that theology is enjoined on faith, out of faith. . . ." But if faith requires theology and theology needs philosophy, does not faith need philosophy? The *"Presupposing"* as well as the mild "enjoining" *(auferlegen)* warn us away from equating this "need" with the (transcendental-) logical necessity in which philosophy is required by theology.

In an early (1929) essay, which is dedicated to Heidegger, Bultmann held that faith had a "practical compulsion" *(praktische Nötigung)* to develop theology. This compulsion stems from the mission of the Church and of faith to communicate the Gospel. The Church's kerygma always builds on a preun-

derstanding of Dasein and effects an explication of existence
which is, at the same time, a disclosure of new possibilities to
existence. In the kerygma *as teaching,* or theology, there is an
*indirect* call to repentance and a promise of forgiveness. But
there is no general rule as to what extent the preunderstanding
of the listener must be explicated in order that there be found
proper expression for the confession of faith and for the communication of the call and promise. Every linguistic expression, theological ones included, is tied to the historical context,
and the elucidation of this contextual matrix for the sake of the
kerygma presupposes obedience to faith. Faith operates along
with and criticizes theological explications. The Christian
(theological) *gnosis* is never an objectifying knowledge possessed by a wise man but an historical self-understanding in
obedience to faith.[41]

When Heidegger employs the Hegelian notion of *Aufhebung,*
which is approximated in English by "sublation" or "overcoming," to describe how, in rebirth, one's prefaithful existence is
raised up and preserved in a new way, we find in all likelihood
a trace of the influence of Karl Barth's *Commentary on Romans.*[42] Bultmann, in an early essay, offers a discussion which
parallels that in "Phenomenology and Theology": Rebirth in
faith is not a magical transformation that removes man from
his humanity. Existence in faith involves an *Aufhebung;* i.e., a
*negatio,* a *conservatio,* and an *elevatio:*

> If, through faith, existence prior to faith is overcome *exis-*
> *tentiell* or ontically, this still does not mean that the exis-
> tential or ontological conditions of existing are destroyed.

In spite of an early appreciation for aspects of Barth's theological writings and Heidegger's cautious discussion of how
Dasein's preunderstanding does not found but only "formally
points out" and "guides" theological explication, Heidegger's
position is ultimately unacceptable to Barth. In fact, it is a form
of hubris in that it sets itself up as a necessary partner of God
and imprisons the word of God. Barth consistently rejected the
claim that any philosophical analysis would provide a necessary a priori scheme of preunderstanding for the elucidation of
the word of God. A schema of thought or a philosophy may be

used when it is subordinate to the pictured object *(Gegen-standsbild)* of the sacred text, which dominates and holds sway over reflection and thought. But *all* philosophical concepts must be subordinated to the power emerging from the object pictured in the text; they can never provide a transcendental or ontological context for its elucidation.[44]

Barth's view implies that revelation creates new, meaningful language games, life-forms, etc., without needing to presuppose and thus stand in a necessary relationship to a linguistic-historical context or the a priori perfect. In this respect, the effect of revelation in faith has similarities to that accomplished by poetic dwelling in Heidegger's later thought. (See our discussion in Part III.) This insight, as developed by Heinrich Ott and others, is the basis for the discussion of *The Later Heidegger and Theology,* edited by James Robinson and John Cobb.

In Heidegger's eidetic of Christian faith in "Phenomenology and Theology," a new creation is admitted, but as an *Aufhebung* of the prefaithful existence. (See also the text of Bultmann quoted above.) To that extent the earlier forms are necessarily presupposed. Without the *conservare* there is no *elevare;* there can be no *elevare* which does not have its preconditions. In Barth's dialectic there seems to be a *coincidentia oppositorum* in history but not a genuine sublation wherein the new reality ineluctably depends on, includes, and overcomes its earlier "moments." In history we have *simul justus et peccator.* Until the *eschaton* there remains the nonresolved antinomy or paradox.[45]

There is doubtless a tension in the early Heideggerian-Bultmannian position that on the one hand states that theology is a positive science and on the other speaks of the necessity of theology to use philosophy for explicating its own basic concepts. If it is true that all theological concepts necessarily refer to that understanding of Being which is constitutive of Dasein, then the theological concepts will be able to be explicated only insofar as the theologian does philosophy (see "Phenomenology and Theology," pp. 18–19). But how can theology still be considered to be a positive science when it essentially must do philosophy, and not just incidentally as a physicist might *also* be an ontologist? The very subject matter of theology demands philosophy (see p. 19) in a more immediate way than other positive sciences. Its basic concepts are always at their frontiers (cf. p. 21) and touching upon philosophy. Granted that ontology does not found theology (and therefore theology enjoys a unique positivity), as a basic paradigm or regional ontology of nature might found physics, nevertheless the ontological elucidation codirects and corrects the science of faith. Because this involves an explication of basic concepts always at their frontiers, and because the explication of basic concepts can never be done by confining these concepts to themselves alone—rather the "original totality" of the ontological context must always be held in view (p. 18)—is it not the case that the theologian therefore *must* be a philosopher and not merely a practitioner of a positive science?

The difficulty of balancing between a positive science founded in Christianness and the insight that this science's basic notions are always at the edges of ontological questions is perhaps the reason for the basic unrest Heidegger indicates with the idea of theology as a science—an issue we have already touched upon in asking whether faith needs (the science of) theology. See pp. 7 and 29, where, in spite of his eidetic-ideal study of theology as a positive science, he still leaves the question open of whether, after all, theology still wants to consider itself a science.

The tension here is clearly between the themes (which Heidegger originally appropriated from Franz Overbeck) of a self-sufficient and self-contained pristine faith (theology as positive science) and the radical scope of *Being and Time* and its implications for hermeneutical theology (Bultmann). It is to some of these themes inspired by Franz Overbeck that we now turn.[46]

## §7. Excursus: Heidegger and "Christian Skepticism"

Hans-Georg Gadamer reports that in the early Marburg years Heidegger owned to adhering to the "Christian skepticism of Franz Overbeck." On this occasion Heidegger held that it was the task of theology, a task with which it must again engage itself, to seek the word which is capable of calling forth and nurturing faith. (Gadamer adds that this was perhaps more an expression of doubt with respect to theology itself than an echoing of Overbeck's criticism of the theology of his day.)[47]

What was Overbeck's "Christian Skepticism"? Overbeck made a sharp distinction between Christianness and Christianity. In his 1873 essay *Concerning the Christianness of Our Contemporary Theology,* Overbeck argued that in early patristic times Christianity gave in to the temptation to be relevant to its surrounding culture. Thereby it forfeited the purity of its faith by trying to be what it could not be. "Modern theology" is a *contradictio in adjecto* and "theology has always been modern and thus constantly the natural traitor to Christianity," i.e., to genuine Christianness.[48] "The first, fresh Christianity is a Christianity without the experience of growing old and it cannot be saved by any theology which does not renounce all of its pretensions: historical, scientific, and theological."[49]

Overbeck sharply separates knowing and believing. The chronic attempts by theology to make of faith a knowing according to prevalent philosophical or cultural standards is deadly to the meaning of the Christian religion, i.e., to Christianness.[50] The essential note of pristine Christianity is a world-denying expectation of the end of the present mode of the world and of the imminent coming of Christ. Later this expectation was transformed into a "more ideal form": the ascetical, faithful *martyrium quotidianum* of monasticism.[51]

A similar distinction between Christianity and Christianness is elaborated by Heidegger in "Phenomenology and Theology" and also when he discusses Overbeck's friend, Nietzsche:

For Nietzsche, Christianity is the historical, worldly-political appearance of the church and her claim to power within the formation of Western humanity and its modern culture. Thus Christianity, in this sense, and the Christianness of the New Testament faith are not the same. A non-Christian life can affirm Christianity and use it as a power factor, just as, contrariwise, a Christian life does not necessarily need Christianity. Thus a confrontation with

Christianity is in no way necessarily a battle with what is
Christian, just as a critique of theology is not itself a critique of faith. . . .[52]

The term *Skepsis* in relation to Overbeck is, according to his
friend Bernoulli (in the Introduction to the posthumous work
*Christentum und Kultur*), the result of acquiring the *habitus*
of doubt, an inevitable consequence of a serious researcher.
However, this doubt and skepticism with respect to Christianity was also a tribute to theology as a science. Only with the
freedom of skepticism could he do justice to theology and confront it completely free of prejudices. His skeptical posture in
no way resulted in his being an open foe of religion. Overbeck
believed that Nietzsche, in his direct battle with Christianity,
had unintentionally become its supporter. The skeptical historical researcher, on the other hand, can, in the course of time,
make Christianity impossible in that he innocuously tran-
scribes its past and thereby shows the incompatibility between
its present identity and its past pristine form.[53] Thus the sense
of "skepticism" in reference to Overbeck's relationship to
Christianity is, following Bernoulli, doubt for the sake of scientific reasons, mixed with motivations of incredibility and respect for the Christian claims.

   Although we see that Overbeck was a skeptic toward Christianity, it is rather clear that he was not a *Christian* skeptic.[54]
The sense of Gadamer's reference might be that Heidegger,
like Overbeck, is committed to bracketing revelation in the
pursuit of the exigencies of philosophical thinking. To determine whether "Christian" skepticism applies, we can turn to
Heidegger's appreciation of theology's task. Heidegger has exhorted theology to consider seriously Paul's statement "Did not
God make the wisdom of this world to be foolishness?" (1 Corinthians, 1:20) and to judge from the experience of Christianness whether it is to theology's advantage to appropriate metaphysical categories.[55] And elsewhere:

There is, to be sure, a thinking and questioning elaboration of the Christianly experienced world, i.e., of faith.
That is theology. Only an epoch which no longer fully
believes in the true greatness of the task of theology can

arrive at the disastrous notion that philosophy can help to provide a refurbished theology, if not a substitute for theology, which will satisfy the needs and tastes of the time. For the original Christian faith philosophy is foolishness.[56]

From these texts "Christian skepticism" might mean the Pauline attitude toward philosophy. But that is not the sense in which it might have been said of Heidegger, for we read in the same place that:

a faith that does not perpetually expose itself to the possibility of unfaith is no faith but merely a convenience: the believer simply makes up his mind to adhere in the future to the traditional doctrine. This is neither faith nor questioning, but the indifference of those who can busy themselves with everything, sometimes even displaying a keen interest in faith as well as questioning.[57]

But what is it for a believer to be constantly exposed to the possibility of nonbelief and to struggle against holding a doctrine in the future? This cannot mean that the believer is full of doubt. Nor can it mean that the believer's faith has no content to which he would want to cling in the future. In the next paragraph faith is described as a form of security with its own way of "standing in the truth." Likewise we learn in the same section that the believer cannot follow philosophy in raising the question, Why are there beings at all and not rather nothing?, without giving up the faith (which is his life) in God the creator—something (a content) presumably the believer *qua* believer wishes to cling to in the future.

It seems that Heidegger's point is intended to be an eidetic one, i.e., a statement about Christian faith as such. The realm of faith has properties distinct from the realm of belief. The negation of believing-that is doubting or not believing. The negation of faith (some sense of believing-in) is not doubt but a cessation of one's being-faithful to that (one) in which one believed. The negation of believing-in indeed subsequently results in doubting things which I believed surrounding that one in whom I believed and to whom I was faithful. So long as I believe-in, my associated beliefs-that remain fairly impregnable. The Christian faith is primarily believing-in, which is a being faithful to. . . . Its negation is not doubt but a loss of faith-in, which may be judged to be infidelity. But in Heidegger's discussions here (EM), the sense of faith is not always clear, i.e., it is not specified whether fidelity, belief-that, or belief-in, or all of these are meant. In "Phenomenology and Theology" it is clear that a way of being-in-the-world, faithfulness, is primarily meant.[58]

To be constantly exposed to nonbelief means that one's fidelity or faithfulness, upon which everything depends, is only through faith-in and available only through this "faith." Even the security of the mighty fortress which God is for faith is not known and possessed; it is not something over which one has charge. Rather it is a gracious gift participated in only through faith, which is itself a matter of faith—a belief-that, but primarily a belief-in and a matter of faithfulness. (See "Phenomenology and Theology," pp. 9–10.)

In these suggestive pages in *Introduction to Metaphysics* Heidegger would thus seem to be calling attention to how easily faith slips into being a secure "knowledge" of some content of faith (a belief-that). Thereby it loses its purifying and faithful character and becomes a convenient defense and security measure as well as a cultural bias. Birault, echoing Barth, relates the condition of continually being exposed to unbelief to the discussion of the abiding tension in the believer subsequent to the sublation or surmounting of the prefaithful existence in the faithful existence. This surmounting and surpassing of prefaithful existence is never a finished, once-and-for-all, matter.[59]

Within the context of philosophy's capacity to raise radical questions and faith's already having an answer to them, Heidegger is making the point that complacency among believers about the meaning of Being is not completely warranted from within their own standpoint. The text's ambiguity, however, is that, on the one hand, the complacency Heidegger clearly wants to challenge is the understanding of the meaning of Being in terms of creation—here primarily a belief-that; but what the believer acknowledges should be challenged is his complacency in his faithfulness, not his believing-that the world is created. But perhaps Heidegger wants also to challenge the complacency that the believer might acquire in thinking that he really believes the revelation of creation (creation *as* creation). That is, the very issue of the believing apprehension of the meaning of creation implicates the believer's faithfulness.

In the same rich text in *Introduction to Metaphysics* another possible sense of "Christian skepticism" is suggested, but in this case there can hardly be any application to Heidegger himself. Heidegger holds that the believer in creation can, after a fashion, raise the question of the meaning of Being, but this is not a genuine raising of the question. The believer accompanies or follows the thinker. It seems that this is, for Heidegger, more than merely going through the motions. But the would-be philosopher pursues the questioning in a conditional form, as if . . . , i.e., as if it were a real question and not already resolved by his faith. Here the skepticism or doubt is not that of Heidegger or Overbeck but that of, e.g., theologians reading Heidegger.

When Heidegger says it is not really questioning which the believer engages in when he does philosophy, he seems to be implying that to do philosophy genuinely one cannot be a believer. Either one is a believer and therefore is not a philosopher, or he is a philosopher and cannot be a believer. For Heidegger this does not seem to be mollified by "at the same time." This interpretation gives a precise sense to the statement in "Phenomenology and Theology" that "faith, as a specific possibility of existence, is, in its innermost core, the mortal enemy of the *form of existence* which is an essential part of *philosophy* . . ." (p. 20).[60]

Is not the proximate philosophical issue here that of Husserl's phenomenological reduction? If one can freely and occasionally reduce the appearances of existing things to the appearing of the appearances as such, without sacrificing anything and without assuming a *(existentiell)* habitus of skepticism or doubt, then the believer can occasionally disengage his mundane and extra-mundane beliefs and do philosophy.

In Heidegger's various remarks on faith and philosophy the standpoint from which he speaks is often in need of elucidation. In "Phenomenology and Theology" we have, from the viewpoint of fundamental ontology, an eidetic analysis of a given region of meanings, of a *positum.* The point of view requires the detachment at least of the eidetic reduction; i.e., the investigation seeks out the "ideal meaning" wherein the essential notes are brought to light and the incidentals are left behind. One need not be a believer to do this, but he must be well acquainted with the mode of existence or form of life of believers. But where does Heidegger stand when he claims that faith is a way of standing in the truth?[61] This statement likewise is to be understood as an eidetic statement from the viewpoint of fundamental ontology because it is about faith as a "form of existence" and every form of existence stands in the truth. Truth here is "unconcealment" and is not to be taken as an affirmation of the validity of the claims of Christianity.

However, when Heidegger on occasion maintains that the metaphysical discussions of God are blasphemy and that theology is religiously dead, the context is such that one can assume he is not speaking as an eidetic phenomenologist. In these cases he is not an analytic outsider commenting on how it must be for the believers.[62] In these cases the sense is that, for Heidegger's own experience, metaphysical theology is blasphemy, and his experience is, in a special sense, normative. What kind of experience is this? We have good reason to hold that Heidegger is not speaking from within the experience of faith but rather from out of what he calls the "experience of thinking." From out of this experience Heidegger gains a "standpoint" from which to judge the holiness and fidelity of theology to the holiness he assumes (believes?) pristine Christianness contains and discloses. Holiness is a primordial phenomenon, which Heidegger assumes to be appropriate to theology but endangered because theology is locked in to thinking of the *causa sui.* The experience of thinking, as the experience of the positive privative of un-concealment, takes up its abode in the uncanny abyss. This, for Heidegger, secures a proximity to the holy. In what sense? The ontic *mysterium tremendum et fascinans* is given ontological moorings as that uncanny abyss which always withdraws from view but which also heals and makes whole. Because the experience of thinking dwells in that which is both uncanny and healing, it is regarded as being preparatory for other "dimensions" of the holy, e.g., the divine or the gods.

How does Heidegger know that the experience of thinking prepares for the divine? If we think of the holy as that which withdraws and yet heals and makes whole, then we may extrapolate: the gods are powers which heal, make whole, and yet are not mortals. But such an account does not do justice to occasional references which point to an experiential preparation for the appearance of the divine. In these cases the evidence is provided by the poets, e.g., by Hölderlin, in whose experiences Heidegger has participated.

Of course to demand that Heidegger make a case for the connection between the experience of unconcealment and the divine might be said to miss the point. The full sense of dwelling in that by which everything comes into view would be collapsed if reduced to a demonstration of the relations between concepts. Perhaps it may be said that Heidegger knows the thinking of unconcealment to be preparatory for the divine because it undoes the thinking which is unholy, i.e., forgetful of the clearing. If there is a more complete and godly sense of the space of the holy, it will be hidden from us so long as we cling to what is present and to be mastered as the meaning of Being.

And even this merely preparatory character of the experience of unconcealment serves as a criterion for judging theology insofar as theology's mode of thinking is a pursuit of what grounds, or what gives an account of the ground, or what calls the ground to account. Such a thinking knows nothing of the uncanny abyss which makes integral—which for Heidegger is the criterion for the piety of thinking. We shall return to these issues in Part III when we discuss poetic dwelling.

## §8. Excursus: *Heidegger and Primitive Mythic Thought*

Heidegger's position toward myth is clearly not "primitivism" in the sense that there is a nostalgia for archaic life-forms. Nevertheless, the most proper mode of human existence, poetic dwelling, attempts to retrieve myth as "that which makes the claim which is in advance of all others and which is most fundamental." Poetic dwelling likewise participates in the establishment of the ideal possible of the actual real. (See Part III of the Commentary.) We can thus distinguish the mythic-utopian aspects of poetic dwelling as a basic human possibility from mythic thought as it is associated with primitives. A brief discussion of the latter helps prepare the way for understanding the former, which is a major theme after *Being and Time*.

Heidegger is convinced that a basic service is rendered ethnologists and comparative-historical phenomenologists of religion by *Being and Time* in that it works out the notion of world as the ultimate context of meanings within which all other meanings, including "world-views," find their place. World is antecedent to world-views and world-pictures or models which can be developed, grounded, improved upon, and of which one can be "convinced." World as the immediate mediation of all innerworldly meanings is always presupposed by world-views.

Heidegger considers the history of science as well as primitive religious phenomena from this perspective. Thus the history of scientific revolutions as well as of religious revolutions is determined by how capable the basic paradigms and notions are of handling the crises and challenges to their coherence and elucidating power. In both cases it is world which is formative of these basic concepts and paradigms. A shift in the manner of being in the world, which is always a coincidence of theory and practice, enables a shift in basic paradigms and thereby makes possible a new way of looking at things, new experimentations, etc.

In primitive human existence the specific form of being in the world is hinted at by the ethnological discovery of mana. Here there is a unique form of thrownness wherein Dasein finds itself delivered over to overwhelming powers which permeate Dasein's reality in every respect. World, under the aspect of mana, is still the immediate mediation, which is invisible with respect to the manifest objects present before primitive Dasein. Yet the objects within the mana-type world can take on extraordinary efficacy because of the antecedent way primitive Dasein finds itself in world. Primitive Dasein sees various objects *as* fraught with mana-power not because the isolated objects manifest a particular awesome aspect in themselves or because Dasein has uncontrolled desires and fears. Rather, the seeing *as,* as well as the specific affects of Dasein, presupposes Dasein's finding itself already in a context which enables the objects and affects to take on their particular meanings. Thus the interpretation of primitive human beings as being endowed with, e.g., "prelogical" powers of thinking wherein there is alleged to be a mystical uniting of incompatible objects (e.g., red parrots and members of a specific tribe in a totemic unity) would not have occurred if one posed the question of whether the natives see the red parrots *as such,* i.e., as the interpreter does, and likewise whether they see themselves as "members of a specific tribe," i.e., as the interpreter sees them.[63] Especially appropriate for the cluster of issues at stake here is Wittgenstein's remark:

> Where now a context is known, which earlier was not known, there was not there an open place, an incompleteness which is now filled out! (One could not at that time say, "I see the matter only so far; from here on it is not known to me.")[64]

The primitive is sensitive to world, as that out of which all meanings arise, in a way the modern is not. His implicit ontology has not yet identified Being with what is present. For this reason reflection on the world molded by mana is important for ontology.[65]

Mana, considered as a conceptualization of a notion enjoying astounding frequency in ethnological research, is perhaps the key notion in the ontology of archaic peoples. But, as Claude Levi-Strauss has suggested, the theme of mana may have relevance for the human spirit as such.[66] Levi-Strauss calls attention to familiar situations wherein we say of someone: "She's got what it takes." "She's got oomph." "He's got the knack." Or the situations wherein we refer to something as "whatchamacallit" or someone as "what's-his-name." These fluid and spontaneous notions represent an indeterminate value of significance which itself is empty of meaning but which nevertheless fills in the difference between signifier and the signified. Or better, on such occasions the inadequation between signifier and signified is established at the expense of the (typical) state of affairs wherein the signifier and signified are in a balanced relation, i.e., wherein the meant-signified saturates or is adequate to the intending meaning or signifier. For Levi-Strauss this inadequation of signified and signifier points to a superabundance of intention or of signifying proper to the human spirit. The "universe," from the beginning of human history, signifies the totality of what humanity expects in coming to know it. Mana "is only the subjective reflection of the existence of a nonperceived totality." The latter is "a totality of signification for which the primitive is quite embarrassed with respect to finding a place among a definite signified."[67] There is always an inadequation between this intention of the totality and the specifications of it in various objects. In his effort to comprehend the world, the human being always disposes of a surplus of signifying intentionality with respect to the signified meanings which he has at his disposal. The mana phenomenon provides an ontology that relates this excess of signification to the structure of things within the world and asserts an original unity between this superabundance and things within world. An example is the magical act of producing smoke in order to raise up clouds and rain. When seen in the light of mana-ontology, it is evident one need not appeal to mana in order to bind smoke to clouds and rain; rather, these discrete things are already the same, at least in a certain respect, and it is this identity which justifies the subsequent association, not vice versa. Mana is not of the order of "real objects" but belongs to a thinking which does not think of what is foremostly in terms of objects.[68]

The notion of mana serves as an instance of a "floating signifier" for Levi-Strauss. In linguistics, the observation has been made that in French, e.g., the zero-phoneme contrasts with all other phonemes in the absence of any distinctive features and of any constant sound characteristic. On the other hand, the zero-phoneme, for its own function, has to be opposed to the absence of any phoneme. Likewise, mana has the function of opposing itself to the absence of meaning without standing in definitive relation to a particular meaning.

Heidegger's concept of Dasein as being-in-the-world is another way of talking about the excess of signifying intention ("of a nonperceived totality"). Furthermore, the unique unity in myth and magic of signified and signifier is likewise to be explained by an original preunderstanding of a unified state of affairs.[69]

Levi-Strauss's discussion of mana as entailing "floating signifiers" points to four basic topics in Heidegger's thought.

1) For Heidegger (cf. the preceding discussion of the phenomenology of religion) "values" are primarily ways world, as that-on-account-of which, urges itself upon us. They are signifiers for that which cannot be specified or presenced by any particular innerworldly meaning.

2) The poet (see the following discussion in Part III), by dwelling in and building from the measure before all measures, opens up world and establishes a realm of meaning which, like mana, is *really real* in comparison with the conventional everyday reality. The task of the poet is the creative discovery of appropriate floating signifiers which let shine the *difference* between that which appears and the immediate mediation.

3) Things endowed with mana present themselves as having a power and density which enable them to be detached from their thingly context (cf. the embarrassment of which Levi-Strauss speaks) and to pack within themselves the full sense of world as, e.g., sacred stones, trees, bread, etc. Likewise, the work of art, which in itself permits world to world, and in its presencing holds open world, is detached from its thingly context and contains within it the context of contexts. (See Parts III and IV.)

4) The notion of a floating signifier occasions postmetaphysical philosophical reflections wherein the quest for presence, ground, and center, around which all structures organize, is foresaken. Absence, play, hiddenness, and free play of substitutions (of, e.g., frames of reference) become leading notions. "The affirmation [of this philosophical po-

sition] determines the non-center otherwise than as loss of
the center."[70] There is neither a sense of loss and nostalgia
nor a resounding affirmation of the negation. But whereas
in a logically consistent explication of basic Heideggerian
themes, as well as in the floating signifier, a sense of paral-
ysis and sterilization threatens to set in, Heidegger's own
explication points to a hopeful poetic existence wherein the
place inhabited by humans is transformed.[71] For Heidegger
the renunciation of presence and a center prepares the way
for the holy and the gods. But for thinking (from out of the
clearing) there is no possible way in which the return of the
god(s) could mean the return of the primacy of presence (as
in *visio beatifica* or *fruitio Dei*). In saying that hopeful
poetic dwelling does not follow from a conceptual explication of the clearing and of the primacy of absence, we are
merely saying it is not *implied ex vi terminorum.* This does
not mean it is a contradiction or is false; such descriptions
imply conceptual contents which have no place in the
clearing. It is "irrational" perhaps in the sense in which
hoping is possible without "compelling evidence."[72]

# Part III · The Changing of the World and the Worlding of World

## §1. The Original Mode of Ex-sistence

The quest after that which is prior and most proximate has its correlates in the attempt to formulate the originating mode of being human. The theme of "equal primordiality" in *Being and Time* and the transcendental imagination in the early work on Kant are attempts at doing justice to the plurality and specialization of human capacities, activities, academic faculties, and distinct disciplines while at the same time locating this plurality in a basic way of being in the world. The early specified sense of being *in* the world as dwelling (see SZ, p. 54) and the early reflection on the originating transcendental imagination merge in the later writings, wherein the most fundamental feature of Dasein is poetic dwelling. We only dwell when poetry occurs, because poetry gives the measure for full human existence. But to consider what poetry is we must first raise the question of what thinking is, because it is in thinking that the most radical sense of measure first becomes a theme.[1]

## §2. The Hortatory and the Utopian

The hortatory character of the discussion of thinking and poetic dwelling, like that of authentic resolve and releasement in *Being and Time,* is a call for human beings to be what they already are. This has two aspects: to retrieve the most basic way of being human which founds all other modalities of being human; to do what we most properly do although we always verge toward undoing what we do because of a fated obfuscation. The exhortation is moral, if this means doing what is "most proper," i.e., our ownmost. Yet it is not toward an action or a goal or even a posture which we have up to now been avoiding but which would be proper to assume. It is not even an exhortation to be "aware," if this means that up to now we have been unaware or that we should be aware of something. It is an exhortation, a call, to come into our own in a way which, on the one hand, presupposes estrangement from our ownmost but, on the other hand, presupposes familiarity in that it is expected that we recognize the propriety of the call and the fittingness of our response. The response to the call is thus a return to what is most original and originating. This is an engagement with the ancient sense of myth. It is also a thematization of the utopian not-yet, if this is understood as a real-possible ideal. (The mythic and the utopian will be treated when we are ready to discuss poetic dwelling, i.e., after we discuss thinking.)

The two aspects of exhortation, to the most basic way of being human as well as to doing what we do most fundamentally, can be brought to light if we review the accounts of the presencing of what is present in *Being and Time* and in the later writings. Both are considered to be ways of being on the way to thinking.

## §3. *Basic Tools*

Heidegger learned from Kant and Husserl that the perception of worldly things involved an intentional unity of a continuous flow of interlacing manifolds of experience and that the primary sense of self was the (temporal) adhesions and affections which unified this manifold. In the language of early Heidegger, Dasein is a synthesis of syntheses and self-affectings. In later writings, there are overtones of these themes when Heidegger employs the notion of "gathering." In this case especially overheard is Husserl's phenomenology of inner-time consciousness, the earliest lectures of which Heidegger himself edited for publication. For Husserl the "living present I" is the fontal source out of which all presencing occurs and is the origination of the continued synthesis of all acts of consciousness in the stream of consciousness. Just as the immediately past note of the melody is retained but is not originally or freshly present—while nevertheless constituting the sense of the present note—so too one's ever-receding and incrementally increasing past is retained in a dark, unlively way and constitutes the sense of the present. And this past is continuously undergoing (passive) synthetic modifications with each presencing act of the living present I. Inasmuch as each retention is a former actual present, the meaning of which is distended to include what just went before it, retentions are always retentions of retentions of retentions. One can awaken a past event in re-presentation, e.g., memory, wherein the past is had as past, only because the constituted meaning is already actually implicit in the background retentional consciousness.[2]

## §4. The Presencing of What is Present in Being and Time

Dasein is a synthesis of gatherings and self-affections on two levels, the inauthentic and the authentic. The proper sense of the presencing of the present depends on whether the proper (authentic) gathering obtains for Dasein. Dasein is essentially in the world in anticipation as always already (a priori perfect), and this anticipation is a form of gathering its thrownness. Although Dasein, as temporal ecstasy, in its inauthentic presencing, is scattered and strewn out, it nevertheless affects, finds, and gathers itself by coming back to itself from its projected possibilities and schemas of meaning—thereby conferring on what is present its particular mode of givenness.

The authentic *(proprius)* appropriating of Dasein's already-having-been-as-a-thrown-project is a gathering of its scattered lostness and fallenness—which scatteredness is still a form of gatheredness and self-affection. Our thrown projections always entail retentions of retentions and syntheses of syntheses. The higher-order exhorted gathering of the gatherings indispensable to ecstatic temporality is a unique form of future possibility to which Dasein is called and by which Dasein gains access to its ownmost being. Its improper scatteredness enables the discrete present to reign as the sovereign sense of time and the meaning of Being. The gathering which is the appropriating of Dasein's ownmost being distends the present into the moment of vision, thereby giving access to that out of which what is present and what is ready to hand come to enjoy their particular mode of givenness.

## §5. *Later Discussions*

The presencing of what is present is a letting be present. As a letting be *present* the focus is on that which is present. As a *letting be* present the focus is on the event of presencing. In the first case the meaning centers on letting the being be free *in the open* with other present beings. Nothing is said of whence and how the open comes to be. In the second case it is not what is present that is stressed but the presencing. The *letting be* present means to *let* it be given, admitted, sent, belong, etc.[3]

The latter emphasis calls attention to what is more fundamental in the order of constitution and in the order of Being. The givenness of what is present or ready at hand has its particular mode of givenness from Dasein's having let it be involved in a context of equipment or significations. This letting-be-involved, which is also a letting-be-given, presupposes Dasein's already being, by way of anticipation, in the clearing, thereby enabling admittance of the given thing to the context of significations and thereby enabling it to be in reach, dealt-with, grasped, and managed. Because of a very early rich and deciding event in Western cultural history, the event of *logos* (as *legein*), that which is placed in reach, grasped, or managed, because it is in the open before us, has held sway over the interpretation of the meaning of Being.

Since this originating decisive epoch there has fallen from view the hidden reserve out of which that which appears is presenced. The thinking which dwells in the gathering is that which is thoughtful of the most worthy of thought; it has, beforehand, in its keeping, the unthought, which hides itself in what is thought. If we understand the essential being of human beings to be the basic gathering of gatherings, or the self-affection of Dasein's ecstatic temporality, we may regard the heart to be the appropriate designation for this being.[4]

## §6. The Thinking which Recollects

All apprehending *(noein)* which unfolds from *legein* is a letting lie in unconcealment. The passive form calls attention to the passive synthetic activity in all presencing, even and especially that toward the present beings which we most actively strive to comprehend, grasp, and master. This passive synthesis in any particular presencing is the gathering of the unrelinquishing intention of all that the heart has ever allowed to become present. This unrelinquishing intention is the basic affection of the self for itself and involves retentions of retentions and gatherings of gatherings, over which the heart has no control and which involve no special enactment. That is why it is a passive synthesis or a passive gathering. Thinking which takes to heart is a thinking which recollects and dwells in the gathering.

This thinking thus involves a *stepping back* and gaining distance from that which first of all comes forth and imposes itself. Thereby does one draw near to what is to be thought, and to the Near itself as that out of which all proximity and familiarity come to be. Thus this thinking does not do anything to what it apprehends; but in its *taking to heart* what is present, it retrieves the original presencing of what is present and the original *letting* lie.

This letting be, whereby something is allowed to come into its essential space, i.e, to come into its own, is through a dwelling in the gathering, which is also an attunement to language. If being in the world as a thrown anticipation is a gathering of gatherings, then the axis of this motion of the heart is a listening to and speaking of language. Thus the called dwelling in the gathering of gatherings can only be an answering to that original listening and speaking.

Although the gathering, to which we return when we take to

heart what is present, is that which is retained by the gathering intentions of the heart, it would be amiss to believe that what is most worthy of thought and withholds itself in the presencing of what is present itself can be reduced to the gatherings which constitute a temporal subject. Dasein, in its gathered gatherings, is itself always already a gathered gathering in that it comes into its own by answering to the call of what discloses itself out of the clearing. All holding and listening are a gathering of what *logos* as language and nature *(physis)* lets lie before us by way of gathering out of concealment. Our bringing to light of all the kept, gathered intentions of the heart would not bring to light that by which these would come to light.

That which is thoughtful of the most worthy of thought and which dwells in the gathering that beforehand has in its keeping what is unthought can be named "taking thought." Taking thought refers at once to the recollective thinking which is taken by what is most worthy of thought as well as to the space within which manifestation out of hiddenness takes place. But this reference is not to two separate entities or events but rather to that out of which all separation and distinction arise. Taking thought, moreover, cannot be reduced to an essence—as if we were able, through free, imaginative variation, to come up with the ideal presence of repetitive sameness in difference proper to "taking thought as such," i.e., of that which is exemplified in each instance of manifestation out of hiddenness. But is there not, nevertheless, a coming into view? Are we not trying to presence the *eidos* of that out of which all presencing occurs? The issue, indeed, is "making present" that out of which all presencing occurs, i.e., of "presencing" absence as absence without thereby destroying its absence and making it something present. But here we do not have one essence among others, because taking thought refers precisely to that which always withdraws from view and within which all collecting into view occurs.[5]

## §7. Poetic Dwelling

On the one hand, the gathering of gatherings, which originates the letting be present, is the *sine qua non* of presencing, but, on the other hand, *dwelling* in the letting presence is called. To achieve this, one recovers what is always already necessarily achieved, but now appropriatingly. This, again, is the step back. The step back recalls the themes of eidetic analysis. To explicate the proper essential legislating space of something, we cor-respond *(responsum cordis)* to the a priori perfect, which is held open by language. We *step back* to that which is prior and out of which things are allowed to come into their own. This is the proper sense of dwelling. Dwelling is not primarily inhabiting but taking care of *(schonen)* and creating that space within which something comes into its own and flourishes. Dwelling is primarily saving *(retten),* in the older sense of setting something free to become itself, what it essentially is.[6]

However, the sense of dwelling is dependent on the "original building" which is poetry. If dwelling is that which cares for things so that they essentially presence and come into their own, and if thinking is that which comes upon the absent and concealed as the measure of the proper space in which things come into their own, it is poetry which makes present this absent, uncanny measure as absent and uncanny, thereby providing for dwelling its measure. Thus Hölderlin's verse "poetically man dwells" characterizes what one always already does insofar as the measure is at work; but the verse is an exhortation as well. The fact that in our technological, unpoetic existence we explicitly seek the measure in what is present and manifest serves as an indirect confirmation of Hölderlin's verse. Only a being with the capacity for sight can be blinded; a being can dwell unpoetically only if it is essentially poetic. The blindness need not come from a lack or a loss; it may also come from excess: "King Oedipus has perhaps one eye too many." It could be that our incapacity for the poetic measure is to be attributed to an excess whereby we are all too certain and well-equipped with measures for calculation and evaluation.[7]

## §8. The Mythic-Poetic Measure

The sense of poetry and poetizing here is not to be restricted to lyric poetry. Rather, it is meant to designate that *poesis* which brings about the overcoming of the forgetfulness and the *opening up* of world and clearing as the unthought immediate mediation.[8] World is necessarily open in an obfuscated way as the a priori perfect; but this obfuscation can be cleared in the event of poetic *works*. Heidegger calls this truth's (i.e., unconcealment's) establishing itself in a work. Such an extra-ordinary work may take a variety of forms: political deeds, works of art, philosophical questioning, heroic and sacrificial acts, and the approach of the god. In authentic poetic dwelling every deed and innerworldly thing can effect the opening of world and the clearing in a way analogous to the way the great poetic art work achieves this opening. Such a work is that by which the everyday for a particular people is held open. It determines what is familiar and wherein things come into their own. Thereby does it also prescribe what realm is uncanny and unfamiliar.[9]

In this respect poetic dwelling corresponds to and articulates the mythic as that which "makes the claim which is in advance of all others and which is most fundamental."[10] Reflection on the poetic measure as the unthought condition for the possibility for thought attempts to overcome the historical circumstance wherein *mythos* and *logos* are separated. This separation rests on the forgetfulness of that which calls for thought. In this restrictive sense myth may be said to be that which enables world to world the way it does "at any particular time."[11] And in this restrictive sense myth and the great work of art are identical in function.

> Just as every great work is itself responsible for the awakening and formation of the generation that will set free the world hidden in that work, the growth of the work in turn must hear ahead to the tradition it is responsible for.[12]

Poetic dwelling is not an attempt to relive or revivify old myths, if thereby is understood sacred exemplary stories of the ancients or the narrative rituals which presence the gods. Nevertheless it is a unique opening up and elucidation of whatever meaning-strata enjoy efficacy in our everyday dealing with what is near and for the most part. Myth as a sacred story surely is among these strata. Nor is poetic dwelling an attempt to create new myths, if that means to propose new sacred stories which presence the gods. Nevertheless, poetic dwelling alone prepares the way for the manifestation of the holy, which itself makes space for the appearance of the gods.

## §9. The Truth of the Poetic Measure (That Which Makes All the Difference in the World)

The poetic work not only determines what is familiar and the space wherein things come into their own (thereby determining as well what is uncanny), but it can also call into question and annul what was proper up until now. This raises the question of whether the measure indeed permits things to "come into their own" in any *proper* sense of what they might or should be.[13]

Initially it might be said that the establishment by the work of what is proper, whether it be the elucidation of the mythic as "that which makes the claim which is in advance of all others" or the calling into question of what was proper up until now, is never capricious, because it opens up that wherein Dasein always already historically finds itself.[14] Hölderlin's verse "poetically man dwells on this earth" calls attention to the dialectical character of the poetic measure: poetizing is what first of all enables man to dwell on this earth, i.e., enables him to allow things to come into their own; but this poetic measure is always an opening up of and measure for things as they always already have been for us; finally, it is the opening up of and measure for things as they *might be* for us. In this sense Heidegger could agree with Theodor Adorno's observation that "reality" (things within world) is not the exemplar for art but rather that "reality" imitates the art work. That is, things receive their space of possibility through the poetic work. The logical and real space-making event of the art work "means what is not could be. The reality of the art work generates the possibility of the possible."[15] Against this background of poetic dwelling a formula of Kant may, *ceteris paribus,* be ascribed to Heidegger: "The conditions of the *possibility of experience* in general are likewise conditions for the *possibility of objects of experience.*" But such a synthesis of ontological and transcendental reflection does not rest in conditions which are principles, grounds, or subjectivity, but in the absence and hiddenness of the clearing disclosed in the work of art.[16]

Two interrelating but distinct themes must be sorted out here. The first is the issue of the truth of the poetic measure; the second is its propriety.

To arrive at the measure we must step back from things as they already are for us. The issue is the profound intention of Kant's transcendental imagination and not an excuse for caprice or fancy. The prior to which one steps back is not "just anything" but is the absence and concealment in what is unconcealed. But because there is no "thing" here but rather that by which things come to presence, there is nothing prior to it as its measure, for it measures all. This measure may not be equated with truth because it is not yet the verifying givenness by which something is *so* disclosed *as* a proposition meant it. This not yet true measure is antecedent to and the mediation of all modes of givenness which verify what assertions mean; it is, as well, antecedent to and the mediation of all assertions which mean to be articulations and mediations of this measure. This measure is the mediating immediacy which, as such, resists being transformed into mediated immediacy; it is the beginning from which everything procedes but which itself never comes to be something which has become.[17]

The charge that poetic dwelling forfeits philosophy to reigning prejudices and that it ultimately is an irresponsible resignation to historical fate may be partially answered by closer examination of its achievements. Although we have no criteria by which we can judge whether things are brought into their ownmost in the sense of their timeless synthetic a priori significance, and although in this sense we have no sure way of telling whether they are being submitted to an ultimately alienating or destructive frame of reference, nevertheless there is a criterion for the proper achievement of poetic dwelling. This may be called the *index of transfiguration,* by which innerworldly meanings are transformed so as to appropriately signify the clearing.

> The poet gathers the world in a saying, whose word [i.e., linguistic embodiment] remains a subdued shining, wherein the world appears in such a way that one looks upon it as for the first time.[18]

Human beings are called upon to establish this "subdued shining," i.e., to see to it that things come into their own by the manifest worlding of world and the gathering of the context of contexts. Heidegger himself has exemplarily elucidated this transfigured relationship of things, i.e., how they might "thing" or gather world. Poetic dwelling lets shine the *difference* borne by things between that which appears and the letting appear or the immediate mediation.[19]

Poetic dwelling makes manifest the struggle between what comes into view and that by which it comes into view, the difference between the absence out of which things come to presence and that which is present. This enables us to look upon things as for the first time. Metaphysics, which thinks of what is in its totality, is obscurely aware of the difference in that it is preoccupied with what is different from things (which bear the difference). It therefore thinks of what is in terms of grounded and grounding, what is accounted for and what accounts for. But metaphysics is unmindful of the difference as such. The way what is present bears the perduring sense of ground or grounded shows how this sense destines the clearing within which Western thought moves. Poetic dwelling steps back from the frame placed around what is present into the coming to presence of this frame, i.e., this side of all grounding and being grounded, and seeks to overcome the forgetfulness of the difference as such. (On the relationship of this metaphysical frame to technology, see Part IV of the Commentary.)

There is a difficulty, however, in saying that poetic dwelling permits the difference *as* the difference to appear. Perhaps poetic dwelling merely lets the difference shine, whereas thinking lets the difference as the difference appear. However, this cannot mean that a new essence appears, i.e., something *as* something within a context of involvements. As we have seen, the authority of the extant claims for an abiding synthetic a priori is undermined when the clearing is taken into consideration. But this does not lead thinking into a paralyzed metaposition which sees all positions and frames of reference as equally hovering over an abyss. Rather, thinking is led into poetic dwelling, which, in seeking out the prior measure, establishes an in-between space wherein things are brought to world and world to things. This index of transfiguration, as we shall soon see, has a utopian project. Not only do we see things as for the first time, but we also are enabled to see their ideal possibilities. To overlook the "subdued shining" of the difference as difference is to miss this project and to truncate Heidegger's thinking.[20]

For the lyric poet the basic task is to say something about the silence out of which and by which all speech and meaning come to be. This does not require a new language but a transformed relationship to the presencing *(Wesen)* of the old language.[21] This transformed relationship which establishes the "subdued shining" parallels the problem in Husserl's transcendental phenomenology of conceiving a language proper to the transcendental ego, i.e., "transcendentalese."[22] The language of the poet, like the language of the transcendental ego, employs an innerworldly speech in order to say something about the nonworldly conditions for the possibility of meaning. The poet appropriates innerworldly meanings, e.g., the sign structure of the signifier/signified, in such a way that these innerworldly sign structures themselves become signifiers of the clearing. This borrowing of signs which have meaning in one sphere or system and using them for another is also found in such metalanguages as ideological myths. Roland Barthes has shown not only how ideological second-level meanings build upon firstlevel proper meanings but furthermore how, by stealing their senses for their own purposes, the first-level meanings are distorted.[23]

How is the gathering of world in the familiar in and of itself not a mirroring, reinforcement, and advertisement for reigning alienating ideologies? How is the appropriation of inner-worldly signs for the purpose of signifying the clearing not itself a form of banality and commercialization? The answer lies in the innerworldly senses of banality and ideology. The great work of art is not something which is able to be placed conveniently and comfortably in our individual and social milieu. Rather, as the relating space in-between which brings things to world and world to things, it calls our whole existence into question. Only in the wake of such a questioning can banality appear as banality and ideology as ideology. Thoreau's "fact" states well the "thinging of the thing" achieved in poetic dwelling:

> If you stand right fronting and face to face to a fact, you will see the sun glimmer on both its surfaces, as if it were a cimetar, and feel its sweet edge dividing you through the heart and marrow, and so you will happily conclude your mortal career.[24]

If language is the "House of Being," its alienated forms can be refuted only by itself. At issue is the proper, authentic use of language and the consequences of being careless and irresponsible in our speech—which is, in fact, being languid about life.

> Our words have for us the meaning we give to them. As our lives stand, the meaning we give to them is rebuked by the meaning they have in our language—the meaning, say, that writers live on, the meaning we also, in moments, know they have but which mostly remain a mystery to us.[25]

This position implies that the clearing and world, as held open by language, always enable speakers to criticize prevailing degenerate uses of language and that language itself can never be merely ideology or banality.[26]

Seeking out the scimitar-like fact of Thoreau, i.e., poetic dwelling, is not merely to search for a style but for a fittingness, a justice, an ecstasy of the appropriateness of words and things coming into their ownmost. The writer and poetic dweller must know at once the propriety of what he brings to presence and, as well, the guiding sense which leads him to allow it to come to presence in the most appropriate way. Thoreau's scimitar-like fact with its two surfaces is a way of talking about the difference: "A fact has two surfaces because a fact is not merely an event in the world but an assertion of an event, the wording of world." The fact that ideology and banality do prevail reveals an absence of poetic dwelling wherein we respond to the call to say what we mean and wherein the experience of the "ecstasies of exactness" feel "like a discovery of the a priori, a necessity of language, and of the world, coming to light."[27]

In the actual performance of poetic dwelling in an unpoetic and estranged epoch, the poetic work is characterized by its uncommonness. The routine everyday is not able to hold world open. Only the unusual can do that *insofar as* its hidden measure is "the oddness of the simple, wherein the reality of the customary lies concealed."[28] The poetic work is thus placing the uncanny in the familiar. Whereas everyday existence involves familiar meanings mediated by world as the uncanny immediate mediation, the poetic work must be comprised of uncanny meanings of the immediate mediated by the familiar: "The poets must leave to the immediate its immediacy but still, at the same time, take over its mediation as the only mediation."[29] This characterization by Heidegger prescinds from the way the uncanny will be manifest in the familiar in any particular period of history.

In an era in which it may be said,

> What times are these, wherein
> A conversation about a tree is almost a crime
> Because it entails silence about untold monstrosities,
> (B. Brecht)

or in an era when there is pervasive commercialization and exploitation of hallowed modes of expression and when degradation shadows all innovations, great works of art may have an index of transfiguration appropriate to such "needy times." Because they are not capable of presenting a substitute, i.e., an alternative vision, they may have recourse to oblique or indirect modes of expression. As a result, they may disclose a regression regressively aware of itself and a stupidity stupid about itself.[30] Thus, of the stupidity presented in Beckett's *Endgame,* it might be said:

The unprotested presentation of omnipresent regression protests against a state of the world that so compliantly obeys the law of regression that it no longer has at its disposal a counter-notion with which it might remonstrate.[31]

Similarly Beckett's lack of differentiation in the presentation of social processes has the effect of avoiding a complexity which could only result in ideology. "In the act of leaving-out [of differentiation] that which is left out survives as that which is avoided, as in the case of a-tonal harmony with respect to consonance. . . ."[32]

Likewise it might be shown that the proliferation of styles and experiments in modern literature is primarily an attempt to surmount prevailing alienated measures and modes of expression. Much modern poetry attempts to get outside of the prevailing norms and patterns and thus is often a mode of writing without content and ideology. For it there are "only styles, thanks to which man turns his back on society and confronts the world of objects without going through any of the forms of history and social life." Thus each poetic word is "a Pandora's box from which fly out all the potentialities of language." The difference, i.e., the uncanny manifest in the familiar, in much modern poetry shows itself as speech "terrible and unhuman . . . full of gaps and full of lights, filled with absences and over-nourishing signs, without foresight or stability of intention. . . ."[33]

With the discovery of language as that by which the signified appears, typical modern poetry interrupts the signifying character of language and reverses the signification process so that language is "foregrounded."[34] Concommitant with the discovery of this "negative discourse" is the temptation to ascribe to language an orphic character, i.e., a magical idealism in which language holds absolute sway over the sense of what is present. For Heidegger, the peculiar character of poetic discourse, even in its negative forms, takes account of the clearing and has, as we shall see, a utopian project which seeks to discover, not create, the most proper possibilities of innerworldly things. In admitting that the sense of innerworldly things is not over against and independent of Dasein and the world-clearing,

Heidegger avoids the temptation, we believe, to exclude any sense of "natural" propriety to innerworldly things. (See our discussion below of "Nature and History.") For this reason the conjunction of political-ethical themes with poetry's negative discourse (by, e.g., Adorno, Barthes, and Cavell), which themes imply a quest of how things ought to be, is not extrinsic to the account of the discovery of negative discourse.

In the negative, indirect, and critical form of much of modern art there is the glimmer of a utopian function insofar as there is the project of the wording of world or the possible recognition of stupidity as such or of ideology-ridden phrases as such. Inasmuch as poetic dwelling and its works of art appeal to the prior measure, they not only open world but open the possibility of alternatives to reigning structures and schemas. The truth of the negative or indirect art work is its "negation of its actual existence; i.e., it points to what might be and criticizes what is."[35] If language is that which foremostly opens up world, it is the art work which holds open the essence of language, inasmuch as its essence is to struggle with the pervasion of language and the forgetfulness of world. In this sense the art work is the utopia of language and the language of utopia.[36]

## §10. The Utopian Poetic Measure

What the world really is—not what one usually thinks about it, but the real, the true, the entire, the integral world, which in no way is evident to all but rather hidden, perhaps today not there, perhaps never there but something futural—that is the proper motivating question in Heidegger's thought.[37]

In the essays "Das Ding" and "Bauen, Wohnen, Denken," Heidegger "thought forward to" how man would dwell if and when another beginning were suddenly to arrive. His characterizations in these essays must be taken to represent his conception of a primordial, genuine, and salutary human state of affairs.[38]

The prior measure, as that which goes in advance of all other measures, is that which is most anticipatingly held as well as what is most originating with respect to all other measures. As that which *enables* all measures and presencings, it itself cannot be identified with any reigning structure or schema of meaning. Although "this side" of any reigning ideology or banality, and therefore, in this sense, exercising a critique of what is, the primary force of its critique is in its project to enable things to come into their ownmost: poetic dwelling is rooted in the hoping of the poet. The nature of this project must now be considered.

"The poet must think about that which first of all concerns the sons of earth if they are to be able to dwell where they are at home."[39] What first of all concerns man, what is most prior, is at the same time that wherein he most properly is at home. This is the uncanny as that which is most originating and anticipatingly apprehended. The poet must fashion ways in which the holy and uncanny can appear among what is familiar in order that the human being and the earth can each come into its own. Out of the uncanny no longer and not yet, the poet must show the not-yet achieved possibilities of human existence on this earth.

The earliest analyses of being-in-the-world pointed to world as "existential" possibility. This is distinguished from possibility as a modal category of what is present before us: the not yet real and the not ever necessary. This is the merely possible, which is less than reality and necessity. Existential possibility, on the other hand, is "higher than reality" insofar as what is actual arises out of this possibility. The ontic paradigm is Aristotle's notion of *hexis:* only a being which *has* a potentiality for something, e.g., reading, can actually have this capacity, and only a being with such a capacity can achieve, e.g., be reading. That the child can actually read presupposes that there was a real possibility for reading; a stone can never read. The possibility goes in advance and is presupposed by the achievement. For Heidegger world and clearing can be considered as real "existential" and "aletheiological" possibility which human beings have, in which they dwell, and out of which the actual "realities" of life take shape.[40] In the project of world there is an exuberance of the possible out of which all disclosure and questioning of present beings arise.[41]

Poetic existence articulates and determines these possibilities. This has two aspects: First, there is the factual claim that it is the poetic work which allows world to world the way it does "in a particular moment in history"—this we have already discussed. Secondly, there is the exhortation to appropriate this utopian poetic dwelling as the most proper way of being human.

The properly utopian aspects of the project and performance of poetic dwelling are discussed as the "golden dreams" of the poet.[42] Dreams are often enough mere fantasies. But what is here in question is the most radical way of posing the measure of the real. Is it not the case that what counts as the real in a particular instance, i.e., what presents itself *as real,* does so on the basis of a not-given measure or criterion? And ultimately such a measure itself is established as validating and legitimizing on the basis of the not-given (and therefore not showing itself *as* real) measure of world. In this case the "unreal" may be said to have a priority (a priori perfect) over the "real." The question can thus be raised whether dreams may serve as the measure for the real. Of course it is evident that the unreality of each and every dream cannot be a measure of the real. But can we not make a special place for the "golden dreams" of the poet which deal with the measure "this side" of all measures?

If we assume the unreal of these dreams to be a not-yet real, then we are in a region between the real and the not real, i.e., the possible.

> In the condition between Being and Non-being the possible becomes real and the real ideal everywhere; and this, in the free imitation of art, is a terrible but divine dream.

This text of Hölderlin is commented on by Heidegger: The essential mode of the poet's dream is the becoming real of the possible as the becoming ideal of the real. It is terrible because those to whom it shows itself are cast by it out of the care-free stay in the familiar real into the frightfulness of the uncanny unreal. But this terrible dream is divine because the possible which approaches the real is made holy upon its arrival through the coming of the holy itself. This extraordinary dreaming enables the possible to *be* more, and that which is ordinarily regarded as being and real appears to have less reality.[43]

The sense of this fore-saying *(propheteuein)* of the real ideal and real possible in the performance of poetic dwelling is not the pronouncement of the certainty of salvation in an otherworldly bliss. Rather, it is the opening up of the place *(Ortschaft)* where historical man dwells on this earth. But this place *(topos)* is defined by ideal (proper) possibilities *(eu-* and *u-topoi).* And because the not-yet proper possibility of the actual historical is a dwelling where man is properly at home, this "dream" shows itself with a density of reality not characteristic of the "real" everyday. Here the themes of transfiguration, difference, and the shining in-between receive new expression when brought into conjunction with "the sting of reality":

> Art lets reality, which in itself is an appearing, appear in the deepest and highest way in the radiance of the transfiguration. . . . Art is the most proper and profound will to let appear, i.e., to illuminate the transfiguring wherein the most eminent legislative structures of Dasein become visible.[44]

In sum, the work effected by poetic dwelling has three characteristics: (1) It is the foundation and beginning which always goes in advance, inasmuch as it is the clearing for a people. (2) As the manifest bearer of the "difference," it not only is the foundation of the actual space of possibility for all things, but it opens up and makes appeal to the most proper possibilities of the actual real. (3) Because it itself is, nevertheless, a work, a "thing," and capable of ontic description, it appears to *be* more than the things around it.[45]

## §11. Hope and the Play of the World

If it is by poetic dwelling that something is established *as* something, and if the most radical measure of poetic dwelling is the golden dreaming of the ideal (or most appropriate mode) of the real, and if this opening up of the proper possibilities as such occurs through the approach of the holy and the divine, does Heidegger ultimately say that the measure of poetic dwelling is the divine?[46]

Initially it may be said that poetic dwelling with its utopian ("golden dreams") project does not involve a *visio deorum*. Rather, the holy and divine become manifest only in the total coincidence of theory and practice which is the effecting of the uncanny in the familiar or the transfiguration of the earth in terms of its proper possibilities. Insofar as the divine may be said to be the prior measure, it is manifest as such in the achievement of poetic dwelling. This is the measure which metes out measures and is not a mere measuring off with a ready-made standard in view.[47]

Assuming that the holy has philosophical and phenomenological legitimacy (see our earlier discussions), what does the philosopher Heidegger achieve or disclose by references to the gods or the divine?

Being in the clearing is not only being-with other mortals but includes the possibility of being with other beings which may be messengers and agents of an integral worlding of world. Only on the basis of this original being-with can the gods be missing and can there be said to be needy times in which the mystery hides its hiding. This being-with-the-gods is, indeed, a strange being-with, because, in needy times, whatever sense this kind of being has is concealed and is manifest only as the uncanny. But this coming to presence of the uncanny makes way for another possible mode of presence.[48]

This other mode, which today is no longer and missing (which includes, e.g., the divine of the Greeks, the prophetic word of Israel, and the sermons of Jesus), is not nothing; rather it is our not-yet, because of the inexhaustible fullness and anticipatory power of its having been. What it might be is, however, hidden.[49] It is a realm of possible being which, though not in Dasein's grasp, is that to which Dasein appeals as providing, in some sense, possibilities for him, and which supports Dasein's hope ("golden dreams") of a relation of world to things and things to world which is most appropriate.

If hope is to describe poetic dwelling, it must take on aspects characteristic of releasing resolve (cf. SZ, p. 341) and the thinking which takes to heart. It cannot be aggressive, because the clearing is not within Dasein's grasp as something over which mortals have control. Nevertheless, it contains possibilities to which mortals may have recourse. Consider the "performative" function of "I hope that's enough" when appended to "I've done all that I can." In saying "I hope," I am not saying (not describing) that I hope but am doing something: hoping (here some sense of appealing). And accompanying this (perhaps tacit) performative there is an expectant compliant posture appropriate to poetic dwelling. This compliance is, of course, neither "obedience to the will of God," nor cringing submission, nor a spineless resignation. One has done all that one can and waits upon that from which demands are senseless. And although the clearing is in no way something which "one counts on," not a "foundation for hope," it can be appealed to and mortals can thereby dream "golden dreams."[50]

The mode of being of the gods provides the occasion for humans to grasp their being toward death. When the abiding immortal being of the gods is held in view, humans are enabled to grasp the fleetingness of their mode of being.[51] The point that the gods are the mode of being by which mortals understand themselves is not homiletic; rather, the deathlessness of the gods sharpens the sense of mortal dwelling because death is the shrine of the clearing: that which never comes to presence as a being or thing and is the abiding horizon within which everything comes to presence.

Mortal dwelling with the gods in the clearing entails being engaged in a play of freedom and necessity. The necessity is the measuredness of everything which comes to presence; the freedom is that abyss of the prior measure out of which all measuring derives. The priority of the clearing as the measure which binds but itself is unbound suggests that play is an especially appropriate characterization of the process of *aletheia* or manifestation out of hiddenness. Heidegger reworks Leibniz's statement, "Cum deus calculat, fit mundus," to "While God plays, world comes to be."[52]

There is something divine about taking thought, not because in taking thought the manifestation out of hiddenness of that-which-is-manifest is itself manifested and thus stands above all else that is manifest as the most fundamental of that-which-is-manifest, but rather because taking thought lets the play between hiddenness and manifestation both bring and come into view without letting itself, taking thought, come into view reduced to the friendly struggle, the play between hiddenness and manifestation.[53]

Play is always an interplay of absence and presence, but if it is to be radically conceived, play must be conceived of before the alternative of presence and absence; being must be conceived of as presence or absence beginning with the possibility of play and not the other way around.[54]

If the process of *aletheia* is a "play" or a "game," the analogy requires that there be some equivalent to the personal agents which "constitute" the "unreal" intentional realm of the play world over against the background of the "real" world. Here the metaphor of the play of world breaks down. The play of world's unconcealment is not that of a god or God. Its primary sense entails no personal player. Nevertheless, humans are called to dwell with the gods in the clearing and they become thereby both the playthings and the players of the world-clearing. They become the latter only by renouncing the nostalgia "for full presence, the reassuring foundation, the origin and end of the game" (Derrida) and by poetically dwelling in hope.

> Much has man learned,
> Much of the heavenly has he named,
> Since the speaking together we are,
> And are able to hear from one another.

This text of Hölderlin's is rendered by Heidegger: "Since the gods have enabled us to speak together, since time is time, since then is the ground of our existence a speaking together."[55] The clearing, as that out of which things are brought to presence, does not begin as a result of man's discovery of language and his subsequent "implementation" of it. Another beginning, the concealment out of which presencing occurs, must go in advance. How does one think of the origin of unconcealment?

"We human beings do not come upon thoughts; thoughts rather come to us mortals, whose being is founded upon thinking."[56] "But thinking is the thinking of Being. Thinking does not come to be. It is insofar as Being presences *(west)*."[57] If mortal thinking means that something already has been thought, then to posit a primordial beginning to thinking would be to posit a thought which is other than mortal; if presencing is a presencing out of absence, the positing of the absence of absence (sheer presence) at the beginning would mean there was never an initial presencing; if all speaking is founded on a prior listening, then the positing of an absolutely first speaking would mean that there was no mortal beginning of language.[58] Mortals can speak and think because they have been addressed. Things come to presence and into their own because there has always been the concealed prior and original measure. And because the original measure is presupposed in all responsible achievements, the recollective thinking of this originating endowment is also called a thanking. The gods are introduced to raise the issue concerning the nature of this original address and measure.

## §12. Nature and History

We have urged that although for Heidegger there is not given eternal material a priori essences of innerworldly things, there is an abiding concern for the most proper meaning of things and thus a project of uncovering a "natural" propriety. Even a cursory examination of the transformations of *physis* into *natura* and the various senses of "nature" affords reasons for skepticism toward an essential "nature in itself."[59] But Heidegger, we believe, must retain a heuristic sense of what has been called nature in order that the clearing be that which enables things to come into their proper fulfillment. The commitment to what is most proper is foremostly to the priority of the clearing in which Dasein ex-sists. Thus Heidegger can ask:

> How long are we still going to believe that there is first a nature in itself and a landscape for itself, which then, with the aid of "poetic experiences," is mythically colored?[60]

Nevertheless, the sense of the clearing is, seen retrospectively, the a priori perfect which always already has let things come into their own; prospectively, it is the immediate mediation which can disclose the most proper possibility of the actually present. The basic sense of nature for Heidegger is that which is brought into its ownmost by poetic dwelling and which, at the same time as its unconcealment, withdraws from view.[61]

Because the issue must be articulated in the light of the prior claims of the clearing, Heidegger chooses to avoid the traditional categories of nature and history and prefers earth and world (later "heaven" or "sky"), which are said to be regionings of (not regions within) the clearing.[62] Earth provides a counter to the temptation to view poetic dwelling in an orphic or magical-idealistic manner. Earth, as that which is to be transfigured and brought into its own, as well as being that whose essential fullness always withdraws from view, must be envisaged in some sense as power or potentiality. (This assertion supplements the earlier discussion of world-clearing as real possibility.) Because, for example, the worlding of world can enable something to appear as . . . for the native Americans but otherwise for modern Americans, earth must have a disposition or capacity which permits this shift. Earth, like the Gestalt reversible picture, appears as determinable, not merely indeterminate. This distinction is necessary because it, on the one hand, enables the worlding of world and the concomitant poetic transformation of the earth to be neither arbitrary nor false, while, on the other hand, it makes room for a more appropriate determination.[63]

Poetic dwelling discloses and determines earth's determinability; it does not create it. Poetic dwelling heuristically intends the most proper real possible determination of earth; otherwise there would be no sense to the project of letting things come into their ownmost and poetic dwelling would be magical idealism. On the other hand, the determination of what is ownmost is never definitive of, although it is attentive to, the real determinability of earth. The uncovering of the possibilities of earth by world/heaven is, at the same time, a concealment: The determinability of earth is manifest in its struggle with world /heaven, which is essentially indeterminate and indeterminable because it withdraws from view in its enabling things to come into their own. But world/heaven is never separate from earth: "The world grounds itself on the earth, and earth juts through world."[64]

## §13. The Changing of the World

The pressing issues of social philosophy draw two considerations from Heidegger: (1) the relationship of philosophy to the task of changing society and changing the world, and (2) the metaphysics behind the modern social philosophical questions.

(1) The enthusiastic endorsement of Marx's statement that the "philosophers have only interpreted the world differently; what is important is to change it" overlooks that a changing of the world presupposes a change in the idea of the world *(Weltvorstellung)*. But the idea of the world is only to be achieved by adequately interpreting the world. Adequately interpreting the world involves a transformation of thinking. Therefore, the demand to change the world must presuppose a transformation of thinking. This means that the task of changing the world implicitly requires not only philosophy but furthermore a transformation of philosophy itself.[65] This exhorted transformation of thinking and philosophy is not something which is to transpire merely in the minds and hearts of philosophers. For example, all social institutions and disciplines of learning are expressions as well as occasions for expressions of the kind of thinking and "philosophy" which holds sway and which is to be transformed. Only the institution of "works" rooted in poetic dwelling is capable of effecting the desired transformation of both institutions and individuals. In this sense all science and politics are to be brought under "the optic of the artist," for it is poetic dwelling which "is the proper legislation for the Being of whatever is" and which makes all the difference in the world.[66]

(2) The proper and adequate interpretation of "the world" which is made possible by a transformation of thinking shows the inappropriateness of any "idea" or representation *(Vorstellung)* of "the world." That is, "the world" must be thought of in terms of the clearing. The question of the change of society

in modern thought is inseparable from the representational understanding of world. Unique to modernity is the position that whatever is in its entirety is regarded as a being, i.e., as something, only insofar as it is the result of the re-presenting and producing human being. World itself is treated as world-view or world-picture.[67]

The basic process of modernity is the conquest of the world as a view or a picture—i.e., a structure resulting from a representing-producing subjectivity. Within this framework the human being struggles for the position which best assures that the human being is the measure and rule for whatever is. The result is the confrontation of world-views. Heidegger places the basic metaphysical issue under the rubric of man as subjectivity or as representing-producing subject. The discussions of individualism over against the We of society, debates whether the human being is a personality within a community or just a member of a group, are meaningful only within the implicit ontology of man as subject. A philosophy which believes itself to have overcome this standpoint of subjectivity hesitates to join in the debate on these terms.[68]

*Ceteris paribus,* Heidegger could say with Aristotle: "It would be strange to regard politics or practical wisdom as the highest kind of knowledge, when in fact, man is not the best in the universe" (1141 a21). Politicality, friendship, and family must be located within the more fundamental mode of dwelling in the clearing.[69] Sophocles, Aristotle, and Hölderlin provide clues for explicating the sparse discussions of the communal character of Dasein. On the one hand, the human being is the most uncanny of beings and therefore he waits upon the gods in reverence, hope, and reserve. On the other hand, we hear only by and from one another, since the time of "a speaking together" which we are.[70] World is only held open because human beings are together in a linguistic-poetic community. Thus human beings can only be where they belong by being with one another. But being with one another does not exhaust the sense of being where Dasein belongs. Aristotle's notion of friendship as a relationship mediated through a life in common is overheard in Heidegger's reference to community. For the other is Dasein as Dasein never merely something within world but always along side of things within world. Dasein as Dasein is never, for Dasein, just along side, but is also poetically dwelling in world and caring for things within world.

In the 1935 lectures on *Introduction to Metaphysics,* Heidegger appropriates the ancient Greek notion of *polis* in order to elucidate what later would be primarily referred to as the clearing.[71] The *polis* is the there wherein Da-sein is most properly himself: This, paradoxically, requires of human beings that they be violently apolitical in the sense of striving to wrest the meaning of their own lives and the meaning of whatever is from obfuscating familiarity and hominess. This means that human beings who most properly dwell in the *polis* habitually place themselves outside of the taken-for-granted established order and its legitimations. This is not done out of any chaotic or asocial predilections but rather because proper "political" life entails foremostly the *hexis* of poetic dwelling which holds open or creates anew the spaces in which the established ways come to be.

> Taking thought makes no public stand, but not because of a private position, its own against public positions, nor because of an opposition to any and every position, but rather because taking thought is the space within which the difference between position and opposition and public and private is played out.[72]

But taking thought, without itself coming into view, lets the space-in-between come into view. And this *difference,* or subdued shining in-between space held open by the friendly struggle between hiddenness and manifestation, is what brings that-which-is-manifest into view and "then itself comes into view as one that-which-is-manifest above or even among others" (Prufer). Heidegger's utopian *polis* would be an "anarchical community" if this meant that mortals would together allow to come to presence the binding conditions and open projects within which everydayness runs its course. But this would always be a letting-be-present which is attendent on the holy utopian possibilities latent in unconcealment and which the works of mortals always presuppose.

# Part IV · Some Heideggerian Pathways to Technology and the Divine

## §1. A Preliminary Note on Method

> This time of technology is a destitute time, the time of the world's night, in which man has even forgotten that he has forgotten the true nature of being. (Albert Hofstadter)[1]

Heidegger's "negative appraisal" of modern science and technology has become notorious, and this notoriety has distracted not only from what he actually says of technology but, more important, from the methods he employs in establishing his position and from the role the analyses of *techne* play in his thinking. Extracted from their context, his critical remarks have a true enough ring to them, but often appear logically arbitrary, without foundation, and hence not a matter which the scientifically educated of our day need take seriously.

It may well be that a variety of approaches best does justice to what Heidegger says of technology and its impact on our "god-forsaken" age. The following essay seeks a direct access to the way Heidegger treats this theme, to the "moves" he makes.[2] For this purpose three texts have been chosen in which the kind of analysis set forth and the role it plays are themselves thematized. A few cross-references to other texts are given to indicate the thematic consistency throughout Heidegger's writings; but references to other philosophical sources are waived.

This direct approach attempts, then, to follow in English

upon what is spoken and thought in German and to arrive at a vantage point from which directives for following the pertinent remarks on technology in other Heideggerian texts might be sighted. The intensive "short path," however, seeks its countermeasure in the preceding parts of this commentary, which offer other accesses and develop the themes much more extensively. It is hoped that through this complementary procedure we will learn not merely to hear the import of what Heidegger has to say but to see how thematizing certain themes becomes a continual task in his thinking, and for our own.

## §2. Being and Time*'s Analysis of the Tool*

Technology *(Technik)* is not an explicit theme in *Being and Time*. What is a theme is the production, use, and manipulation of things as tools—the human activity often thought to be the source of technology. Heidegger's analysis will eventually reveal the unquestioned basis of this commonplace opinion; it will command us to rethink the position that technology is a matter of human doing. In the meantime, we shall pursue the theme of instruments and equipment, under the heading of tools, long enough to anticipate their peculiar grip on our usual thinking and speaking about technology.

The analysis of tools in *Being and Time* is an exercise in hermeneutical phenomenology (cf. §7c). Accordingly, its task is first to exhibit the "as-structure" of the phenomenon (cf. §33): how we always produce, use, and manipulate things *as* tools in an irreducible instrumental context; and then to interpret this using as a fundamentally *existential,* i.e., *temporal,* structure, with its own mode of understanding beings. It remains for us to give at least a preliminary account of the role of this analysis in *Being and Time:* how it brings into view the horizon of this and all modes of understanding.

ANALYSIS

In *Being and Time* §14–§18, Heidegger discusses the Being of tools as an access to the sense of world proper to human beings. We can follow the analysis by asking how we are to catch sight of what always withdraws into unobtrusiveness (the tool in its operative matrix; the world in its "there"), which means to catch sight of our own being-in-the-world (the nearest access to the proper sense of world).

The discussion begins with what is first off and usually there for human beings: what is there for . . . *(zuhanden)* within the world-about-us *(Umwelt)*. Both the world-about-us and what is there for . . . within the world-about-us are first off and usually undiscovered as such; and the comportment of human beings toward what is there for . . . is unthematic. The world-about-us, though undiscovered as such, is not removed from the view of our everyday comportment; and this comportment is not blind: It sights *(Umsicht)*, but does not thematize, a whole matrix of relations, within which it finds "this" usable for "that," "this" applicable to "that." But the relation which ties "this" with "that" (both unobtrusively embedded in the world-about) and the world-about as such do not spring into view until what is with . . . is severed from its being . . . in the world-about (as happens when the tool breaks). This de-worlding *(Entweltlichung)*[3] of the piece of equipment lights up the priority of the equipmental context and so betokens an already disclosed world, wherein human beings exist.

In §69, the discussion of the Being of tools is recapitulated to expose the temporality of everyday comportment and its thematic (theoretic-scientific) modification. The analysis of the temporal horizons of such being-in-the-world clears the way for a glimpse of the Being of the world in the proper sense. According to the previous analysis, the tool always shows up as a reference to an equipmental context projected whenever we let "this" be usable for "that"—and use it as such—unobtrusively. §69 exposes how our "letting be for" is derivative of the way world and what is within the world are presented whenever we keep "this" (in mind) for "that" *(ein behaltendes gegenwärtigendes Gewärtigen)*. It further exposes the shift from everyday comportment to the thematic stance: "this" or "that" is released from the proximate world-about *(Entschränkung)* and kept (in mind) as just there *(vorhanden)* to be discovered, i.e., as object, to be held against the questions we direct to it. Thus the presentings accomplished by scientific thematization derive but are distinct from the presentings of everyday comportment, as "nature" derives but is distinct from the world-about. The world-about (caught sight of when the tool obtrudes as tool) and "nature" (kept in view by scientific thematization) come about as the horizons of everyday and theoretic presentation. Human beings keep "this" (in mind) for "that" within a whole matrix of relations, and the world-about is presented; human beings thematize this or that within a system of meanings, and the world is made present; human beings exist in the world, and world is temporalized: human-being-in-the-world, and the Being of world.

INSTANCING

*(a)* We can illustrate the foregoing discussion by reflecting on the broken tool, for example, in the context of gardening.

Absorbed in the rhythmical fall of the shovel while digging in the garden, I take no notice of the shovel itself. It functions best when it is as inconspicuous as possible. The handle suddenly breaks off; the intention of the activity is interrupted. I notice that the joint between the crescent-shaped handle and the stock has rotted out; I think how the broken shovel will cause me delay in planting the garden and how my planting a garden has been dependent upon that particular tool. The shovel now shows itself to me as a shovel; before, it was lost, as it were, among the pattern of things concerned with planting a garden. It shows itself as not just this one thing, by itself, but as a part in a whole chain of intentionality: the shovel is for digging, which is for planting, which is to provide our daily food, which is for ourselves, for . . . a possibility of our Being. This whole context is presented with the shovel, now—with its broken handle—just there *(vorhanden)*.

The "same" shovel, when used for the construction of a school building, for example, will have a different proximate context to delimit its meaning as a shovel. It is not that the particular proximate context constitutes something present in order to . . . *(zuhanden);* rather there can be something present in order to . . . only because, with the world already there, human beings can discover intentional contexts which give things their place. This unthematic placing is an act arising out of a possible mode of human temporality: throwing myself into gardening, I attend the harvest and keep it (in mind); I am waitful even for a sign of the first sprouts, and keep them (in mind) while digging. Being attentive to and retentive of a whole design for the world about me, I let something be present in order to . . . until an interruption holds up the immersion of its presence in the design, and further deliberation brings nearer and holds up to view: a broken shovel.

My being attentive to and retentive of . . . is never reducible to a particular purpose in mind or to an expectation of the finished product. Rather, it is a basic way of letting-be-present, and what is presented is presented within the horizon of what I am attentive to and retentive of. My being attentive *to* and retentive *of* . . . is a unified transporting toward . . . *(ekstatische Einheit)* enabling me to let "this" be present for "that" (unthematically) or "this" be present as "this for that" (deliberately). This existing is a way of being temporal and of temporalizing. Only thus am I ever in a position to find myself presently planning the future or doing something as a means to a goal.

Is this account not a subjectivistic reduction of tools, their production, use, and manipulation? Only if we ignore that within which the tool first shows up, the horizon of all that we are attentive to and retentive of. It is world, and not some mere subject, out of which the tool emerges.

*(b)* In what manner world is there prior to our being a designer, maker, and user of tools is further exemplified by the scientific stance, for theoretical discovery is only a modification of our being concerned with the world-about-us in a way that views it for our sake. Let us return to the world of gardening for an introduction into theoretical discovery.

While shoveling, the handle now repaired, I come across a small white larva in the earth and wonder whether it be friend or foe of my garden. The entomologist, freed from this local concern, would let the insect appear differently, in a "universal" context, and would see it as a member of a species of a genus, with such and such characteristics. He does not assert that my larva in itself is harmful or beneficial; it is simply there for him, whereas for me it is there so as to. . . . In order to discover the larva in itself he has thematized it, defining its context in terms appropriate to letting it show itself purely as an object of his investigation, irrespective of the place I have given it in the context of my gardening. "Thematizing modifies and articulates the [prior] understanding of Being."

As a science, entomology first discovers the larva in the environment, but it views the environment as something for the sake of discovery, as it were. The questions it asks release the larva and the environment from proximate contexts of human concerns into "objectivity." It does not have an eye for the world-about-us—this it has transformed, i.e., de-worlded, into "nature"; its theme is the universe of whatever is there to be discovered within its project of relevance; and only after discovering the larva in a region of like beings can it investigate any potential harmfulness or benefit to my garden.

*(c)* It cannot be said that my concern about the insect is of a practical nature, while the entomologist's activity is purely theoretical. For the thematic stance has its own *praxis,* guided by its own sight—which is theory, not the *Umsicht* of existing in the world-about. The advice the entomologist can give me concerning the larva is blind without his theoretical constructs, just as his theorizing is helpless without experimental tools. The whole scientific stance is a shift from my way of looking at the insect while gardening. Science comes equipped, as it were, with an articulate way of understanding beings within a defined region and a selected terminology. Science can thematize because human beings can project, i.e., understand, a world of things to be discovered in their simple thereness. Mathematical physics, for example, can quantitatively describe things because it has already discovered certain *(a priori)* constants and variables, e.g., energy/matter.

Attentive only to the discovery it will accomplish, science makes things present as there to be discovered in themselves. The "truth" of the exact sciences lies not in "pure facts" but in discovering beings the only way they open themselves to discovery: by projecting (understanding) beforehand their kind of Being and making this explicit, e.g., as being quantitatively there. This "truth" rests on our already being-in-truth, on already being disclosed to ourselves *(Gelichtetheit).*

*(d)* The exercise in hermeneutical phenomenology thus finds the ontological genesis of science in an authentic mode of human existence, specifically in the way human beings can make something explicitly present for the sake of their investigation. Is this account a psychologistic reduction of the validity of science? Again, only if we ignore what every thematizing presupposes: world. Always disclosed with us, without us it is not "there." Never "there" the way a tool is for the gardener or the insect for the scientist, world transcends these and casts them back upon human understanding.

Hence, any design to "change the world" or improve it through technology, as well as any notion of progress within science itself, would be derivative of the world upon which we cast beings whenever we design to "change the world" or to make progress. Hermeneutical phenomenology lets technology be seen not merely as the willed transformation of nature; what technology is can only become visible out of how world is already there for it. How world is already there is what enables technology to forecast (understand) whatever is as transformable nature.

RETRIEVAL

*Being and Time*'s analysis of the tool broaches but does not congeal Heidegger's account of technology. The account, as we have rendered it thus far, is preliminary on two counts. First, our way of thematizing hovers all too close to an eidetic phenomenology of a specific region when we suggest that a tool (or instrument or piece of equipment) is such and such a kind of being, something there in order to . . . (e.g., the shovel is for digging, which is for planting, which is for harvesting, etc.), or that it is first something and subsequently placed in some intentional context, which is then recast by the scientific stance that has a new look at the thing. These terms do not yet make it clear in what manner "things" like shovels always emerge out of world, itself always prior and never reducible to a region of beings.[4] Our account removes the interpretation of instruments and the like from the terms supplied by the region called "the world of science and technology," but does not yet collect the terms proper to naming tools and technology together. The *logos* commensurate to the phenomenon, and hence the collective phenomenon itself, remains obscure.

Second and consequently, if the analysis has shown how the ordinary tool can coalesce the world of our everyday comportment and upon disruption bring it into view, or how the scientific stance can shift the view, disperse the everyday world, and discover nature, it has not yet clarified the one sense of world that allows us to speak of world-announcement (in the de-worlding of the disrupted tool) *and* world-retraction (in science's de-worlding of the everyday world of tools). This sense is given neither by the crisis in everyday comportment (when the tool breaks), nor by the scientific shift, nor even by traditional ontology: Unlike everyday comportment, science and traditional ontology have a thematic grasp of beings within the world and supposedly of the world as the totality of just such beings (e.g., as nature), but they fail to take into account everyday comportment (a mode of being-in-the-world) and what everyday comportment finds within the world (this being for that). Hence the proper sense of world eludes both everyday comportment (which is unthematic) and science and traditional ontology (which do not thematize the unthematic as such).

World announced but not thematized (i.e., the world-about) and world thematized but not as unannounced (i.e., "nature") can differ from each other only from out of the mutual source which announcement, retraction, and thematization can never exhaust, which abounds in the unannounced and proffers countless themes. This is the sense of world precisely as it is forgotten *in* the tool (most itself when used, unannounced, unthematized) and *by* technology (a thematization, but not of unthematic use). The proper sense of world, it would seem, must account for the forgottenness of that proper sense; the world must "include" withdrawal of world. Only then can "things" like tools draw out of "the world" the uses human beings find latent "in it."

In spite of these shortcomings, a hint has been given of how Heidegger will come to speak of a thing as a gathering of world, and of the essential nature of technology as *Ge-Stell:* the gathering of (instrumental) placings. From there it is not difficult to foresee the connection between framing "the world" (all that is) in instrumental terms and finding that the divine is missing *(Fehl des Gottes)*.

## §3. Techne *and* Ge-Stell *in the Setting of "The Origin of the Work of Art"*

SETTING

In "The Origin of the Work of Art" (1936), Heidegger treats *techne* and *Ge-Stell* as models of the way world and world-withdrawal are brought out. We can retrieve the discussion by inquiring how things fashioned by the hand of man (works of art and pieces of equipment) can disclose this worlding of world or close it off from view.

Coming across works of art and pieces of equipment as actual things, we inquire first into the opaque sense of concrete things, in which fine art or instrumental networks supposedly reside. This sense is not clarified by a linguistic survey of all the ways the word "thing" gets used, or by recourse to traditional metaphysical determinations of a thing (as bearer of qualities; subject of predications; unity of perceptions; formed matter), or even by a phenomenological description which, for example, finds that what makes something be a piece of equipment is casting it in an instrumental context. We let the opacity of the concrete thing stand as that which withdraws where the piece of equipment is being used or where the work of art is at work as art. Where this happens, the piece of equipment gets lost in a matrix of relations, but the work of art opens a whole expanse of relations and openly shelters them in its being there.

The earthly setting of a world which is van Gogh's painting of a peasant woman's shoes, in Heidegger's example, lights up how the reliable shoes unfold a world and fold it back into themselves, and shelters this world-emergence and world-withdrawal. All things fashioned by the hand of man,[5] whether works of art or handiwork, arise from *techne:* they give refuge to world (the shoes being worn; the worn shoes being depicted in the painting) and give rise to world-withdrawal (the shoes worn out; the painting sold on the market); but the working of art in the painting sets the shoes in a frame which lights up and shelters this unfolding and folding back into . . . by letting the two confront each other (as the depicting of shoes having been worn confronts the picture of worn out shoes). Lighting up and sheltering such disclosure and closure, the work of art is essentially the working of truth: clearing *(Lichtung)* in its full sense. Setting the confrontation of disclosure and closure into an autonomous frame *(Gestell),* the working of art collects *(Ge-Stell)* the frameworks into which men cast beings. The most originary clearing of beings is the collection or condensation of speech called poetry *(Dichtung).*

In an Addendum written twenty years later, in 1956, Heidegger relates this original sense of *Ge-Stell* (bringing world out of earth by way of *techne;* bringing out their difference by way of the working of art) to the later derivation of *Ge-Stell* (calling out and making demands on the earth to yield a secure world; refusing world-withdrawal and forgetting the refusal; losing sight of the difference). The latter kind of disclosure is the epochal sway of modern technology.

ILLUSTRATION

Heidegger cites several examples to elucidate the working of truth in the work of art: van Gogh's painting of the peasant woman's shoes; C. F. Meyer's poem "Roman Fountain," quoted in full; the ancient Greek temple, which brings out the breadth of the sky, the ground on which men dwell, and the presence of the god giving man to himself.

Perhaps the surest way for us to illustrate the theme is to prescind from copying Heidegger's manner of citation and let an artist speak for himself—not in *propria persona* but through a work which sets any such personal speaking on its own, in an ironic interplay with what is "spoken" by this very setting.

A passage from a modern Japanese novel, Natsume Sōseki's *The Three Cornered World,*[6] thematizes the author's own inquiry into the nature of art by first setting art into the framework of thoughts of the novel's speaker and then setting the speaker back into his world to release the novel as art:

> Going up a mountain track, I fell to thinking. . . . Strip off from the world all those cares and worries which make it an unpleasant place in which to live, and picture before you instead a world of graciousness. You now have music, a painting, or poetry, or sculpture. I would go farther, and say that it is not even necessary to make this vision a reality. Merely conjure up the image before your eyes, and poetry will burst into life and songs pour forth. Before even committing your thoughts to paper, you will feel the crystal tinkling, as of a tiny bell, well up within you; and the whole range of colours will of their own accord, and in all their brilliance, imprint themselves on your mind's eye, though your canvas stands on its easel, as yet untouched by the brush. It is enough that you are able to take this view of life, and see this decadent, sullied and vulgar world purified and beautiful in the camera of your innermost soul. Even the poet whose thoughts have never found expression in a single verse, or the painter who possesses no colours, and has never painted so much as a single square foot of canvas, can obtain salvation, and be delivered from earthly desires and passions. They can enter at will a world of undefiled purity, and throwing off the yoke of avarice and self interest, are able to build up a peerless and unequalled universe. . . . It was just as my meandering thoughts reached this point, that my right foot came down suddenly on the edge of a loose angular rock, and I slipped.

The "world of graciousness" unfolded in the imagined work of art, as aesthetically pleasing as it is, finds its bounds *(peras)* and is folded back into the mundane world of the speaker. Art at work in the shape of this passage from a novel explicitly sets the emergence of the speaker's imagined world of art in confrontation with the world he lives in. What we have called world-withdrawal and world are lighted up and sheltered within the framework of the passage: "Going up a mountain track, I fell to thinking . . . just as my meandering thoughts reached this point," I slipped on a rock.

Another passage evokes the contrast between two senses of *Ge-Stell* (giving shape to; placing under control) and then revokes their difference back into the one framework of the novel:

> Once again I returned to my thoughts. . . . There in the mountains, close to the delights of Nature, everything you see and hear is a joy . . . looking at the landscape, it is as though you were looking at a picture unrolled before you, or reading a poem on a scroll. The whole area is yours, but since it is just like a painting or a poem, it never occurs to you to try and develop it, or make your fortune by running a railway line there from the city. You are free from any care or worry because you accept the fact that this scenery will help neither to fill your belly, nor add a penny to your salary, and are content to enjoy it just as scenery. This is the great charm of Nature, that it can in an instant, discipline men's hearts and minds, and removing all that is base, lead them into the pure unsullied world of poetry. . . . It was just as I had come to this conclusion, that I glanced up and saw that the sky looked threatening.

Clearly, this passage intimates, aesthetic appreciation is no more "true" in the revealing and concealing of what is than are technological projections. These two (subjectivist) senses of *Ge-Stell* dirempt into the forgotten sense, here recalled by the very framework of the passage, which includes the "pure unsullied world of poetry," the projected "railway line," and the "threatening sky." The worlding of world suggested in this passage is visible neither in the speaker's viewing of Nature as art nor in his non-viewing of Nature as material resource, nor even in his opposing the two, but rather in the setting which unfolds these as the viewing of a speaker, then folds them back into a translated, quoted, and detached speech, said to be spoken in the opening of a novel.

TRANSITION

Phenomenological analysis had shown how a pre-disclosed world is brought to light through a broken (de-worlded) tool, but could not adequately clarify how world is there when it (with the tool) is both unannounced and unthematized. If be-ing-in-the-world means having beings disclosed to us, and us to ourselves, there is still a sense of refusal to be all-disclosed hinted in the many modes of uncovering world (using the tool; deliberating on the broken tool; measuring its weight; reflecting on all these modes) and in the many worlds uncovered (the world lived in; the world objectified; the lived-in world withdrawn in the objectified world, and the objectified world drawn out of the lived-in world). We have called this sense of refusal world-withdrawal.

The notion of earth allows Heidegger to name world-withdrawal as such, to speak of the disclosure of the undisclosable as undisclosable. This speaking is borrowed, as it were, from what is "spoken" by the work of art, from the disclosure of earth and the sheltering of world that the work of art shows itself to be. It is not a matter of merely having Heidegger's word that this is what happens in the work of art, but of finding a *logos* commensurate to a phenomenon which withdraws from disclosure while disclosing its own withdrawal, which uniquely reflects the very process of truth. We actually come across this phenomenon in works of art and are exhorted to learn the proper *logos* from them directly—most properly and most directly from poetry, the working of art in language. The words *"techne"* and *"Ge-Stell"* are spoken not as this *logos,* but as terms suggested to help us rethink such "things" as works of art and technology. The "strategic place" of the work of art in Heidegger's thinking corresponds to its place as a "thing" in the world: clearing the twofold truth of all things and so lighting up the worlding of world. The earthly settings which are originally gathered under the name *Ge-Stell* shelter the disclosed while letting the undisclosable emerge as such.

Derivative from this is another way world worlds: in the half truth, as it were, which occurs in the kind of disclosing that demands complete disclosure with nothing left over, mastery, control. Heidegger hints that the relentless framing of the universe in calculative terms not only discloses a world (objectified nature) that gives no stay to "the god"; more fundamentally, it precludes this absence from view. Technology is a theme be-

cause it supplies an unquestioned frame of reference for thinking about all things today. But in what "frame of reference"
then does the true nature of this framing (the *Ge-Stell* of modern technology) come to light? And what is "the god" that it
withdraws before such setting which collects the world and
sets the measure of all things in calculative terms?

## §4. *In Quest of Technology and the Divine*

In "The Question of Technology" (1955), Heidegger returns to
poetry to reveal the *Ge-Stell* of modern technology as the worlding of world which dangerously precludes withdrawal from
the sense of truth. Inquiring into the foundation of the terms in
which modern technology is usually spoken about, we come to
see technology as a form of truth. Seeking to inquire into the
measure of this form of truth, we come to the related notion of
poetry which reveals the danger of modern technology and
therewith the source of its rescue.

In a technological age we are used to thinking about technology in terms of means to an end (the shovel is for digging . . .) set in motion by means of human agents, made precise
by means of instruments. Technology, means and end, instru-
mentality—themselves frames of reference—have been and
continue to be thought of in terms of causality. Watching the
turns this term has taken in the course of our tradition, we see
through such instrumental speech to ("by means of") the
"frame of reference" in which the Greeks spoke *aition:* that
which a thing owes its presence to, that which lets it be what
it is, which brings it out as something and hence lets it be
disclosed for what it is. Taking our clue here, we rethink technology as a manner of disclosing (as *aletheia*), recalling all the
while the way we have uncovered technology to be such.

A similar uncovering showed handiwork, works of art, poetry, nature herself (as *techne, poiesis, physis*) to be ways the
world is brought out. In defiance of them, the demanding disclosure of modern technology is uncovered as *Ge-Stell:* install-
ing in all things a demand to supply *(herausforderndes bestel-
len auf . . . Bestand)*. Installed in man himself, the demand to

supply conceals its own duplicity and compels man to think technology is merely a human instrument and to speak about it in instrumental terms.

The uncovering of this duplicity is itself an attempt to retrieve the various senses of world within the one worlding of world: technology, uncovered as not merely something present, is a presencing, issues from *Ge-Stell; Ge-Stell,* uncovered as not all of presencing, is an issuance of the sense of world governing history itself *(eine Schickung des Geschicks); Geschick* underlies history *(Geschichte)* as the occurring worlding of world which makes our historical retrieve and uncovering possible. Accordingly, recovery from the danger of disclosing all things as supply is already enclosed in *Ge-Stell,* thought of as the *Geschick* which also includes lighting up the worlding of world in works of art, above all in poetry. How are we to speak of what is recovered in the clearing of poetry?

In a sequel piece called "The Turn" (published in 1962 though composed as early as the first drafts of "Technology" and of "The Thing" in 1949), a connection is made which draws our pathways to a certain plateau. It is suggested that in bringing the danger of technology to light as a danger, the forgotten sense of withdrawal turns to an event of appropriation *(Ereignis)*—which is: the preservation of the truth of presencing as distinct from what is present *(Wahrnis des Seins).* This is a return to the full sense of the worlding of world which appropriates forgottenness as forgottenness, withdrawal as withdrawal. It is said to be the worlding of world which flashes in the thing as the "fourfold mirror-play of heaven and earth, mortals and divinities."[7] Here the confrontation of world and earth ("Origin of the Work of Art") is restated to distinguish the full sense of world from each of the many emergent worlds of man and each of the many worlds historically withdrawn and presently forgotten. If "earth" allows us to speak of the withdrawal appropriate to the worlding of world, "heaven" or "sky" permits us to name an appropriated forgottenness, the presence of an absent. The "friendly struggle" between earth and sky gives play to presencing and absencing, and the presencing of an absent. Whatever be the full implications of "the gods" in Heidegger,[8] we may ask whether the strategic sense of "the divine" in this struggle is not first of all a move to recall that which is present as forgotten, to name the presence of an absent as absent *(Gegenwart des Fehls).*[9] This is perhaps what moves Heidegger to the questioning which is "the piety of thinking" *(die Frömmigkeit des Denkens),* compliant to the covering and uncovering of truth.[10]

# NOTES

## Translators' Preface

1. Martin Heidegger, *Vorträge und Aufsätze,* I (Pfullingen: Neske, 1967), p. 36. This work has been issued in three (I-III) parts. Hereafter it will be referred to as VA.

2. Martin Heidegger, *Unterwegs zur Sprache* (Pfullingen: Neske, 1971), pp. 175–176, 179–180; translated as *On the Way to Language* by Peter Hertz (New York: Harper and Row, 1971), pp. 71–72 and 75–76; hereafter referred to as US. As this work goes to press numerous translations of Heidegger's writings are in various stages of preparation for publication. See the "Heidegger Bibliography of English Translations," compiled by Keith Hoeller, *The Journal of the British Society for Phenomenology* V (1975).

3. See especially Part II of the Commentary.

## THE PIETY OF THINKING: ESSAYS BY MARTIN HEIDEGGER

## *"Foreword"* to the German Edition of Phenomenology and Theology

1. *Phänomenologie und Theologie* (Frankfurt am Main: Klostermann, 1970). Heidegger dedicated this work to Rudolf Bultmann "in friendly remembrance of the Marburg years, 1923–1928." Cf. Bultmann's "Autobiographical Reflections" in *Existence and Faith: Shorter Writings of Rudolf Bultmann,* ed. and trans. Schubert M. Ogden (Cleveland: Meridian, 1960), pp. 283ff.

2. Throughout this book Heidegger's *Being and Time,* trans. John Macquarrie and Edward Robinson (New York: Harper and Row, 1962) will be referred to in the notes as SZ and the page numbers will be from the seventh German edition, *Sein und Zeit* (Tübingen: Niemeyer, 1963), which appear in the margins of the Macquarrie-Robinson translation.

3. In the German text the French editors' expression of gratitude to Professor Heidegger appears along with best wishes for his eightieth birthday. The editors also call attention to the "excellent commentary" of Henri Birault, "La foi et la pensée d'après Heidegger," *Recherches et Débats* 10 (1955), pp. 108–132.

4. In Franz Overbeck's *Über die Christlichkeit unserer heutigen Theologie* (Reprint, Darmstadt: Wissenschaftliche Buchgesellschaft, 1963), pp. 14–19, the beginning years of the friendship and the simultaneous publication of their "little writings" are recounted. The kind of exploration required to evaluate Heidegger's conviction concerning the philosophical and theological merits of the "little writings" of the two friends reaches beyond the scope of this work. Concerning the influence of Overbeck's "Christian skepticism" on Heidegger, see the translators' Commentary, Part II, §7.

5. *Holzwege* (Frankfurt am Main: Klostermann, 1963), pp. 193–247; hereafter referred to as H.

6. *Nietzsche* II (Pfullingen: Neske, 1961), pp. 31–256 and 335–398. Both essays appear in a separate volume, *Der Europäische Nihilismus* (Pfullingen: Neske, 1967).

## *"Phenomenology and Theology"*

1. This is a translation of the 1927 and 1928 lecture to which Heidegger refers in his Foreword and which appears in *Phänomenologie und Theologie,* pp. 13–33.

2. We have translated *Sein* almost without exception as "Being." *Das Seiende* is variously translated as "whatever is," "being(s)," "entity," etc. The task of philosophy is the question of Being. What does that mean? It is that "which withdraws itself from the way it comes into view within any other horizon." (From an unpublished manuscript, "Toward Beginning *Being and Time,*" by Thomas Prufer.) Heidegger's life work is a sustained attempt to speak about "Being." Cf. the translators' Commentary.

3. The translators have followed the practice of other translators and have usually left untranslated the technical term "Dasein," for man as the openness and question of Being. This term is also connoted by "existence" (or ex-sistence), which points to human being as being-in-the-world, or being in that context of contexts which "withdraws itself from the way it comes into view within any other horizon" or context. The marks of this basic structure of human being are *existential* and the inquiry is called *ontological.* The point of departure for such an inquiry begins with categories and phenomena that are to be placed within the ontological context. This initial inquiry is called *ontic* and the phenomena of human life which serve as this necessary point of departure are called *existentiell.* See SZ, pp. 12–13, 184–185, 302–303.

4. It is to be noted that all positive sciences in this account begin with beliefs-that, which comprise the guiding paradigms, procedures,

laws, etc. taken for granted by the science, and which open up the realm to be investigated. The positive science of theology, as we shall see, is uniquely inaugurated and sustained by belief, but primarily a belief-in.

5. How is theology enjoined *(auferlegt)* upon faith? Does faith intrinsically need theology? The text is very hesitant. See the translators' Commentary, Part II, §6.

6. This seems to draw near to Karl Barth's understanding of theology. However, in the light of the subsequent discussion, such an interpretation is unwarranted. See the translators' Commentary, Part II, §6.

7. The notion of "formally free operations of reason" must be interpreted in the light of later discussions such as "Principles of Thinking," which is translated in this volume. Heidegger's view would be that what goes for "reasoning" (according to the prevailing rules of logic) occurs in theology, even though theology (or any science) does not properly (i.e., in Heidegger's technical sense) *think.* Cf. the "Discussion with Martin Heidegger" in this volume, as well as the translators' Commentary, Part II, §7.

8. Cf. the translators' Commentary, Part II, §6.

9. Heidegger's note: "All theological concepts of existence which are centered on faith intend a specific transition of existence, in which pre-Christian and Christian existence are united in a unique way. This transitional character is what motivates the multidimensionality of theological concepts—a feature we cannot examine more closely here."

10. Heidegger's note: "Cf. *Sein und Zeit,* §58."

11. Heidegger's note: "It should not require extensive discussion to show that it is a matter here of a basic (existential) confrontation of two possibilities of existence which does *not exclude,* but *includes,* a factual, existentiell, and reciprocal acknowledgment and earnestness."

## "The Theological Discussion of 'The Problem of a Non-Objectifying Thinking and Speaking in Today's Theology'—Some Pointers to Its Major Aspects"

1. From *Phänomenologie und Theologie;* see Heidegger's Foreword at the beginning of this volume.

2. Ideas, for instance, that derive from traditional Western metaphysics. Augustine's *fruitio Dei* is an example cited by Heidegger in his 1921 lectures on Augustine and neo-Platonism (according to Otto Pöggler, *Der Denkweg Martin Heideggers* [Pfullingen: Neske, 1963], pp.

36 ff.): to expect to enjoy God (as *summum bonum*) in the "beatific vision," to seek in God rest from the disquietude of life, is precisely to forget the original Christian experience of *kairos:* despite the approaching hour of God, life must continue to be lived—in watchfulness, not in expectation of the day and hour. (On the other hand, one might ask whether Augustine's quietude is not already an example of non-objective thinking.)

This exhortation, in the context of 1 Thessalonians, 5:1–12, was evidently influential in the formation of Heidegger's notion of the facticity of Dasein (see Pöggler's brief account of the 1920/21 lectures "Introduction to the Phenomenology of Religion," in *Der Denkweg*). But the general implications of this reading were farther reaching, for Augustine's *frui,* viz. *praesto habere* (cf. H, p. 338) meant for Heidegger another instance of historical interference to be cleared away ("destroyed"): on the one side, the Greek metaphysical dis-covery of Being in whatever lies present (before our eyes) and the concomitant (Aristotelian) dis-covery of time in the measure of whatever comes upon us and passes away; on the other side the original Christian experience: Now is the time to live our life in sober vigilance of God, without a past to rely upon or a future at our disposal; the *confusio* of the two sides in Augustine: the Being (presence) of God thought in terms of a steadfast being-before-our-eyes, even if now the interior eye of the mind or heart was meant (cf. Pöggler, p. 42); finally, out of the latent tension between the two sides, a partial revelation for the young Heidegger that the horizon within which the meaning of Being discloses itself had been forgotten. This entire discussion can be seen as an example of the "onto-theo-logic" Heidegger finds in the tradition; cf. the Commentary, Part II. However, Heidegger's existential interpretation of Paul and the pristine Christian experience here (as Pöggler reports it) is not without its difficulties when it assigns a specific content to this experience. Compare "Excursus: Early Heidegger and Early Bultmann" in Part II, §6 of the Commentary.

For a critique of the early Heidegger's understanding of the Christian experience of history, *kairos,* and *fruitio,* see Karl Lehmann, "Christliche Geschichtserfahrung und ontologische Frage beim jungen Heidegger," *Heidegger,* ed. Otto Pöggler (Cologne-Berlin: Kiepernheuer & Witsch, 1969), pp. 140–168.

It is significant that Heidegger, both in the addresses in this volume as well as in the exhortation to theologians in "Einleitung zu'Was ist Metaphysik?'" (in *Wegmarken,* hereafter W [Frankfurt am Main: Klostermann, 1967], p. 208; trans. by Walter Kaufmann, "The Way Back to the Ground of Metaphysics," in his *Existentialism: from Dostoevsky to Sartre* [New York: Meridian, 1972], cf. p. 218), refrains from mentioning specific instances of ideas or categories which are alien to the experience of faith; such cases are, rather, left to the theologian's discrimination. But see the discussion of Heidegger's reproof of God as "causa sui" in Part II of the Commentary; see also his criticism of the view of the world *(ens creatum)* in (borrowed, alien) terms of matter and form, in H, p. 19.

3. Despite the apparent and now notorious discord between the positions of Carnap and Heidegger, there is good reason to suspect a common intention in their dealing with the conditions for the possibility of language. See especially Karl-Otto Apel, "Heideggers philosophische Radikalisierung der 'Hermeneutik' und die Frage nach dem 'Sinnkriterium' der Sprache," in *Die hermeneutische Frage in der Theologie,* ed. O. Loretz and W. Strolz (Freiburg: Herder, 1968), pp. 86–152; also in Apel's *Transformation der Philosophie,* Vol. I (Frankfurt am Main: Suhrkamp, 1973), pp. 276–334.

4. Bergson offers us another variation of this opinion in the introduction to *Creative Evolution,* trans. Arthur Mitchell (London: Macmillan, 1920), pp. ix ff.:

> We shall see that the human intellect feels at home among inanimate objects, more especially among solids, where our action finds its fulcrum and our industry its tools; that our concepts have been formed on the model of solids; that our logic is, preeminently, the logic of solids. . . . But from this it must also follow that our thought, in its purely logical form, is incapable of presenting *(représenter)* the true nature of life, the full meaning of the evolutionary movement.

It is noteworthy that (at the other end of the spectrum from the "philosophers of life") the philosopher Augustine, criticized earlier by Heidegger for articulating the experience of faith in alien Greek categories, is also criticized by Wittgenstein in the beginning of the *Philosophical Investigations* for implying that language consists only of thing-naming words, i.e., grammatical substantives. Heidegger has pointed out elsewhere how such grammatical classifications, as noun and verb, derive from Greek metaphysics. See, e.g., *Was heisst Denken?* (Tübingen: Niemeyer, 1971), p. 134 and passim; trans. by Fred D. Wieck and J. Glenn Gray (New York: Harper and Row, 1968), p. 228; hereafter referred to as WhD. Many of Heidegger's own "nouns" seem at first sight to tend toward verbal meanings, e.g., *Sein* (Be-ing), *Wesen* (essence/presencing). Yet the non-objective speaking called for by this address is neither verbal nor noun-dominated speech, but rather an attending to . . . which is not pre-determinable by grammar or linguistics. It has, perhaps, the nature of song, thanks-giving, or commemoration. See "Addition to the Pointers" at the end of the address.

5. In the address there are several passages which seem to support the "myth of the given" discussed in Part I of the translators' Commentary. For example: "It is invariably easier to set forth a proof in a given case than, in a differently presented case, to venture into catching sight of and holding in view *(hinnehmendes Erblicken)*"; and: "Insight into the proper nature of thinking and saying comes about only by holding phenomena in view without prejudice *(in einem vorurteilsfreien Erblicken der Phänomene),*" p. 29, this volume. This seems to echo Goethe's notion of "primordial phenomenon" *(Urphänomen),* of which early phenomenology made use: "One seeks nothing behind the phenomena; they themselves are the doctrine" (*Maxims and Reflections,* n. 993). Upon which text Heidegger has commented: "The phenomenon itself, in this case the clearing, presents us with the task of questioning the phenomenon, to learn from out of it, i.e., to let it say something to us" (our translation). *Zur Sache des Denkens* (Tübingen: Niemeyer, 1969), p. 72; trans. by Joan Staumbaugh as *On Time and Being* (New York: Harper and Row, 1972), pp. 65–66; hereafter referred to as ZSD. The clearing is called "a primordial phenomenon"—but it seems Heidegger would mean *the* primordial phenomenon, i.e., the only one which would approximate the definition of Goethe or early phenomenology's intuited and unmediated *eidos.* The examples of the primordial phenomena in this essay, thinking and speaking, bear out this interpretation if one reads the essay in the light of Heidegger's more basic discussions. Furthermore, the passages suggesting a primordial phenomenon use a *terminus technicus: erblicken.* See *Die Technik und die Kehre* (Pfullingen: Neske, 1962), pp. 44 ff., and *Identität und Differenz* (Pfullingen: Neske, 1957), pp. 24–25; the translation by Joan Stambaugh, *Identity and Difference* (New York: Harper, 1969), p. 36, justifiably shies away from Heidegger's etymological excursion; *Identität und Differenz* shall hereafter be referred to as ID. *Erblicken,* translated here as holding in view, has reference to the clearing in which Dasein dwells and out of which things come into their own. There is not some *given* object held in view, cut off from the process by which it comes into view; the holding in view holds on to the *letting* be present, which Heidegger has also called a "letting-go." Both speaking and thinking are this letting be present out of the clearing and in this sense are "primordial phenomena." This essay, therefore, is not a lapse into the "myth of the given."

6. This briefly-sketched distinction between object *(Objekt)* and

that-which-is-standing-against *(Gegenstand)* receives technical elucidation in Heidegger's various discussions of Kant. See Hansgeorg Hoppe's "Wandlungen in der Kant-Aufassung Heideggers," *Durchblicke* (Frankfurt am Main: Klostermann, 1970), esp. pp. 304 ff. The following text from *Satz vom Grund* (Pfullingen: Neske, 1957) may serve as a further elaboration of Heidegger's point:

> For the Greeks what is present discloses itself, indeed, in the character of the over-against—but never in the sense of the that-which-is-standing-over-against *(Gegenstand)* as this word is now used in its modern conceptual sense of object *(Objekt)*. Over-against *(Gegenüber)* and (the modern) that-which-is-standing-over-against *(Gegenstand)* are not the same. In the that-which-is-standing-over-against the against is determined from out of the representing-projecting-against of the subject. In the over-against, on the other hand, the against discloses itself in that which comes upon the perceiving (viewing-listening) human being—befalls that one who never has conceived of himself as a subject for objects. Accordingly, that which is present is not that which a subject projects unto itself as an object, but what comes to perception and what human viewing and listening places and presents *as* having come upon it. The Greek statue *(Stand-bild,* standing likeness) is a view [*Anblick*] of one standing whose stand has nothing to do with a that-which-is-standing-over-against in the sense of an object. The Greek *antikeimenon,* the over-against—or more exactly, that which in being over-against lies before us—is something completely different from the that-which-is-standing-over-against in the sense of object. In the presencing (looking-in) of the gods the Greeks experienced the most uncanny and enchanting over-against: *to deinon.* But they knew nothing of that-which-stands-over-against in the sense of an object.

*(Satz vom Grund,* hereafter referred to as SG, p. 140; see also, p. 141.)

Nevertheless, the talk of the blossoming rose in this paragraph (of the translated text on non-objective thinking) is not without its ambiguities when Heidegger first says we do not make a *Gegenstand* of the rose, then opposes the blossoming rose as a *Gegenstand* to the redness of the rose. The opposition seems to be between the eidetic properties of the two phenomena ("redness" being an "ideal object" without spatial-temporal properties in the world of perception). But in *both* cases there is reference to a non-objective thinking to which the modern sense of object does not do justice.

7. Here again the point is that all saying is, first of all and only, a presencing. See US, pp. 252–262; trans. pp. 122–131.

8. This "belonging together" *(Zusammengehörigkeit)*, with the emphasis on *belonging,* is clarified in ID, pp. 16 ff.; trans. 29 ff.

9. "Ein Hauch um nichts." "A breath for nothing" stands at the end of the sonnet quoted from Rilke. Cf. the elucidations in H, pp. 292 ff.; translation by Albert Hofstadter in *Poetry, Language, Thought* (New York: Harper and Row, 1971), p. 139; hereafter the texts which appear in Hofstadter's collection of translations will be referred to as PLT.

## Review of Ernst Cassirer's Mythical Thought

1. The German original was entitled *Philosophie der symbolischen Formen,* 2. *Teil: Das mythische Denken* (Berlin: Bruno Cassirer, 1925). Heidegger's review appeared originally in *Deutsche Literaturzeitung,* 21 (1928), pp. 1000–1012. The translators have correlated the page references in the review to those of the English translation of Cassirer's work by Ralph Manheim (New Haven: Yale University Press, 1955).

Shortly after this review was published there appeared (1929) Heidegger's *Kant und das Problem der Metaphysik,* which has been translated by James S. Churchill, *Kant and the Problem of Metaphysics* (Bloomington: Indiana University Press, 1969). The fourth edition of this work (Frankfurt am Main: Klostermann, 1973) contains a protocol of the 1929 conversations between Cassirer and Heidegger at Davos, Switzerland. A translation of a protocol of these conversations is to be found in Nino Langiulli, ed. *The Existentialist Tradition* (New York: Doubleday Anchor, 1971), pp. 192–203, "A Discussion between Ernst Cassirer and Martin Heidegger," translated by Frank Slade. For Cassirer's review of Heidegger's early book on Kant, see Ernst Cassirer, "Kant und das Problem der Metaphysik," *Kant-Studien,* XXXVI (1931), pp. 1–26. In Heidegger's *Being and Time* reference is made to the work of Cassirer on mythic thought and Heidegger's reservations, which he develops in this review, are hinted at. Reference is also made to an earlier 1923 discussion between the philosophers in which they agreed to the necessity of an "existential analytic." See p. 51 of SZ and p. 490 of the Macquarrie-Robinson translation.

2. Heidegger's position toward a regional ontology and essence-analysis of religion ("the phenomenology of religion") is the same as toward regional ontologies in general: They are ineluctable because presencing is always a presencing of something as something within a generic meaning-space. Nevertheless such analyses hover and tend to be without philosophical moorings until they are founded in an

account of the meaning of Being and in the analytic of the questioner of Being. (See "Phenomenology and Theology," in this volume, as well as §3 of SZ.) Thus with respect to the task of working out a "natural conception of the world" by recourse to the history of religions and ethnology, Heidegger says:

> The rich store of information now available as to the most exotic and manifold cultures and forms of Dasein seems favorable to our setting about this task in a fruitful way. But this is merely a semblance. At bottom this plethora of information can seduce us into failing to recognize the real problem. We shall not get a genuine knowledge of essences simply by the syncretistic activity of universal comparison and classification. Subjecting the manifold to tabulation does not ensure any actual understanding of what lies there before us as thus set in order. If an ordering principle is genuine, it has its own content as a thing *(Sachgehalt)*, which is never to be found by means of such ordering, but is already presupposed in it. So if one is to put various pictures of the world in order, one must have an explicit idea of the world as such. And if the 'world' itself is something constitutive for Dasein, one must have an insight into Dasein's basic structures in order to treat the world-phenomenon conceptually. (SZ, p. 52; we have followed the Macquarrie-Robinson translation here.)

Thus the comparative-historical "phenomenologies" of religion are faulted insofar as they are conceptually naive about the guiding notions which enable them to compare religions A and B with respect to X; nevertheless, the regional ontology of religion has its own measure of naiveté. See Part II of the translators' Commentary.

3. Heidegger's (1929) *Kant and the Problem of Metaphysics* attempts to show that the meaning of the "Copernican turn" was to move the question about the possibility of ontic knowledge back to the question about the possibility of ontology itself.

4. In SZ Heidegger remarks that we should not confuse everydayness with a primitive mode of Dasein; even primitive Dasein has its own kind of everydayness. There is something to be gained for the analytic of Dasein by study of the ethnological material because primitive Dasein is often "less concealed and complicated by extensive self-interpretation." Primitive Dasein might be of special interest to philosophers because "primitive Dasein often speaks to us more directly in terms of a primordial absorption in 'phenomena' (taken in a pre-phenomenological sense)" SZ, p. 51. Other discussions of interest

to phenomenologists and historians of religion are on pp. 81–83, 247–249, 313, 380, and 394–395. Cf. also the translators' Commentary, II, §8: "Excursus: Heidegger and Primitive Mythic Thought."

5. In SZ (p. 192) care is argued to be the way the Being of Dasein primarily discloses itself because it is the unity of Dasein's existential structures. Care is characterized as Dasein's being already ahead of itself in the world by being along side the beings which it lets be by its being in the world. One of the structures which comprise care as the unified mode of Dasein's disclosure is "thrownness." In everydayness Dasein's being always already ahead of itself entails a mooded being "there," the whence and whither of which are obscure. The expression "thrownness" is used by Heidegger to suggest "the facticity of its being delivered over" to the power of innerworldly beings, traditions and heritages, collective structures, social pressures, etc. Cf. SZ, p. 135.

6. The moment of vision *(Augenblick)* is the authentic mode of temporal understanding in which Dasein holds in view the coming into view (presencing) of what is present (at hand or ready to hand) and does not allow the present to be identified with the "now." The releasing presencing of the moment of vision is an appropriation of one's own past (retentions and habitualities) and future (protentions, concerns, and projects), out of which the present at hand and ready to hand are constituted. Nothing occurs "in" the moment of vision; but by means of it, as the appropriating holding in view and waiting-towards, we are enabled for the first time to encounter what can be "in a time (era)" as present at hand or ready to hand. See SZ, pp. 337–338. The inference we seem permitted to draw is that what is "authentic" (i.e., proper) temporal understanding within the context of the mana-representation and the thrownness of mythic Dasein is a unique holding in view, releasement, and openness for what is surprisingly extraordinary. (See the text.) In SZ (p. 355) being surprised is founded upon the fact that the presencing of something ready to hand involves a non-expectancy of something other which, nevertheless, stands in a possible context of involvements with the presenced ready to hand. The primitive "moment of vision" holds in expectancy that the awaited context of involvements need not be the case and that unexpected concatenations and contexts are possible. This moment of vision establishes the "natural" as the wonderful without thereby routinizing it to the "uniformly surprising."

7. This reference to a "unique survey of possibilities which does not overlook any of them" *(auf Grund eines eigentümlichen Nichtüberschauens der vielen Möglichkeiten)* seems to be a reference to Cas-

sirer's (Freud-influenced) position that for mythic thought there is an omnipotence of desire:

> Thus in the magical world-view the I exerts almost unlimited sway over reality: it takes all reality back into itself. . . . Through the magical omnipotence of the will the I seeks to seize upon all things and bend them to its purpose; but precisely in this attempt it shows itself still dominated, totally "possessed," by things.

See Cassirer, pp. 157–158.

8. In *Kant and the Problem of Metaphysics* (1929) there is an attempt to show that for Kant the transcendental imagination, as the capacity for synthesis, is proximate to the notion of "original temporality" in *Being and Time*. The Kantian and Husserlian notions of self-affections and passive syntheses of "the heart" *(Gemüt)* are basic tools for Heidegger's reflections throughout his life. (Cf. Part III of the translators' Commentary.) In the latest edition (1973) to *Kant and the Problem of Metaphysics* Heidegger again recommends the 1930 work of one of his students, Hermann Mörchen, *Die Einbildungskraft bei Kant* (reprint, Tübingen: Niemeyer, 1970). This book carries the analysis of the imagination beyond the *Critique of Pure Reason* to other writings. Heidegger also recommends Hansgeorg Hoppe's essay, "Wandlungen in der Kant-Auffassung Heideggers," in *Durchblicke* (Frankfurt am Main: Klostermann, 1970), pp. 284–317, for an instructive and critical examination of the transformation of Heidegger's interpretation of Kant.

9. The meaning of myth is never systematically discussed in Heidegger's writings, but a case can be made that some sense of myth is close to the center of his thinking. For example, already in *Being and Time* in the context of discussing *aletheia,* Heidegger remarks, "in citing such evidence we must avoid uninhibited word-mysticism. Nevertheless, the ultimate business of philosophy is to preserve the *force of the most elemental words* in which Dasein expresses itself, and to keep the common understanding from leveling them off to that unintelligibility which functions, in turn, as a source of pseudo-problems" (SZ, p. 220). And later, in the course of a commentary on a text in Sophocles' *Antigone,* mythology is described as "primordial history," "not a ferreting out of primitive lore or a collecting of bones," neither partially nor totally science. It is not something primitive and backward, weak and helpless, but "the opposite is true. The beginning is the most uncanny and the mightiest." Human beings exist, as the most uncanny of beings, by harboring "such a beginning in which everything all at once bursts from superabundance into the overpowering which

itself is to be mastered." *Einführung in die Metaphysik* (Tübingen: Niemeyer, 1966), p. 119; translation (here modified) by Ralph Manheim, *An Introduction to Metaphysics* (New York: Doubleday Anchor, 1961), p. 130; hereafter referred to as EM.

In 1951–52 Heidegger brought together these notions in relation to "thinking" (a *terminus technicus,* see the translators' Commentary, Parts II and III):

> Myth means the telling word. For the Greeks to tell is to lay bare and to let appear—both the coming to appearance and that which is present in the coming to appearance, in the epiphany. *Mythos* is that which becomes present in its telling, namely, that which appears in the unconcealedness of its claim. For all human beings *mythos* makes the claim which is in advance of all others and which is most fundamental. It is the claim which permits thought about that which appears, about that which becomes present. *Logos* says the same; *mythos* and *logos* have not, as the current history of philosophy believes, come into opposition through philosophy. On the contrary, the early Greek thinkers (Parmenides, *Fragment* 8) use *mythos* and *logos* in the same sense. *Mythos* and *logos* became separated and opposed at the point where neither *mythos* nor *logos* could maintain their original essential-presencing *(Wesen).* This happened already with Plato. It is the prejudice of history and philology, founded in Platonism and taken over by modern rationalism, to imagine that *mythos* was destroyed by *logos.* Nothing religious is ever destroyed by logic; it is destroyed only by the god's withdrawal. (WhD, pp. 6–7; trans., here modified, p. 10.)

This text, wherein a mode of thinking is envisaged which is antecedent to the fragmentation of *mythos* and *logos,* provides a context for interpreting a 1938 statement:

> Philosophy has not originated out of myth. It originates only out of thinking and in thinking. But thinking is the thinking of Being. Thinking does not come to be. It is insofar as Being presences *(west).* But the fall of thinking into the sciences and faith is the ill-fated historical destining disclosure of Being *(böse Geschick des Seins).* (H, p. 325.)

Here myth is understood in a (popular) derivative sense and is not equated with thinking. The overcoming of the fragmentation of *mythos* and *logos* receives its most significant explication in the discussion of "poetic dwelling." See the translators' Commentary in Part

III; see also the attempt at an integral view of primitive mythic thought in Part II, §8.

## *"Principles of Thinking"*

1. "Grundsätze des Denkens," *Jahrbuch für Psychologie und Psychotherapie,* VI (1958), pp. 33–41.

2. Here, as in all of his writings, Heidegger distinguishes between history in the proper sense *(Geschichte)* and the current study of history and all the events, dates, etc., it entails *(Historie).* The latter term has been variously translated as "scientific history," "historiography," "historiology," etc.; but it is clear that what is generally referred to as the historical disciplines is meant, and we choose to use this more familiar expression in translating *Historie* and *historisch.* The distinction between *Geschichte* (with its cognate *Geschehen* or occurrence) and *Historie* is made clear in the following discussion by Heidegger.

3. Kant's role in this revolution of thinking is discussed in *Die Frage nach dem Ding* (Tübingen: Niemeyer, 1962), pp. 144 ff.; trans. by W. B. Barton and Vera Deutsch, *What is a Thing?* (Chicago: Regnery, 1967), pp. 184 ff.; hereafter referred to as FD.

4. The theme of the work and its relation to world is amplified in Heidegger's essay "The Origin of the Work of Art," in H (trans. in PLT). Cf. also Parts III and IV of the Commentary. Especially to be noted here is the sense of "growth" *(Hervorbringung)* of the work, which Heidegger relates to the ancient Greek sense of bringing forth by way of *techne* or of *physis.*

5. Hegel's notion of reflexivity, Husserl's transcendental reduction, and Heidegger's "step back"—each in its own way—indicate the irreducibility of thought to a "series of representations in the human consciousness." Cf. the Commentary, III, §6 and §7.

6. Heidegger's remarks here on the questionable foundation of the laws of thought reflect his position in *Being and Time* that his phenomenological (i.e., fundamental-ontological) analyses are prelogical, hence not to be uncritically founded upon logical premises. For an attempt to bring Heidegger's analyses under the validity of the logic which governs statements *(Konsequenzlogik),* see Thomas Seebohm, "Über die Möglichkeit konsequenzlogischer Kontrolle phänomenologischer Analysen," in *Kant-Studien,* 63 (1972), pp. 237–246. Seebohm's circumspect conclusion is that Heidegger's critique of logic (in *Being and Time*) forgets that logical analysis too is intrinsically open to clarification of its foundations, including its very axioms.

"Principles of Thinking" sheds some new light on Heidegger's position in this regard and amplifies the remarks on logic and dialectic in WhD, p. 101; trans. pp. 156 ff. See also the extended reflections in SG (especially p. 38 on the principle of contradiction and p. 147 on dialectic and the history of thought); finally, see ID, passim.

7. For clarification of the link between the principles of thinking and the epochal reign of modern technology, cf. SG, pp. 196 ff.

8. For a development of these remarks see Part IV of the Commentary.

9. This "uneasiness" is a variation on the theme of the "uncanny" *(das Unheimliche);* see Part II of the Commentary.

10. See also Heidegger's interpretation of this text in *Erläuterungen zu Hölderlins Dichtung* (Frankfurt am Main: Klostermann, 1971), pp. 119 ff.; hereafter referred to as EH.

### *"Conversation with Martin Heidegger"*

1. We wish to thank Professor Heidegger, Professor Noack, and the Protestant Academy of Hofgeismar for granting us permission to translate Professor Noack's report. Because of the nature of the publication in which the report appeared (*Anstösse: Berichte aus der Arbeit der Evangelischen Akademie Hofgeismar,* Vol. I, 1954, pp. 31–37) Professor Noack, in response to our request for his permission, obtained the approval of Professor Heidegger on Dec. 17, 1973, to translate the report for this volume. Professor Noack mentioned in his letter to us that before the text was published (1954) he had sent it on to Professor Heidegger and all the other participants. Professor Heidegger did not find anything in the text or in Professor Noack's concluding summary with which he chose to take exception. It should be noted at the outset that the participants in the discussion seemed to be unaware of Professor Heidegger's (1927) lecture, "Phenomenology and Theology," as well as the discussion in the early pages of EM, discussed in II, §7 of the Commentary.

2. See W, p. 208; trans. in Kaufmann, p. 218.

3. In Professor Noack's report there are occasional references to technical terminology which pose difficulties for translators. We have rendered "Schickung des Seins" and "Seinsgeschick" as "historical destining disclosure of Being." The German *Schicken* and *Geschick* enable the reader to hear overtones of *fate* or *destiny* as well as the verb for "to send" *(schicken);* in addition, the "historical" *(geschichtlich)* may likewise be faintly echoed. Whereas this is unfortunate for translators it enables Heidegger to fashion a precise reference to the

process of unconcealment and the most fundamental dimension of the clearing. Thereby he calls attention to the silent concealed formative historical matrix for all life and thought. Cf. the discussion of the clearing in the translators' Commentary, Part I.

4. See "Letter on Humanism," trans. by Edgar Lohner in *The Existentialist Tradition,* ed. Nino Langiulli, p. 234. The original is in W, pp. 181–182; the translation here is our own.

5. See W, 159; trans., "Letter on Humanism," in Langiulli, p. 216.

6. This appears in VA, III, pp. 27–52 as "Moira (Parmenides VIII, 34–41)." Noack refers to but does not review this lecture in his report because the lecture was soon to be published.

7. We have taken the liberty here of rendering *Offenbarkeit* ("openness" or "manifestness") with "unconcealment" *(Unverborgenheit),* which in the discussion were made equivalent. The advantage is that the "positive privative," i.e., the concealment out of which all manifestation occurs, is not lost from view. (See the translators' Commentary.) This makes clearer the opposition Noack seems to be describing between Heidegger and those who hold for a manifestation to which the (alleged) essential historicity and hiddenness belonging to all *un*-concealment does not apply. Furthermore, such a view, when theological, would depend on a metaphysics which holds that the meaning of whatever is (a being) is in its being-created. (Cf., e.g., the Thomist case for the veiled reference to *ipsum esse subsistens* by every *ens* insofar as it participates in *esse simplex et absolutum sed non subsistens* or *ens commune.*) For this theological view the meaning of Being does not intrinsically involve concealment but only *quoad nos.* However, such a line of thinking goes against Heidegger's own philosophical position as well as his understanding of what theology should be. The summary, therefore, does not always successfully keep separate the divergent views.

8. In spite of Heidegger's not taking exception to Noack's summary, this statement is capable of being misleading. As the report shows, Heidegger does not think theologians should be wrestling with "Being." And inasmuch as Being is for Heidegger the hiddenness which makes space for all that appears and which, in no way, is to be considered as ground and cause, the statements brought together by Noack do exclude one another. That is, the sense of "manifestness," equated with the "truth of whatever is," seems to mean something completely and incompatibly different in the two cases. Here, however, is the place where the "Thomist-Heideggerians" (e.g., G. Siewerth, J.-B. Lotz, and K. Rahner) would like to enter into the discussion. For Heidegger's polemic against understanding Being as ground see Part II of the

translators' Commentary. Jean Beaufret has reported another statement from a 1952 address to a Swiss audience which reiterates the
incompatibility of "Being" and theology; but it also adds another puzzling piece to the difficult mosaic which is Heidegger's relationship to
theology:

> Certains d'entre vous savent peut-être que je sors de la théologie,
> que je lui garde un vieil amour, et que j'y entends même quelque
> chose. Si j'entreprenais d'écrire une théologie, à quoi bien sou-
> vent je me sens incliné, alors en elle c'est le mot être, qui ne
> saurait intervenir. La foi n'a pas besoin de la pensée de l'être.

*La Quinzaine littéraire,* 196 (1974), p. 3.


TRANSLATORS' COMMENTARY

*Part I: Hermeneutical Phenomenology and Eidetic
Phenomenology*

1. US, p. 95; trans., p. 9.
2. See SZ, pp. 149–158. Cf. the discussion of G. N. A. Vesey, "Seeing and
Seeing As," in *Perceiving, Sensing, and Knowing,* ed. Robert Swartz
(Garden City: Anchor, 1965), especially pp. 73 and 83. Wittgenstein
provides precision to this discussion. Although all seeing involves seeing in a certain respect (and in this sense it is interpretative), there is
a level of tacitness for the "hermeneutical as" which makes it inappropriate to say of this situation that it involves a seeing as. . . . We say
we see something as . . . when we can see it differently and are aware
of this possibility—which is not characteristic of the situations exem-
plifying the "hermeneutical as"; it is proper, however, for the author
of *Being and Time* when he, from his (non-everyday) situation, describes everyday being-in-the-world. See *Philosophical Investigations*
II (New York: Macmillan, 1965), pp. 193–216.
3. See Edmund Husserl, *Ideen* I (The Hague: Nijhoff, 1950), p. 160:

> What is initially given is surrounded with a fringe of indetermi-
> nate determinability which has a way of bringing one closer to
> the issues through the results of the imaginative attempt to bring
> the object to givenness. We are initially in darkness, but then the
> object enters the realm of givenness and finally it comes forth
> encircled luminously with perfect givenness. . . . It is as if (in the
> single average case) the most general, the genus (color as such,
> sound as such) were fully given but not yet the difference. This
> is offensive talk but I do not know how to avoid it.

In free imaginative variation one is thus not completely free:

> It is a general essential-insight that every imperfect given (every inadequately given noema) contains a rule for the ideal possibility of its perfect realization. . . . We are bound by a legal space as a frame which the idea, e.g., of a possible thing as such, strictly prescribes.

*Ibid.,* p. 366. (James Hart's translation). Cf. the English translation by W. R. Boyce Gibson, *Ideas* (New York: Collier, 1962), pp. 181–182 and 381. Although the metaphors of "fringe" and "horizon" are appropriate with regard to *essential* meanings, the implied (spatial) extrinsicality is misleading. See Eugene Gendlin, *Experiencing and the Creation of Meaning* (Glencoe: Free Press, 1962), pp. 65–67.

4. For this account of what is representative of the Munich-Göttingen Circle we depend on Jean Hering's 1921 essay, *Bemerkungen über das Wesen, die Wesenheit und die Idee* (reprinted, Darmstadt: Wissenschaftliche Buchgesellschaft, 1968).

5. A basic statement of the orientation of the Munich-Göttingen Circle can be found in Adolf Reinach's *Was ist Phänomenologie?* (Munich: Kösel, 1951) with a foreword by Hedwig Conrad-Martius. This lecture was first given in 1914. Another important account is Dietrich von Hildebrand's *What is Philosophy?* (Milwaukee: Bruce, 1960).

6. Compare Husserl's discussions in *Ideen* I, pp. 21 ff. (trans. pp. 55 ff.), as well as in *Ideen* III (The Hague: Nijhoff, 1952), pp. 21–37, and 93 ff. with Heidegger's in SZ, §3 and §10, and, in this volume, "Phenomenology and Theology."

7. See Heidegger, VA I, "Wissenschaft und Besinnung."

8. Cf. Heidegger's Preface to W. Richardson, *Heidegger: Through Phenomenology to Thought* (The Hague: Nijhoff, 1963), pp. xii ff.

9. For the following see FD as well as SZ, pp. 9–10. The proximity of Heidegger's thinking to Thomas Kuhn's on the nature of scientific revolutions is well known. See T. Kisiel, "Zur Hermeneutik naturwissenschaftlicher Entdeckung," in *Zeitschrift für Allgemeine Wissenschaftstheorie,* 2 (1971), pp. 195–221. See as well Kisiel's earlier statement "Scientific Discovery: Logical, Psychological, or Hermeneutical?" in David Carr and Edward Casey, eds., *The Phenomenological Horizon* (Chicago: Quadrangle, 1972).

10. See FD, pp. 129–131; trans., pp. 165–166. The problem of the circularity of interpretation and discovery when they arise from the dictates of the paradigms or horizon of the interpreter, i.e., the question of how anomalies and revisions do, in fact, occur, is answered by reference to the *de jure* and *de facto* posture of science which attempts to direct its gaze to "den Sachen selbst" and to protect itself

from narrowness and caprice. See SZ, p. 153, and H.-G. Gadamer's commentary in *Wahrheit und Methode* (Tübingen: Mohr, 1960), pp. 250 ff.

11. See FD, p. 130; trans., p. 166. Cf. Husserl: "Blindness with respect to ideas is a form of blindness of soul; one has become, through prejudice, incapable of bringing into the field of judgment what one has in the field of intuition." *Ideen* I, p. 49; trans. p. 80. This is developed explicitly in terms of moral presuppositions of knowing by Scheler and von Hildebrand. See especially *Sittlichkeit und ethische Werterkenntnis* (1922) by Dietrich von Hildebrand (reprinted Darmstadt: Wissenschaftliche Buchgesellschaft, 1969). Heidegger, as we shall see, cannot agree that there are eternal essences of value qualities toward which impurity of heart causes us to be obtuse, but he does exhort to a proper mode of existence and "logic of the heart" which alone enables us to see things properly and without which we suffer from a form of blindness.

12. Cf. Part IV of the Commentary for a more detailed account of the relation of tool, *pragmata,* and world.

13. SZ, p. 169.

14. For the "a priori perfect" see SZ, §18. Cf. Husserl's late (1927) critical remarks on his early division of world into regional ontologies without a thorough examination of world as such in *Ideen* I, pp. 389–390 (*Beilag* VI).

15. Cf. US, e.g., pp. 176–179, 232–233; trans., pp. 72–75 and 151.

16. US, p. 161; trans., p. 59.

17. Cf. W. Sellars, *Science, Perception and Reality* (New York: Humanities, 1968), pp. 161–162.

18. The continuity of the views is not to be overlooked: Dasein is a thrown project, i.e., the projection of possibilities is always an anticipation out of the historical-cultural context in which one finds oneself. Furthermore, though it is maintained that the understanding of meaning is prior and then comes to linguistic expression (or words accrue to meaning), even here (SZ, p. 161) it is cautioned that there are never word-things which become equipped subsequently with meanings. A careful discussion of the role of language in *Being and Time* is Richard Schmitt's, *Martin Heidegger on Being Human* (New York: Random House, 1969), Chapter Three.

19. Thomas Prufer, "Welt, Ich und Zeit in der Sprache," *Philosophische Rundschau,* 20 (1973), p. 240.

20. See the writings of Eugene Gendlin, e.g., "What Are the Grounds of Explication?" *The Monist,* 49 (1965), pp. 137–164.

21. For this discussion of the relationship of the views of Heidegger

to linguistic philosophy and Wittgenstein, we are indebted to Karl-Otto Apel, *Die Transformation der Philosophie,* vol. I, *Sprachanalytic, Semiotik, Hermeneutik* (Frankfurt: Suhrkamp, 1973), and to (James Hart's former teacher) Eugene Gendlin's various writings, especially, "What are the Grounds of Explication?"

22. See Allan Janik and Stephen Toulmin, *Wittgenstein's Vienna* (New York: Simon and Schuster, 1973), p. 194, which is a translation of a remark recorded by Friedrich Waismann, *Ludwig Wittgenstein und der Wiener Kreis* (Oxford: Blackwell, 1967), pp. 68–69. It can be noted that the example chosen by Wittgenstein hits the mark exactly for Heidegger, who has always pursued that which makes possible the Why as such, which is the question of the origin of world. See for example *The Essence of Reasons,* trans. Terrence Malick (Evanston: Northwestern University Press, 1969), pp. 112–116; in W, p. 64.

23. The habitual feeling for language, which makes possible eidetic variation because it holds world open, is not sufficient for essence-analysis because a word hardly ever "shakes off its etymology and its formation" (John Austin). Familiarity with the language must be supplemented with historical-lexical studies. See VA II, pp. 20 and 47, for example. However, the historical-philological approach by itself is closed off from the phenomenological mode of thinking which lets the essential meanings unfold. That the elucidation of essential meanings necessarily makes references to historical perspectives is founded for Heidegger in the claim that the world is temporality.

24. L. Wittgenstein, *Philosophical Investigations* I, §583; cf. Dietrich von Hildebrand, *Christian Ethics* (New York: David McKay, 1953), pp. 241–242.

25. Hedwig Conrad-Martius sought to mediate between Heidegger and early phenomenology with a sense of world as that within which everything comes to light and which is an a priori perfect founded on the atemporal meaning network of the *kosmos noetos.* See *Schriften zur Philosophie,* III (Munich: Kösel, 1965), pp. 404–442, and *Das Sein* (Munich: Kösel, 1957), pp. 76 ff. This view finds its earliest statement in writings of Max Scheler. See especially, *Die Stellung des Menschen im Kosmos* (Munich: Francke, 1928 and 1966).

26. See our later discussion of the phenomenology of religion.

27. See W. F. Sellars, pp. 318–319. A modification of a basic framework involves the approach of anxiety. See our later discussion in Part II.

28. Otto Pöggler discusses this criticism by Oskar Becker in "Hermeneutische und mantische Phänomenologie," in *Heidegger,* ed. Otto Pöggler, pp. 321 ff.

29. W. F. Sellars, pp. 316 and 320.

30. The question of whether Heidegger has disposed of the "abstract series of nows" finds an important discussion with a negative verdict in Thomas Seebohm, *Zur Kritik der hermeneutischen Vernunft* (Bonn: Bouvier, 1972).

31. The issue of constitution is the proper focus for the debate between the Munich-Göttingen Circle and the students closer to the Husserl of the Freiburg years. The Munich-Göttingen phenomenologists grant that a realm of meanings does not disclose itself without the corresponding intentional acts. But they resist accepting the mode of intentionality as explicated by Husserl's eidetic analyses of the perception of a cube or a melody as paradigmatic for realms of ideal objects, essential states of affairs, or mathematical objects. Although this essay attempts to present Heidegger's case, the debated issues are not settled. Some of them are alive on American soil. The proto-phenomenological realism of the Iowa School (Gustav Bergmann and his students) holds for a standpoint proximate to that of early phenomenology, whereas the critique of the "myth of the given" by followers of Wittgenstein, Neo-Marxists, and Wilfred Sellars approximates the position of later phenomenology. This writer finds his own unsettledness reflected in Frege's answer to a question put to him once by Wittgenstein: " 'Don't you ever find *any* difficulty in your theory that numbers are objects?' He replied, 'Sometimes I *seem* to see a difficulty—but then again I *don't* see it.' " Cited in G. E. M. Anscombe and P. T. Geach, *Three Philosophers: Aristotle, Aquinas, Frege* (Oxford: Blackwell, 1963), p. 130.

32. Wilfred Sellars's critique of the "myth of the given" and of the entire framework of givenness approaches Heidegger's a priori perfect:

> For if the ability to recognize that x looks green presupposes the concept of *being green,* and if this in turn involves knowing in what circumstances to view an object to ascertain its color, then, since one can scarcely determine what the circumstances are without noticing that certain objects have certain perceptible characteristics—including colors—it would seem that he could not form the concept of *being green,* and, by parity of reasoning, of the other colors, unless he already had them. ... And while this does not imply that one must have concepts before one has them, it does imply that one can have the concept of green only by having a whole battery of concepts of which it is one element. It implies that while the process of acquiring the concept of green may—indeed does—involve a long history of acquiring *piece-*

*meal* habits of response to various objects in various circumstances, there is an important sense in which one has no concept pertaining to the observable properties of physical objects in Space and Time unless one has them all—and, indeed, as we shall see, a great deal more besides.

See Sellars, pp. 147–148. Here Sellars synthesizes early and late Wittgenstein. Cf. the *Tractatus Logico-Philosophicus* (New York: Humanities, 1963), 3.42.

33. SZ, p. 35. Heidegger was to later reject the view that by having established world as the ultimate criterion for meaning a ground or reason was established. See our presentation of Heidegger's critique of a metaphysics of grounding in Part II, §2 of the Commentary.

34. "Principles of Thinking," p. 56 in this volume.

35. W, pp. 143–144; cf. the translation by John Barlow, "Plato's Doctrine of Truth," in *Philosophy in the Twentieth Century,* vol. III, ed. W. Barrett and H. D. Aiken (New York: Random House, 1963), pp. 269–270. For this turn from the transcendental-ex-sistential to the aletheiological-ex-sistential position see A. Rosales, *Tranzendenz und Differenz* (The Hague: Nijhoff, 1970), pp. 313–314, and F. W. von Hermann, *Die Selbstinterpretation Martin Heideggers* (Meisenheim am Glan: Anton Hain, 1964), pp. 64–68 et passim.

36. For the theme of the clearing see especially ZSD and VA III.

37. For the following see Thomas Prufer, "Welt, Ich und Zeit in der Sprache," pp. 236–237.

38. "A sign of the pervasiveness of the teleology of presencing: the very absence of a signifier can be used as signifier of whatever is signified and thus presenced-in-absence by the signifier." Prufer, idem. For example: "If I don't call, you know I won't be there."

39. An especially forceful way to characterize this turn-about in the phenomenological movement is to say that there has occurred a "cosmological" turn. This has been emphasized in the various works of Eugen Fink. The sense in which this thinking is "cosmological" merits discussion. Cf. Fink's brief explanation and Heidegger's noncommittal response in Martin Heidegger and Eugen Fink, *Heraklit* (Frankfurt am Main: Klostermann, 1970), pp. 174–177. A way of pursuing the legitimacy of "cosmological" as applied to the world-clearing would be to contrast the cosmological phenomenology of Conrad-Martius with that of Fink. The ways part not only on the issue of the status of essences but more specifically on the topics of world-space and world-time. It is especially in the interpretation and critique of Kant's discussion of these topics that the issues focus.

*Part II: Phenomenology and Religion*

1. Although one must fault the essence-analysis of "the feminine" as undertaken at first by Scheler and then more elaborately by Buytendijk for provincialism, the merits of these studies as explications of our (European) habitual orientations (forms of seeing as . . . ) should not be overlooked. See F. J. J. Buytendijk, *Die Frau,* trans. Auguste Schorn (Cologne: Bachem, 1953). Paul Ricoeur's writings on evil and the will are the most methodologically refined continuation of the phenomenology of religion. Ricoeur's method involves eidetic analyses of essential (ideal-typical) meanings and cultural and transcendental hermeneutics of what constitutes these essential meanings. There is always a tension between, on the one hand, a transcendental-universal philosophic project and, on the other, the awareness that the point of departure of this project is historically and culturally mediated meanings. Ricoeur's relationship to Heidegger's thought is briefly discussed in *Le Conflit des Interpretations* (Paris: Seuil, 1969), pp. 96–97, 222–232, and passim.

2. Rudolf Otto, *The Idea of the Holy,* trans. John W. Harvey (New York: Oxford University Press, Galaxy, 1958). Max Scheler, *On the Eternal in Man,* trans. Bernard Noble (New York: Harper, 1960), pp. 161 ff.

3. Scheler's reaction to Heidegger's *Being and Time* will soon be made public in Vol. IX of the *Gesammelte Werke* of Max Scheler.

4. SZ, pp. 99 and 150.

5. H, pp. 93–94. Here Heidegger would seem to receive partial explication in C. I. Lewis, *An Analysis of Knowledge and Valuation* (La Salle: Open Court, 1971), Book III, Chapter XVI; in this volume cf. "The Problem of a Non-Objective Thinking and Speaking in Today's Theology."

6. See SZ, pp. 63–64. Cf. SG, pp. 34–35; also Eugen Fink, *Nietzsches Philosophie* (Stuttgart: Kohlhammer, 1968), p. 186.

7. "Letter on Humanism," in Langiulli, pp. 232–233; trans. of W, pp. 179–180. Cf. also EM, p. 151; trans. p. 151. "We should not forget too soon the remark of Nietzsche made in 1866: 'In the refutation of God it is only actually the moral God that is rejected.' For reflective thought, this means the God thought of as value, even if he be the highest, is no God." From *Aufzeichnungen aus der Werkstatt,* taken from Pöggler, *Der Denkweg,* pp. 261–262.

8. H, p. 33, our translation; cf. the translation in *Poetry, Language and Thought,* by Alfred Hofstadter (New York: Harper and Row, 1971), p. 44; hereafter cited as PLT.

9. See in this volume Heidegger's discussion of Cassirer's study of mythic thought and see also Part II, §8 of the Commentary for a more specific discussion of some issues within the phenomenology of religion.

10. ID, p. 51; trans. by Joan Stambaugh, pp. 54–55.

11. ID, p. 70; trans. (slightly modified), p. 72.

12. Wherein lies the philosophical merit of this "story" of Western thought? The argument is double-pronged: in the case for the clearing, and in the merits of Heidegger's studies of Western philosophers.

13. See especially, SG, ID, and VA III.

14. ID, p. 55; trans., p. 58.

15. SG, p. 185.

16. Apparently even in Heidegger's own thinking, though it is not clear to what extent Heidegger would admit this. Cf. Heidegger's discussion of Being *as* "appropriating-event," i.e., as that which enables whatever is to come into its own. Here Heidegger excludes the appropriating-event from being a species of the historical senses of Being. Rather, Being is considered to be a species of appropriating-event. This means that Heidegger's discussion claims for itself a status which is of more than epochal significance. See ZSD, p. 22; trans., p. 21. Cf. also US, pp. 127–128; trans., pp. 33–34. A "perspective" is reached which does justice to Being as the clearing or as appropriating-event but which is exempted from being seen *as* such within the history of the disclosures of Being, because all seeing *as* within . . . finds its sense only in this "perspective." Heidegger's question remains the question of Being, i.e., of B̶e̶i̶n̶g̶.

17. VA III, p. 77.

18. W, pp. 5–10, and SZ, §40.

In the middle of enjoying something a wave of nausea can come upon us; in the midst of intensively being busy an inexplicable boredom; and in the middle of the familiar surroundings of our everydayness a sudden strange ill at ease: *Media in vita in morte sumus.* . . . But what is eerie here is that the ground that normally supports us can open up—that we can sink into the abyss. The eeriest thing about this eerie event is not the suddenness of its appearance, not the unexpected transformation of a familiar landscape into an inexplicable strangeness, but rather: we always already knew about this possibility. But we have repressed, held down, and violently forgotten this knowledge. The strangeness of this [innerworldly] being is not a moment which suddenly arises and sets aside the familiarity of things. This strangeness always waited in ambush under the thin cover of a superficial familiarity, ready to spring into the light of our superficial life. In truth we at all times are familiar with this strangeness which the [innerworldly] "given" being in its wrappings conceals from us. We know it as we know death. And we also are at pains to chase death away, to get rid of it at the edge of our life, out of the human settlements into the cemeteries before the town gates— but still it sits at every dinner table and lies in every storage room, is operative in every deed, and waits at all our joys and sorrows. In like manner the dark puzzling strangeness of the Being [of innerworldly beings] flows under the daily familiarity of our intercourse with things. In philosophy, then, this strangeness is experienced as such and in explicit poignancy.

Eugen Fink, *Sein, Wahrheit, Welt* (The Hague: Nijhoff, 1958), pp. 19 and 29.

19. "Death is the shrine of Nothing *(des Nichts)*, that is, of that which in no respect is ever a mere being but which nevertheless presences even as the mystery of Being itself." VA II, p. 51; see PLT (here modified), p. 178. We shall return to the sense of "mystery" shortly.

20. SG, p. 187. See Eugen Fink, *Spiel als Welsymbol* (Stuttgart: Kohlhammer, 1960), for a development of the sense of play and game as they are used by Heidegger to explicate Heraclitus' *Fragments* 32 and 50. See also our later discussion in Part III.

21. EM, pp. 112 ff.; trans. pp. 123 ff.

22. VA III, p. 77.

23. *Der Europäische Nihilismus,* p. 293, and *Nietzsche* II, p. 395.

24. W, pp. 181–182 (our translation); "Letter on Humanism," in Langiulli, p. 234. Cf., in this volume, "Conversation with Martin Heidegger," pp. 59–71. In another text Heidegger maintains this order of essential-presencings but gives the historical-metaphysical *(seinsgeschichtliche)* genesis of homelessness:

When the unconcealment of Being as such stays away *(bleibt aus)* everything salutary disappears among that which is [or beings]. With the disappearance of the salutary the open space of the holy is occluded. This occlusion of the holy darkens any radiance of the divine. And this darkening seals and conceals the absence [or missingness] of God. The dark absence leaves all beings stranded, not at home; while that which is, as the objective in the limitless act of objectification, appears to be in certain possession and familiar everywhere and in every respect. The unhominess of what is as such [or beings] brings to light the homelessness of historical man within the totality of beings. . . .

*Der Europäische Nihilismus,* pp. 292–293, and *Nietzsche* II, pp. 394–395.

25. See H, pp. 70 and 196–204. See the following discussion (§7) on "Heidegger and Christian Skepticism." We can here note the direction in which Heidegger is *not* moving. With the loss of power of official Christianity and of the "beyond true world" it does not follow that the basic structure dissolves and homelessness is overcome. Both Christianity and its opponents result from the historical-metaphysical constellation of Being. Thus the displacement of power and authority from the trans-worldly to "conscience" or to collective-historical progress, wherein creativity, once the exclusive property of the biblical God, is now a characteristic of human action, is still a form of estrangement and inauthenticity. Whither Heidegger? Sophocles and Hölderlin point the way. The remark of the Christian philosopher Gabriel Marcel, who pursued a kind of thinking very close to Heidegger's, merits reflection: "Heidegger is a Greek." In this conversation with Marcel, Paul Ricoeur comments: "I am always somewhat disturbed by what I might call the prudence with which Heidegger circumvents this [i.e., Judaeo-Christian] tradition. . . . Heidegger's metaphors are Greek, your own [Marcel's] are biblical." See Gabriel Marcel, *Tragic Wisdom and Beyond,* trans. Stephan Jolin and Peter McCormick (Evanston: Northwestern University Press, 1973), pp. 242–243.

26. H, p. 248; PLT, p. 91. We have taken liberties with Hofstadter's beautiful translation here and have rendered the expression of Hölderlin, *Fehl Gottes,* with the clumsy "missingness of God"—as in *Du fehlst mir*—because the sense Heidegger wishes to give is not *(a)* a defect *(der Fehl der Tasse),* nor is it *(b)* merely a mistake *(Fehler)* of God, nor is it *(c)* his sheer absence, because it is an absence which properly should be felt, i.e., the god should be missed when not present. The *Fehl Gottes* as a characteristic of the experience of world is indeed an experience of a marred, unintegral world. See EH, passim, but especially pp. 27–28 and 110. Cf. Helmut Danner, *Das Göttliche und der Gott bei Heidegger* (Meisenheim am Glan: Anton Hain, 1971), pp. 72 ff. Hofstadter's translation might, nevertheless, capture the sense of *Hölderlin's* meaning, which is perhaps not to be identified with God's being missed and staying away. Ruth-Eva Schulz-Seitz contends that *Fehl Gottes* refers to a mistake and incapacity (default!) which the god and poet have in common. See "Bevestigter Gesang" in *Durchblicke* (Frankfurt am Main: Klostermann, 1970), pp. 78–80.

27. H, p. 248f; PLT (here modified), p. 92.

28. EH, p. 87, et passim. This theme will occupy us in Part III.

29. W, p. 169(from "Letter on Humanism," our translation). What is a dimension? Cf. "Principles of Thinking" in this volume, pp. 49f. Cf.

also Danner, pp. 72ff. In an interview Heidegger is reported to have said: "I do not deny God. I state his absence. My philosophy is a waiting for God. Here is the problem of our world. Not in gloom." *Partisan Review,* April (1948), p. 511.

30. Cf. the etymological ties between "whole" and "holy." They closely parallel Heidegger's working with *Heil* and *das Heilige.* See EH, p. 63. A text of Catherine of Genoa points to this wholesome and healing power of the holy (clearing):

> O that I could tell you what the heart feels, how it burns and is consumed inwardly! Only, I find no words to express it. I can but say: Might but one little drop of what I feel fall into Hell, Hell would be transformed into a Paradise.

See Otto, p. 38. Although this is a description which Heidegger perhaps would call ontic, "genuine" mysticism, like poetic dwelling and aspects of primitive mythic thought, involves a kind of thinking which is mindful of the clearing. In discussion of a text of Angelus Silesius, Heidegger suggests that this mystic's reflections on the sense of "why" ("The rose is without why; it blooms because it blooms") is to be placed not *in* thinking but rather *before* thinking, i.e., it belongs to that which is prior to the kind of thinking which seeks to ground things in sufficient reasons. A careful study of mystics might lead one to believe "that proper to genuine and great mysticism is the utmost acuity and depth of thinking." See SG, pp. 68–71; cf. also VA II, p. 49; trans., PLT, p. 176. Is the merit ascribed to the apprehension of the rose by Angelus, which is presenced in such a way as to be free from the search for foundations or reasons, also to be ascribed to the nonobjective apprehension of the rose in the garden (see, in this volume, p. 26)? It would seem so. The brief discussion of the apprehension of the rose in the garden can be clearly distinguished from a vacuous gaping when it is placed in the context of the discussion of Angelus' perception of the rose.

31. There are several examples wherein the holy is identified with the experience of the clearing. See, e.g., US, p. 44; trans., p. 165. And VA II, p. 71; trans., PLT, pp. 222–223. Cf. James M. Demske, *Being, Man and Death* (Lexington: University of Kentucky Press, 1970), pp. 124–126, and also Jörg Splett, *Die Rede vom Heiligen* (Freiburg: Karl Alber, 1971), p. 173. Cf. Mircea Eliade's (ontic) observation: "When something of the sacred manifests itself (hierophany), at the same time, it hides itself, it becomes cryptic. This is the true dialectic of the sacred: By the very fact of showing itself it conceals itself." *Fragments d'un journal,* trans. into French by Luc Badesco (Paris: Gallimard, 1973), p. 506.

32. For example, W, p. 89, and US, p. 148; trans., p. 50.

33. *Nietzsche* II, pp. 369 ff.

34. ZSD, p. 72; trans. pp. 65–66.

35. "The Historicity of Man and Faith," in *Existence and Faith: Shorter Writings of Rudolf Bultmann,* trans. Shubert Ogden (Cleveland: World, 1966), pp. 93–94; from "Geschichtlichkeit des Daseins und der Glaube: Antwort an Gerhardt Kuhlmann," in *Heidegger und die Theologie,* ed. G. Noller (Munich: Kaiser, 1967), pp. 73–74.

36. See Ogden, p. 97; Noller, p. 79.

37. See especially Otto Pöggler, *Der Denkweg,* pp. 36 ff., and Karl Lehmann, in *Heidegger,* ed. Otto Pöggler, pp. 140 ff.

38. See the 1929 essay "The Concept of Revelation in the New Testament," in Ogden; from "Der Begriff der Offenbarung im Neuen Testament," *Glauben und Verstehen,* III (Tübingen: J. C. B. Mohr, 1965). Cf. "Phenomenology and Theology," pp. 9ff.

39. Ogden, p. 304; Noller, p. 78.

40. After Heidegger moved from the transcendental-existential phenomenology of *Being and Time* to the later themes of the clearing and unconcealment, the differences between the thinkers became more pronounced. The differences have seemed so great that some theologians have claimed to see greater proximity between Karl Barth and the later Heidegger. See the discussion in James Robinson and John Cobb, *The Later Heidegger and Theology* (New York: Harper and Row, 1963). An energetic caution against this interpretation is given by Helmut Franz, "Das Denken Heideggers und die Theologie," in *Heidegger,* ed. Otto Pöggler, pp. 179 ff.

41. "Kirche und Lehre im Neuen Testament," in *Glauben und Verstehen,* I (Tübingen: J. C. B. Mohr, 1954), pp. 153–176.

42. See the entire section of "the New Man" where the reformation theme of *simul justus et simul peccator* is dialectically orchestrated. We are told in N. Languilli's *The Existentialist Tradition,* p. 187, that Bultmann suggested to Heidegger in the early Marburg years (1923) that he look at Barth's *Commentary on Romans.* The reading of this work made a strong impression and, because of the presence of Kierkegaard felt there, Heidegger went on to study the Danish thinker. Heidegger's debt to Kierkegaard is acknowledged in *Being and Time.* Sometime later Heidegger was to write: "Kierkegaard is not a thinker but a religious author. And indeed not one among many but the only one who measured up to the destiny of his era. In this lies his greatness, if in so speaking there does not already lie a misunderstanding." H, p. 230. We take this to mean that Kierkegaard, especially in his edifying writings (because, for Heidegger, in the others he is captured

by the metaphysics of Hegel), we find a paradigm for theology. In these writings a mode of discourse and expression is sought which does justice to the exigencies of faith. Such a discourse not only combats what is foreign to faith but is fully aware of how this discourse on faith, out of faith, for faith is imperiled by unfaithful ingredients, e.g., modes of expression, which nevertheless are ineluctable.

43. See Ogden, p. 96; Noller, p. 78.

44. See Karl Barth, *Church Dogmatics* I,2, trans. G. T. Thomson and Harold Knight (Edinburgh: T. & T. Clark, 1956), pp. 731–736; *Kirchliche Dogmatik*, I,2 (Zollikon-Zurich: Evangelischer Verlag, 1960), pp. 820–825.

45. Cf. Henri Bouillard, *Karl Barth* I (Paris: Aubier, 1957), pp. 72 ff.

46. Relevant to this discussion is Karl Barth's appreciation of Franz Overbeck. See "Unsettled Questions for Theology," in *Theology and the Church,* trans. T. F. Torrance (New York: Harper and Row, 1962); from "Unerledigte Anfragen an die heutige Theologie," in *Die Theologie und die Kirche* (Zurich: Evangelischer Verlag, 1928).

47. See Gadamer, "Martin Heidegger und die Marburger Theologie," in *Heidegger,* ed. Otto Pöggler, p. 169. The article appeared originally in *Zeit und Geschichte: Dankesgabe an Rudolf Bultmann zum 80. Geburtstag,* ed. Erich Dinkler (Tübingen, 1964), pp. 479–90.

48. See *Über die Christlichkeit unserer heutigen Theologie,* pp. 24–29, 42, 85, 216–217, et passim.

49. *Christentum und Kultur* (reprint, Darmstadt: Wissenschaftliche Buchgesellschaft, 1973), p. 8.

50. *Über die Christlichkeit,* pp. 25 ff.

51. See *Über die Christlichkeit,* pp. 83–88. Cf. Otto Pöggler's account of the 1920–21 lectures on the "Introduction to the Phenomenology of Religion," where the Pauline notion of *kairos* is explicated by Heidegger in terms of a life of faith concentrated on the in-cision of eschatological decision. *Der Denkweg Martin Heideggers,* pp. 36 ff. Cf. also the Notes (n.2) to "The Problem of a Non-Objective Thinking in Today's Theology."

52. H, pp. 202–203.

53. See Bernoulli's Introduction to *Christentum und Kultur,* pp. XV–XVIII.

54. A fuller study of the relationship of Heidegger to Overbeck might well examine the latter's theme of primordial questions and truths as the subject matter of religion; likewise the relationship of death to life and inquiry. Otto Pöggler has sketched some possible ties in "Hermeneutische Philosophie und Theologie," *Man and World,* 21 (1974), pp. 3–19.

55. See W, p. 208; trans. in Kaufmann, p. 218.

56. EM, p. 6; trans., p. 6 (slightly modified).

57. EM, p. 5.

58. This discussion partly reflects Henri Birault, "La Foi et la Pensée d'après Heidegger," *Recherches et Débats,* 10 (1955), pp. 114–116.

59. See Birault, pp. 123–124.

60. See in this volume "Conversation with Martin Heidegger," where Heidegger states that if he were addressed by faith he would have to close his philosopher's (i.e., thinker's) shop. But if this is Heidegger's position, what is the kind of theology toward which he is inclined? i.e., what sense should we give to the text quoted in n. 8, p. 183?

61. EM, p. 6; trans., p. 6.

62. See especially W, pp. 179–180; "Letter on Humanism," in Languilli, pp. 232–233; H, p. 240; and ID, pp. 45 and 64; trans., pp. 54–55 and 72.

63. See here Hans Lipps, *Die Wirklichkeit des Menschen* (Frankfurt am Main: Klostermann, 1954), p. 32.

64. *Philosophische Bemerkungen,* ed. Rush Rhees (Frankfurt am Main: Suhrkamp, 1964), p. 187.

65. Cf. SZ, p. 51.

66. For the following, see Levi-Strauss's Introduction to Marcel Mauss, *Sociologie et Anthropologie* (Paris: PUF, 1966), pp. XLI–LI. For clues we are indebted to remarks of Mikel Dufrenne, *Jalons* (The Hague: Nijhoff, 1966), p. 143.

67. The Introduction to M. Mauss, p. XLVI

68. The Introduction to M. Mauss, p. XLVII

69. See, along with the "Review of Cassirer's *Mythical Thought*" in this volume, SZ, pp. 81–83.

70. Jacques Derrida, "Structure, Sign and Play" in *The Structuralist Controversy,* ed. Richard Macksey and Eugenio Donato (Baltimore: Johns Hopkins, 1972), p. 264.

71. See the above-cited essay by Jacques Derrida as well as the transcript of the discussion following his lecture. See also his *Speech and Phenomena* (Evanston: Northwestern University Press, 1973), trans. David B. Allison, especially pp. 129 ff.

72. Readers familiar with the writing of Mircea Eliade will recognize in our presentation affinities of themes and formulations. Central for our presentation is the common conviction that the mystery (or the "holy") hides its hiddenness and that the remedy is to be found in poetic dwelling, the initial task of which is specified by Eliade as the elucidation of the camouflage of mystery in the events of immediate reality:

How to sort out, consequently, the ambivalence of every 'event,' in the sense that every apparently banal 'event' is capable of revealing a universe of transcendent meanings and that an apparently extraordinary or even fantastic event is able to be accepted as commonplace and as something which it would never occur to anyone to be astounded at. (*Fragments d'un journal,* p. 443.)

## Part III: The Changing of the World and the Worlding of World

1. See WhD, p. 163; trans., p. 162, and VA II, p. 76; trans. PLT, p. 227.

2. See Edmund Husserl, *Zur Phänomenologie des inneren Zeitbewusstseins* (The Hague: Nijhoff, 1966); trans. by J. Churchill, *The Phenomenology of Internal Time Consciousness* (Bloomington: Indiana University Press, 1964). Heidegger merges the themes of Husserl's inner-time consciousness with the process of unconcealment in his discussions of *logos* as *legein:* to lay together, as in gleaning and harvesting. To accomplish this Heidegger sketches an eidetic analysis of reading (in German, gleaning and reading have the same root verbal form: *lesen*) which points to a passive synthetic sense of gathering. See WhD and VA III. As Thomas Prufer has observed, Husserl's formulation of the "living present" as a "temporalized, pre-temporal temporality" is "comparable but not equivalent" to Heidegger's themes of the disclosure of the two-fold of letting-be-present and that which is present. Like Heidegger, Husserl sought that which mediates the experience of worldly being. He placed it in the primordial *fungor* of *Strömen-stehen (Quellen),* which is "even more fundamental than *both* the synthesis, through 'the standing form' of the temporality of experience, of *Urimpression* (verbal not nominal) and distention (retention and protention), *and* the reflection, open to indefinite iteration, and self-objectification made possible by this synthesis." Thomas Prufer, revision of "Reduction and Constitution," in *Studies in Philosophy* V (Catholic University of America, Washington, D.C.), 1970, p. 343, n.11. See also Prufer's "Welt, Ich und Zeit in der Sprache." Despite the possibility of comparison, Heidegger has insisted on the difference: "My question about time was always determined by the question of Being. It went in a direction which was always alien to Husserl's investigation of inner-time consciousness." Martin Heidegger, "Über das Zeitverständnis in der Phänomenologie und im Denken der Seinsfrage," in *Phänomenologie—lebendig oder tot?,* ed. Helmut Gehrig (Karlsruhe: Badenia Verlag, 1969; publication of the Catholic

Academy of the Archdiocese of Freiburg, n. 18), p. 47.

3. ZSD, p. 40; trans., p. 37.

4. WhD, pp. 91–97, 157–159; trans., pp. 139–151.

5.Thomas Prufer:

Taking thought is non-public not simply out of difference to the public: it is the space of *aletheia,* the space within which manifestation *out of (a-)* hiddenness *(lethe)* takes place, a space irreducible to any repetition-in-difference of the tension between the matrix hiddenness and the process of manifestation out of that matrix: taking thought is irreducible to manifestation out of hiddenness of manifestation-out-of-hiddenness, this in turn reduced to one that-which-is-manifest above or even among others.

There is no *eidos* of taking thought, no collectedness into view, but it is not thereby hidden from view: taking thought has neither visible character nor secret teaching.

Taking thought is the space within which the friendly struggle, the play between hiddenness and manifestation takes place and brings into view that-which-is-manifest and then itself, the play between hiddenness and manifestation, comes into view as one that-which-is-manifest above or even among others.

This is an excerpt from Thomas Prufer, "Taking Thought," an unpublished manuscript. How "the friendly struggle" brings into view that-which-is-manifest is the question of poetic dwelling, to which we next turn.

6. VA II, pp. 23–24; trans., PLT, pp. 149–150.

7. VA II, pp. 76–77; trans., PLT, pp. 227–228.

8. Nevertheless poetry in the narrower sense retains an essential priority because it is language which first of all opens world and enables things to appear as. . . . See H, p. 61; trans., PLT, p. 74.

9. H, pp. 49–50; trans., PLT., pp. 61–62.

10. WhD, pp. 6–7(our translation). Cf. Heidegger's "Review of Ernst Cassirer's *Mythical Thought"* in this volume; also see II, §8 of the Commentary.

11. World is "historical," "withdraws," "dissolves," "comes into being," "makes place," "lets things come into their own," etc. That is, it does something and is modified. But these innerworldly descriptions are treacherous. Therefore world most properly simply "worlds."

12. "Principles of Thinking," in this volume, p. 48.

13. We have already considered this issue in terms of the synthetic material a priori. Insofar as there can be said to be a synthetic mate-

rial a priori for Heidegger it is not that of already finished, eternal essential meanings proper to things.

14. H, p. 62; trans., PLT., p. 75. See our discussion below (§12) of nature and history.

15. Theodor Adorno, *Ästhetische Theorie* (Frankfurt am Main: Suhr-kamptaschenbuch, 1973), p. 200. For another fruitful parallel, cf. John Dewey, *Art as Experience* (New York: Capricorn-Putnam, 1958), pp. 344–349.

16. Thus Heidegger says of this text of Kant:

> Whoever understands this principle understands Kant's *Critique of Pure Reason*. Whoever understands the latter does not only know one book among the writings of philosophy, but masters a fundamental posture of our historical Dasein, which we can neither avoid, leap over, nor deny in any other way. But we have to bring this position, by an appropriate transformation, to its full bearing for the future.

FD, p. 143; trans. (here modified), p. 183.

17. See ZSD, pp. 76–77; trans., pp. 69–70; whether intended as such or not, these pages are relevant to Ernst Tugendhat's critique of the identification of disclosedness and, later, the clearing with truth. See *Der Wahrheitsbegriff bei Husserl und Heidegger* (Berlin: de Gruyter, 1967).

18. *Hebel der Hausfreund* (Pfullingen: Neske, 1965), p. 19.

19. See the discussion of the difference and *Austrag* in ID, pp. 40 ff. and 56 ff.; trans., pp. 50 ff. and 64 ff. See also US, pp. 22–30; trans., PLT, pp. 199–208. For Heidegger's exemplary account of bringing world to thing and thing to world, the "thinging of the thing," see VA II; trans. PLT, pp. 143–186 and 211 ff.

20. Jacques Derrida's discussion of the difference, especially in *Speech and Phenomena,* p. 158, calls attention to the text in H, pp. 336–337, where Heidegger says the difference as such does not show itself. But then Heidegger goes on to say that "nevertheless, in the presencing as such the relation to what is present may announce itself in such a way that the presencing is expressed *as this relation*." Derrida does not take this into account, nor does he refer to the discussion in ID. However, he sees the utopian side to Heidegger's discussion: "the other side of nostalgia, which I will call Heideggerian *hope*," *Speech and Phenomena,* p. 159.

21. Preface to Richardson, p. XXIII.

22. See Thomas Prufer, "Welt, Ich und Zeit in der Sprache."

23. See Roland Barthes, *Mythologies* (New York: Hill and Wang, 1972), p. 15; trans. Annette Lavers. Barthes' basic schema is:

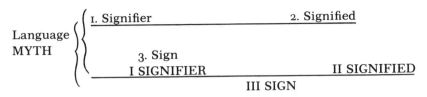

24. Walden II, p. 22. Text taken from Stanley Cavell, *The Senses of "Walden"* (New York: The Viking Press, 1972), p. 11. I find Cavell's little work to be, in part, a beautiful explication of Heidegger's notion of poetic dwelling and his meditations on Hölderlin.

25. Cavell, pp. 90–91. See also Robert Sokolowski, *Husserlian Meditations* (Evanston: Northwestern University Press, 1974), pp. 34–42, 218–221, 225 n. 11.

26. Where would one stand to be able to say the contrary? Does the sense of "language enables us always to say what needs to be said" imply a sense of transcendentalese within language itself? See Prufer, "Welt, Ich und Zeit in der Sprache."

27. Cavell, ibid., p. 43.

28. EH, pp. 102–103. It would seem that the unalienated and authentic poetic epoch would not usher in a state of affairs wherein the uncanny became ordinary and thus destroyed. The difference can never be surmounted. But its manifestness can be secured through a poetic *hexis*.

29. EH, p. 71.

30. One might well be skeptical about the effectiveness *today* of the indirectness of modern art, i.e., whether it can bring world to things and things to world: "What else have we had, in major art of the past hundred years, but indirectness: irony, theatricality, yearning, broken forms, denials of art, anti-heroes, withdrawals from nature, from men, from the future, from the past. . . ." Stanley Cavell goes on to observe that in our day, "which not only does not know what it needs, but which no longer even demands anything, but takes what it gets and so perhaps deserves it; where every indirectness is dime-a-dozen, and any weirdness can be assembled or imitated on demand—the thing we must look for, in each case, is the man who, contrary to appearance, and in spite of all, speaks." For Cavell, the "difference" is exemplarily manifest in a work like Kierkegaard's *Fear and Trembling,* not because of the presentation of the inevitability of Abraham's silence but because of "the continuous awareness of the pain, and the danger, of that silence—of the fear of the false word, and the deep wish that the right word be found. . . ." See Stanley Cavell, *Must We Mean What We Say?* (New York: Scribner's, 1969), pp. 178–179.

31. Theodor Adorno, *Noten zur Literatur* II (Frankfurt am Main: Suhrkamp, 1965), p. 198.

32. Idem.

33. Roland Barthes, *Writing Degree Zero and Elements of Semiology* (Boston: Beacon, 1967), trans. Annette Lavers and Colin Smith, pp. 52 and 48 of *Writing Degree Zero.*

34. Recently the relevance of Heidegger's discussions to the self-understanding of poets has been demonstrated in detail. See Gerald L. Bruns, *Modern Poetry and the Idea of Language* (New Haven: Yale University Press, 1974). This paragraph is indebted to Bruns's work and purports to offer some precision in the conception of Heidegger's "orphism."

35. Theodor Adorno, *Ästhetische Theorie,* p. 200.

36. Barthes claims that even modern poetry, with its uprooted proliferation of styles and forms of expression, may be said to have the project toward a "utopia of language": "It hastens as towards a dreamed-of language whose freshness, by a kind of ideal anticipation, might portray the perfection of some new Adamic world where language would no longer be alienated." Roland Barthes, p. 88. This reading of Heidegger is both supported by and indebted to Gianni Vattimo, "Sprache, Utopie, Musik," *Philosophische Perspektiven* IV (1972), especially pp. 160–162.

37. Walter Bröcker, *Dialektik, Positivismus, Mythologie* (Frankfurt am Main: Kostermann, 1958), p. 35.

38. Werner Marx, "Poetic Dwelling and the Role of the Poet," in *On Heidegger and Language,* ed. Joseph J. Kockelmans (Evanston: Northwestern Universtiy Press, 1972), p. 245.

39. EH, p. 123.

40. Cf. SZ, pp. 38, 142–143. However, cf. Roman Ingarden's critique of Heidegger's view that "the Being of Dasein is its possibility" as not allotting to human existence an abiding actual essential-core: "Whoever has been busy at all with the problem of real possibility knows that it can obtain only from real actual being and can be transformed into reality only out of this full being." *Der Streit um die Existenz der Welt,* I (Tubingen: Niemeyer, 1964), pp. 234–235. Prescinding from the important anthropological issues at stake here, we merely note that "real possibility," when ascribed to world or the clearing, intends to be another way of talking about that out of which all presencing in any modality occurs. The clearing is "what enables" all modes of presencing and it itself is not *something* actual or possible. To apply to the clearing the position that all real possibility presupposes that there be a prior actuality with respect to the being in question is a "category

mistake" because world or clearing is a unique "class." See Heidegger's discussions of "es gibt..." in the essay "Time and Being," in ZSD. Eugen Fink has attempted to deal explicitly with this issue in *Alles und Nichts* (The Hague: Nijhoff, 1958).

41. See W, pp. 64 ff. The translation, *The Essence of Reasons,* p. 115, misleads with "the project of world outstrips the possible."

42. For what follows, see EH, pp. 112 ff.

43. EH, p. 113. This recalls the proper sense of the phenomenon of "values." Values, insofar as they present world in a more urgent way than ordinary things, may be said to have a unique "density" inasmuch as they are charged with world as that on account of which and the clearing is that within which all meaning finds its place. This is the sense to be given certain beings as more real or more being. Heidegger elsewhere mentions a way in which unconcealment is established: "the nearness of that which is absolutely not a being but the beingest of a being"—which we take to be a reference to "the god." H, p. 50 (our translation); PLT, p. 62. See in this volume also Heidegger's discussion of mana in the "Review of Ernst Cassirer's *Mythical Thought*"; cf. also II, §8 of the Commentary.

44. *Nietzsche* I, p. 249.

45. A text in "The Origin of the Work of Art" brings these considerations together:

> In the midst of beings as a whole an open place occurs *(west)*.
> There is a clearing, a lighting. Thought of in reference to what
> is, to beings, this clearing is in a greater degree than are beings.
> This open center is therefore not surrounded by what is; rather,
> the lighting center itself encircles all that is, like the Nothing
> which we scarcely know. ... Only this clearing grants and gua-
> rantees to us humans a passage to those beings that we ourselves
> are not, and access to the being that we ourselves are.

H, p. 41; trans., PLT, p. 53.

46. Any judicious comments on these strands in Heidegger's texts may not be any less cautious and tentative than the texts themselves. Furthermore, because Heidegger's references to the gods are, for the most part, in texts dealing with Hölderlin and other poets, it is difficult to separate Heidegger's thinking about poetic dwelling from the form poetic dwelling takes in particular poets.

47. VA II, p. 76; trans., PLT, p. 227.

48. See VA II, p. 71; trans., PLT, pp. 222–223.

49. See VA II, p. 57; trans.(modified), PLT, p. 184. Here Heidegger is quite clear that he is not joining ranks with "traditionalists" or "classi-

cists." "Since Being is never merely just what is actual, to guard Being can never be equated with the task of a guard who protects from burglars a treasure stored in a building. Guardianship of Being is not fixated upon what is present before us."

50. See VA II, p. 25; trans., PLT, p. 150, and *Heraklit,* pp. 242–245. This hoping would not seem necessarily to imply an *actual* divine mode of being. To get clear on the status of the gods one must be prepared to explicate: "Whether the god lives or dies is not decided by the religiosity of humans or, even less, by the theological aspirations of philosophy and the sciences. Whether God is God finds its proper place from out of the event of the constellation of Being and within it." *Die Technik und die Kehre* (Pfullingen: Neske, 1962), p. 46. If Dasein is the being which holds open the clearing, does the annihilation of Dasein imply the annihilation of the gods? If not, the god is god independent of the constellation of Being or the event of the clearing; if so, other aspects of the gods become unintelligible. See below. On the destruction of human beings and the clearing, cf. the remarks in "Principles of Thinking," this volume, pp. 52f.

51. For the fullest discussion of the "existential ontology" of the gods and the mortals, in connection with texts of Heraclitus, see M. Heidegger and E. Fink, *Heraklit,* pp. 158 ff. Although this discussion is by Fink, Heidegger (p. 177) states his agreement with the interpretation.

52. SG, p. 186.

53. Thomas Prufer, from the unpublished manuscript, "Taking Thought."

54. Jacques Derrida, "Structure, Sign, and Play," p. 264. We have modified the English translation which justifiably translates "jeu" as "freeplay." Cf. Fink, *Spiel als Weltsymbol,* p. 240.

55. See EH, pp. 38–42.

56. "Principles of Thinking," in this volume, p. 53. This essay is an extended meditation on the origin of unconcealment.

57. H, p. 325.

58. Note that these alternatives, understood, e.g., in a creationist context, might be acceptable to some theologians.

59. See W, pp. 309 ff.

60. EH, p. 21.

61. See VA I, pp. 54 ff., where the objectifying thinking of the natural sciences is held to be especially ill-suited for apprehending the "essential fullness" of nature; cf. also Pöggler's discussion in *Der Denkweg Martin Heideggers,* pp. 254–258.

62. Heaven and earth, along with the mortals and the gods, are not ontic regions within world but are the four-fold non-innerworldly, not

mutually-excluding but internally-relating constitutive regions of the world-clearing. The sense of world-clearing requires that each of these be taken into account; and taking account of each of these implies an account of the other three. See H, pp. 7–68, and VA II; trans., PLT.

63. We are ascribing to earth a sense of power proximate to that found in Andrew P. Ushenko's *Power and Events* (Princeton: Princeton University Press, 1946; reprint by Greenwood, 1968). Ushenko summarized his view in the following way:

> First, knowledge must conform to real or objective tendencies, i.e., to dispositions that make up the world whether or not singled out in true statements. Second, an objective tendency or disposition must be actualized or manifested, and therefore transformed, in order to be discernible and accessible to public knowledge. This is so because the latent state and the manifestation of a tendency are different modes of being; and transition from one state to the other must be a transformation. The instrument of cognitive transformation is a perspective. For to be actualized a tendency must be entangled from a complex of alternative or competing tendencies. And the fact that a perspective can present only one aspect of a complex thing is equivalent to a disentanglement, and manifestation, of a certain tendency. Hence a cognitive perspective means conformal transformation.

*Dynamics of Art* (Bloomington: Indiana University Press, 1953; reprint by Kraus, 1969), p. 196.

64. H, p. 37; trans., PLT, p. 49. Cf. W, pp. 351 ff., where Heidegger shows that for Aristotle something can be said to be suited for . . . or have its proper possibility only subsequent to the transforming disclosure of the thing, i.e., a specific determinability of earth is manifest only subsequent to a ("historical") letting appear as . . . , which is achieved in a work.

65. See W, pp. 274–275, and *Martin Heidegger im Gespräch*, ed. Richard Wisser (Freiburg: Alber, 1970), pp. 68 ff.

66. See *Nietzsche* I, pp. 248–254.

67. See Heidegger's anticipation of the (Protagorean) objection that man is the measure in H, pp. 94 ff. See, in this volume, Heidegger's address on "The Problem of a Non-Objective Thinking in Today's Theology" for a discussion of modern objectifying thinking.

68. See H, pp. 83–87; cf. the trans. by Marjorie Grene, "The Age of the World View," *Measure* II (1951), pp. 269–284.

69. See W, p. 54; trans., *The Essence of Reasons,* p. 87.

70. Cf. EH., pp. 38–39.

71. EM, p. 117; trans., p. 128.

72. Thomas Prufer, from the unpublished manuscript, "Taking Thought."

## Part IV: Some Heideggerian Pathways to Technology and the Divine

1. See the Introduction to PLT, p. XV.

2. The gesture of an inquiring thinking is "to pay attention above all to the way, not to be caught on individual statements and titles." *Die Technik und die Kehre* (Pfullingen: Neske, 1962), p. 5. Compare: "The point is not to listen to a series of propositions, but rather to follow the movement of showing." ZSD, p. 2; trans. by Joan Stambaugh, p. 2.

3. This "de-worlding" does not, of course, take the tool "out of" the world; it remains always in the world, but now removed from the equipmental context of the world-about. "De-worlding" here and in the following must be taken in its restricted sense of a fundamental shift; cf. SZ, pp. 65 and 112.

4. Heidegger makes an indirect criticism of the phenomenological notions of "region" and "intentionality" by indicating their derivative character: the determination of a region hinges upon how and how well the Being of the regional beings is understood, e.g., as things merely present *(vorhanden)* (SZ, p. 362); the "intentionality of consciousness" is grounded in the ecstatic temporality of Dasein (SZ, p. 363n). See also Part I of the Commentary.

5. "Only a being who can speak, that is, think, can have hands . . . the hand's gestures run everywhere through language." WhD, p. 51; trans., p. 16.

6. Natsume Sōseki, *The Three Cornered World*, trans. Alan Turney (London: Peter Owen Ltd., 1965). The following passages (quoted with permission of the publisher) are taken from pp. 12–14, 18, 24. Sōseki (1867–1916) at one point has the speaker say: "An artist is a person who lives in the triangle which remains after the angle which we may call common sense has been removed from this four-cornered world." This passage, giving the English translation of the novel its title, recalls the theme of the uncanny *(das Unheimliche)* presented in Part II of the Commentary. In his Introduction the translator, Alan Turney, writes of the novel: "Sōseki's method of describing both Nature and his other physical surroundings is that of the painter. Every scene he presents is in perfect proportion, as though he were reproducing it on canvas. He also makes detailed allusion to colours, shapes and textures. In-

deed, so graphic is his description that a certain Japanese artist, having read *Kusa Makura* [i.e. *The Grass Pillow,* the Japanese title of the novel], actually painted the scenes which appear in it" (p. 11). The concrete working of truth here is untouched by any difference between Sōseki's notion of "Nature" and Heidegger's inquiry into the meaning of *physis* as a process of unconcealment.

7. The fourfold *(Geviert)* mentioned in "Die Kehre" is explicated in VA II; trans. PLT, pp. 143–186 and 211 ff.

8. On the "friendly struggle" and the full implications of "the gods" in Heidegger, see the previous discussion in Parts II and III of the Commentary.

9. Compare the discussion in "Wozu Dichter?": "God's appearance through the sky consists in a disclosing that lets us see what conceals itself, but lets us see it not by seeking to wrest what is concealed out of its concealedness, but only by guarding the concealed in its self-concealment. Thus the unknown god appears as the unknown by way of the sky's manifestness." Translated by Albert Hofstadter in PLT, p. 223.

10. *"...fromm, prómos, d.h. fügsam dem Walten und Verwahren der Wahrheit."* See *Die Technik und die Kehre,* p. 34.

# INDEXES

INDEX OF TOPICS